Rowan
Atkinson

Rowan Atkinson

BRUCE DESSAU

ORION

Extract from We Bombed in New Haven
by Joseph Heller copyright © 1967
by Scapegoat Productions, Inc. Reproduced
by permission of the author c/o Rogers,
Coleridge & White Ltd., 20 Powis Mews,
London W11 1JN.

First published in 1999 by Orion Media
An imprint of Orion Books Ltd
Orion House, 5 Upper St Martin's Lane, London WC2H 9EA

A CIP catalogue record for this book
is available from the British Library.

ISBN 0-75280-088-4

Filmset by Selwood Systems, Midsomer Norton
Printed and bound in Great Britain
by Butler & Tanner Ltd,
Frome and London

Contents

Acknowledgements

This is a book about a showbusiness paradox – an enduring individual in a flash-in-the-pan world. He comes into millions of homes on a regular basis and yet gives away little of himself. He remains a private person, drawing a sharp line between the personal and the professional. The key to this book was decoding the art to discover where the artist came in.

At times during the writing I have felt like a minor character in a particularly Kafkaesque *Blackadder* episode. Just as I thought I had everything worked out Atkinson would slip through my fingers again. Imagine trying to carry an octopus in a string bag. It is fair to say that over the last two years Rowan Atkinson has made me laugh and made me cry. There have been frustrating moments and euphoric moments, both onscreen and off.

Over the last 25 years Rowan Atkinson has created a substantial body of work. He has been involved in the creation of two characters that will certainly outlive him. It is this body of work that this book sets out to examine. The personal is always there, but the professional is very much at the forefront. In this quest to understand something about Atkinson, I have been assisted by a number of people. Some gave interviews off the record. Some gave interviews on the record. Some refused to acknowledge requests for interviews. Some refused to speak when contacted by telephone. Some could not see a problem. Many thanks to those that offered advice and support. The nicest refusal of all undoubtedly came from Griff Rhys Jones.

Other sources include the national UK newspapers and my employers *Time Out*, as well as specialist magazines, particularly *Cult TV*, *Radio Times*, *Broadcast*, *Vox*, *TV Zone* and *Car*. Local publications *The Oxford Mail*, *The Newcastle Journal* and the *Newcastle Evening*

Chronicle also helped me to join the dots. American and Australian publications are credited in the text where quoted directly. The newspaper agency Cutting It Fine was an invaluable saviour when it came to tracking down Atkinsonobilia, as was the British Library, Westminster Reference Library, the National Sound Archive and the British Film Institute. The BFI's ever-enthusiastic Dick Fiddy excelled at delivering soundbites on the state and history of television comedy. *Time Out* magazine's library, run magnificently by Jill Tulip, also turned up some priceless goodies, while HMV in London's Oxford Street filled in the video gaps.

Where books have been quoted they have been acknowledged wherever possible in the relevant places, but the one invaluable reference book that only ever left my desk to accompany me to the toilet was Mark Lewisohn's *Radio Times Guide to TV Comedy*. If a long-forgotten sitcom title threw me, Lewisohn's impeccably accurate and comprehensive tome put me back on track. I started this book before Lewisohn's book came out, but without him I wonder if I would have ever finished it.

Cath Greenwood provided both emotional support and administrative skills while Brandon Robshaw offered wisdom on a regular basis and John Dugdale completed the picture of Oxford in the 1970s. My agent Lisa Eveleigh did what the best agents do, she left me alone when I needed to be left alone and reassured me when I needed reassurance. Trevor Dolby, my editor at Orion, was so full of brilliant ideas I frequently felt that he should be the author.

The greatest and strangest acknowledgement of all, however, has to go to Rowan Atkinson himself. He did not co-operate with the biography. Yet without him it could not have been written. If that is not the ultimate showbusiness paradox I'm a Dutchman.

Bruce Dessau
Amsterdam
May 1999

1

Nobody's Fool

Six identical leather-trimmed tweed jackets, a size too small, are hanging up on a rail in the sunshine. Twelve Marks and Spencers shirts hang next to them. On the ground is a line of black brogues. There are umpteen pairs of socks with a Winnie the Pooh logo on them. The scene is California. The weather, naturally, is hot, although it has been changeable. But whatever the weather, who on earth would wear clothes like these?

The answer is probably nobody on earth. Maybe on some distant planet where they worship Mr Bean everybody dresses like this. Maybe to them it seems perfectly normal to strut around Venice Beach resembling a deputy English teacher at some minor public school in the 1980s, while bronzed figures rollerblade past. Maybe, in fact, out there somewhere is a whole planet populated by Mr Beans. Maybe the reason he has such difficulty fitting in is because he does not come from round these parts. Maybe, as the opening title sequence to his television show has often hinted, Mr Bean has been sent down to earth, just like the *Star Trek* crew get beamed down to various planets.

Having arrived though, he is not always Mr Bean. Sometimes he seems to use the name of Rowan Atkinson, and to blend in he dresses rather better. The question is, what has this alien been doing among us? Why does he visit our living rooms each night in a little box? Is he trying to take us over?

There is no shortage of strange people in California; it attracts oddballs like a magnet. It is easy to find – go west across America and then stop before you topple into the Pacific – less easy to make sense of. And yet people have always flocked there. An average of 320 days of sunshine a year is a pretty good selling point, but if you stay out in it too long you might just become even nuttier than when you first arrived. Early settlers used to prospect for gold; more recent ones seek their fortune in Hollywood.

Some try to explain the California phenomenon; they say it's as if America has been tipped on one side and all the fruitcakes have slid down into the south-western corner. But back in late 1996 on Venice Beach, a place where oddballs are a dime a dozen, one figure stood out among the assorted cyclists, joggers, rollerbladers and muscle-bound hunks in trunks the size of postage stamps. You couldn't miss him – while everyone else was sporting lycra and muscles the size of a small British county, Atkinson was wearing a tweed jacket and getting into difficulties with a skateboard. It was Mr Bean, or rather Rowan Atkinson, filming the first Mr Bean movie.

Mel Smith, cigar close at hand when draconian health regulations allowed it, was directing the scene. Frequently fans had to be eased out of shot. It could be tough going. America had embraced Rowan Atkinson. This didn't come as a surprise; what did come as a surprise was that it took them so long. Atkinson had been a top billing star for nearly two decades in Britain, having created not one, but two memorable long-lasting franchises. America, after some false starts, had finally found a place in its heart for the quintessential modern clown.

But if you want to understand how Atkinson got into this enviable position, the answers are closer to home. Rowan Atkinson's roots are a world away from south-west America, in the north-eastern corner of England. It might be easy to forget, given his Home Counties casual clothing and locationless accent – well, not completely locationless, you can find lots of people who speak like him in the upper echelons of the civil service and the BBC – but Rowan Atkinson is Geordie. The accent, he told Sarah Ward on Capital Radio in 1981, had been 'thrashed out'. The River Tyne might not be coursing through Rowan Atkinson's veins, but the region had undoubtedly left its mark. You just have to look a little harder to uncover it. And when you do, you will find that Rowan Atkinson is not the first member of his family to find fame and fortune on the other side of the Atlantic.

Rowan Sebastian Atkinson was born in a nursing home in Gosforth on 6 January 1955. His father, Eric Atkinson, was a gentleman farmer; his mother was Ella Atkinson. They lived in Stocksfield, one of the swisher parts of the north-east – some bright spark once dubbed it 'the Bel Air of Newcastle' and the epithet stuck – and used to commute down the A68 to Hole Row Farm, 12 miles south-west of Newcastle, overlooked by Consett steelworks. It was a pretty spectacular spread, a 400-acre beef, dairy and arable farm on both sides of the Derwent Valley.

The family was a prosperous one, thanks, in no small part, to Rowan Atkinson's paternal grandfather, Edward Atkinson. He had been one of the early settlers in Saskatchewan in western Canada, where he bought 200 acres of land for $6. He farmed the land for a decade before returning to the north-east of England. Once there, his entrepreneurial spirit flourished and his investments always seemed to make a profit. His farm was productive and he had a fruit wholesale business, but he was always prepared to diversify. There was a brisk charabanc business that bussed people around. And then there was property. But Edward Atkinson had seen the future. He realized that mass entertainment was coming. Shrewdly he invested in the entertainment boom in the early part of the century, opening up theatres and cinemas. By spreading his interests around, he even thrived during the Depression. By a quirk of comedy fate, one of his cinemas was managed by the father of Stan Laurel – another north-eastern comic icon who made it big in Hollywood.

By the time Edward's son, Eric Atkinson, was ready to start a family, after studying at Oxford, marrying and learning the family business, money was not a problem. Rowan was the youngest of three boys. Rodney was born in March 1948; Rupert was born in 1950. The third 'R', Rowan, was substantially younger, but he quickly learnt how to muck in. In the summer holidays they all helped with the harvest and cleaned out the barns, which would be swarming with field mice. According to Rodney, quoted in the *Daily Mail* in February 1998, even when Rowan was only about five he would happily squash them with a spade, or 'whatever was handy'.

The family's roots may have been in the north of England – Atkinson was a local derivative of 'Adam's Son' and there were references to Atkinsons in the area over 700 years ago – but Rowan was a decidedly Gaelic name, coming from Ruadhan, a colloquial version of the Irish word for red. Just to confuse things further, his middle name could be traced back to a character in Shakespeare's *Twelfth Night* – one of his farce-like comedies. There was as much logic as sentiment to giving him the name of Sebastian. Rowan had been born on the twelfth night after Christmas.

Life was comfortable for the Atkinsons, but not without the kind of character-building privations that were considered normal for the middle to upper middle classes in the 50s and 60s. At home there was no television. The emphasis was placed on academic advancement. Pre-prep school would be followed by prep school, then public school, then university. Rowan's path had already been set out for him by Rodney and Rupert: St Elizabeth's in Stocksfield, the Chorister School in Durham when he was eight, and finally boarding at St Bees in Cumbria on the coast. He barely had his own identity. Inevitably he became known among masters simply as Atkinson Three. As it would turn out, classmates had rather more personal epithets for this strange-looking boy.

And there was no getting away from the fact that he looked strange. While his brothers had relatively normal Caucasian complexions, Rowan's skin was of a more unusual hue. Some might have even said it was greenish. Top this off with a larger than average nose and you have someone strange, someone who does not quite seem right. It was as if Rodney or Rupert had been photocopied and then that copy had been photocopied and so on a number of times until the quality of the reproduction started to deteriorate. It was still recognizable but a number of stages beyond the original. There was something alien about Rowan Atkinson's appearance.

As his brothers headed for predictable careers in business and finance, it looked as if Rowan's fate would be to take over Hole Row Farm. The young boy with the unruly mop of black hair and the unearthly visage was resigned to his inheritance, as he went through the education system. But he also had extra-curricular interests. At St Elizabeth's in Stocksfield he first acted in plays. The drama continued and whenever he returned home from Durham Chorister School, what he saw made him think about his future. Every now and again he would wander around the grounds of the farm in the shadow of the nearby slag heaps and notice a sinister red dust. Was this what he wanted to be covered in for the next 50 years? But there were avenues of escape. Without a television at home, the theatre and cinema were an inevitable draw.

When he was nine he was taken to see comic actor Terry Scott in pantomime at Newcastle's Theatre Royal. But cinema was to become his real love. The Empire Theatre in Consett was one of his grandfather's chain, and Rowan would see the latest films there. He would also visit his grandfather at home and watch television there. But showbusiness still never seemed a means of avoiding his middle-class fate. It just was not how people like him earned their money. There was something magical, yet foreign about showbusiness. Television might as well have been shot down to earth on a beam of light from another planet. As a budding scientist he knew this was not the case, but the strange flickering images were light-years away from his own life. He later recalled that 'acting was a strange job. Television was something people in the south did.'

As Atkinson's adolescence progressed, however, there weren't initially that many outward signs of future fame. He appeared in plays, but so did many of his peers at Chorister School, a place staffed by the kind of vicars and eccentric clergymen who would help to shape Atkinson's uniquely bizarre portrayals of the priesthood. Canon John Grove, Atkinson's headmaster at the time, remembers the nascent clown as a regular performer in plays, most notably, George Bernard Shaw's *Saint Joan* in 1966 when Atkinson of Class 5B was still only 11. He was cast as the rather fey Dauphin, and judging by parts of Shaw's description of the character, it could almost have been a dry run for a prototypical Mr Bean: 'He is a poor creature physically ... the expression of a young dog, accustomed to be kicked, yet incorrigible and irrepressible. Just at present he is excited, like a child with a new toy.' The funny thing is that one might have imagined the Dauphin – the future King Charles VII – to be a child in this play. In fact, Shaw points out that he is 26. This was the one contrast: where Bean would be a small child trapped inside a man's body, in this production Atkinson was a boy playing a man – who had the demeanour of a small child.

Others came to see the production, and Atkinson was certainly beginning to make an impression. According to another master, Dr Brian Crosby, one aspect of Atkinson's performance stuck out in particular: 'There was an interesting comment from an English master from St Pauls who came up to review the play. He said that Atkinson was splendid in the petulant role but tended to look a bit bored if he wasn't actually speaking.'

Dr Crosby, a doctor of musicology, used to teach Atkinson mathematics, but at that stage Atkinson didn't seem to shown any particular scientific promise, nor did he stand out. According to Dr Crosby: 'He is somebody I don't really remember much about at all, except that he was one of three brothers whose Christian names all began with the letter R. He was the youngest, but the problem was remembering what order they came in.'

Dr Crosby can recall only one notable Atkinson misdemeanour, and he is not actually sure which of the two younger brothers was the culprit. The story has, however, been immortalized as the Fire Practice Incident. 'During fire practice boarders used to have to go across the cathedral precincts to the Deanery, which was the assembly point. When we did a roll-call Atkinson wasn't there, so I went back and had a look for him and found him fast asleep in bed. His dorm monitor assured me that he had been the last out of the room and that by then Atkinson had already left. We can only assume he got as far as the toilets and then went back to bed.'

Others had better, more significant memories of Atkinson. Drama teacher Cyril Watson called him 'odd', according to the *Daily Mirror* of 6 August 1997. In the same feature headmaster Canon John Grove recalled Atkinson as 'shy with a slight stutter and a slightly rubbery face just like the one he has now ... he had a cheeky sense of humour and always got his own way.'

Durham Chorister was a strict, traditional prep school, which provided the groundwork for a conventional public-school education and from there university and a career in one of the professions. It was in the heart of the city but was fortunate to have its own games fields a short walk away. Atkinson, however, wasn't a great one for games, which helps to explain why Dr Crosby had such a faint memory of young Rowan: 'If he had been keen on rugby or cricket or athletics I would have remembered that. I'm afraid he made no impression on me.' It was Rowan's swarthy, unearthly appearance that stuck out more than his personality.

Atkinson Three seemed more interested in the gardening club, run by Roger Kirkham, than in games. Perhaps this was in preparation for taking over Hole Row Farm; perhaps it was just his way of avoiding anything too physically demanding. Apart from Tony Blair, who was a couple of years ahead of Atkinson, the only other notable alumnus from that period is James Fenton, the writer and critic and now a poetry professor at Oxford. Even though Atkinson's family lived only about ten miles away, Rowan was a full-time boarder who was allowed only four or five home leaves each term. It was a disciplined life that taught a child all about independence. It left its mark.

It has become a cliché in comedy biographies to pinpoint pivotal events in the comedian's early life. The usual cliché trotted out is that the comic was bullied and used jokes to deflect punches like some kind of quick-witted verbal Superman. In Atkinson's case there seems to be little evidence that he was picked on any more than any other gawky adolescent. His comic genius was simply in there waiting to come out. It did not need to be kicked out of him. It just emerged down a flight of stairs in the changing rooms when he was about 11. Jumping up and down, pulling faces, he entertained his classmates and found the ensuing laughter not unsatisfying. It is unclear, however, how much he had to be coaxed into this impromptu early gig and how much he set out to get the attention. It really seemed to be mainly for his own benefit. Either way though, the event was an undoubted success and it established Atkinson as a character at school. This was his party trick and it helped to get him known – not that he seemed to crave fame; he was a simple, self-contained child who didn't really need a lot of friends and seemed to garner the most fun from amusing himself.

Occasionally the mimicry would be spotted by a member of the staff. In August 1997 Atkinson's art teacher Margaret Till told the *Daily Mail*: 'I remember once coming to the art class and finding a small, funny-looking brown-haired boy standing at my desk and being me, much to the amusement of his classmates.' If this sort of behaviour made Rowan quietly notorious at school, his family was rather more dismissive of this new habit, assuming it was just a phase he was going through.

In 1968 by the age of 13 he had attained a degree of academic excellence and won a modest scholarship, known as an exhibition, worth £75 a year, to St Bees, an expensive public school on the bleak, windswept west Cumbrian coast, not that far from Sellafield Nuclear

Power Station. There was no doubting that St Bees was a school with history behind it. It had been founded way back in 1583, motto, 'await the lord!'

There was still little about Atkinson Three that marked him out for future greatness. Nor was St Bees a school with a great history of creating famous people. The comic character actor Bryan Pringle was an old St Beghian; that was about the extent of the school's contact with the performing arts. Luckily there were changes afoot in the Atkinson household that would point him in the right direction. When Rowan Atkinson was approaching 15, his parents finally acquired a television. It was pretty good timing. It was the late 60s and BBC comedy was at its peak. There were acutely scripted sitcoms such as *Steptoe and Son* and *Till Death Us Do Part* and the inspirational ensemble brilliance of *Dad's Army*. If there wasn't much humour to inspire him at home, there was plenty on the box.

One comic stood head and shoulders about the others for the young Atkinson, in both a literal and a metaphorical sense. The gangly John Cleese had already made his televisual mark on *The Frost Report*, where he would invariably be cast as the upper-class bowler-hatted gent in satirical pieces. Atkinson, however, had come across him on the radio, listening to *I'm Sorry I'll Read That Again*, the anarchic radio show that was a precursor of *Python*'s brand of bombastic madness. *I'm Sorry* had started out on the Home Service in 1964 before moving to the new-fangled Radio 4 in 1968. Atkinson was riveted by the sound and fury of Cleese even before pictures came along.

Monty Python's Flying Circus started just as the Atkinson household plugged in their first television. Cleese's resident toff from *The Frost Report* continued, although there was a more surreal spin to it now. He might be playing a tuxedoed BBC announcer, but he would be behind a desk in a zoo or in a swamp. He might be an army officer, but he would be holding a fish. Most famously, he was a civil servant. He might have really been a civil servant in a parallel universe, but he would never have been employed by the Ministry of Silly Walks. Maybe in Cleese, Atkinson saw a potential comedy role model for someone from the middle classes. Cleese proved you could be a comedy superstar with received pronunciation and without spending your formative years slogging around the working-men's clubs in the north of England.

Atkinson developed an obligatory interest in *Monty Python*, but by the early 70s *Python* was virtually a compulsory subject at British public schools, so it hardly made him unique. But it did have a huge impact on him. When, that is, he was able to watch it. The school seemed to do its best to isolate its pupils from popular culture. Getting information from the outside world was rather similar to the way the Russians managed to obtain Western information under communism. Records and music were the main sources of inspiration for the young boys, who would huddle together, trying to avoid the wind, at the side of the school's red sandstone buildings, discussing the relative merits of Cream, Captain Beefheart and The Grateful Dead.

A decade later Atkinson would be invited to record an audio version of *Tom Brown's Schooldays*. The similarities between Rugby in the nineteenth century and St Bees in the 1960s may have been few and far between, but the British public-school experience is a distinctive, character forming one, and one that had a lasting effect on Atkinson. Like Rugby in Tom Brown's days, there were certainly privations that went with attendance of St Bees. The simple fact that the school was so geographically isolated made it seem cut off from civilization. Fell walking and long-distance running were often imposed as punishments. Rowan became something of a loner, internalizing his thoughts as a way of coping with the regime.

St Bees may have been a seaside town – and it did have its sunny days – but the tourist trade seemed to have passed it by. It was more like a scenic picture-postcard village, complete with green fields and grass-chomping sheep. For a quiet, contemplative boy like Atkinson, even though he was following the family tradition and his two older brothers to the school, there was an all-pervasive sense of isolation about the area. The school was rather like a production line, turned on some time in the middle of the century to produce captains of industry. They went in as interchangeable children and emerged as identikit future members of the establishment.

Then again, Atkinson did stand out in a crowd. It was no surprise that at the school he started to attract nicknames. By his early teens his appearance marked him out. His features became more prominent; his eyes bulged, his ears stuck out and his lips and nose seemed to go on for ever. His nostrils seemed wider than the Mersey Tunnel. Gone was the tamed mane of black hair that had been trimmed back in his pre-teens, replaced by a proverbial floor-mop. It was as if puberty was making him mutate into a comic character. Or maybe it had something to do with the fact that St Bees was in such close proximity to the nuclear power station that in 1957, when known as Windscale, had been at the centre of a notorious disaster. There had been worries about radiation seeping out. Whatever the reasons for his complexion, it earned Atkinson a collection of affectionate nicknames – Dopie, Zoonie, Moonman, Green Man and Gruman – stemming from the fact that his friends felt that he looked like an alien.

Despite that early burst of natural comedy in the changing rooms, adolescence seemed to push any showbusiness aspirations into the background. There were exams to pass and qualifications to acquire. He also showed hitherto untapped sporting prowess of sorts, becoming reasonably proficient with a rifle. In the past he had shown little interest in rugby: 'It was as if the touch line was the only part of the field that he was at all prepared to commit himself to,' remembers contemporary Richard McCaw. And of course, it simply wasn't done for someone from his class to become a comedian. On the other hand, though, there were occasional flashes when he seemed to sense his destiny. With a penchant for sciences he ended up on the technical team for a school play one year. But as he recalled in *The Observer* in 1984: 'I remember looking down from the lighting gantry onto the stage during the performance and thinking, I've made the wrong decision, I'd prefer to be down there.'

But he was torn between performing and tinkering. He was always fascinated by electrical science and would often be spotted wandering around the school with a screwdriver sticking out of his blazer pocket. He was also very good at sorting out problems. He could often be found adjusting the sound in the Memorial Hall; he would play Led Zeppelin's *Stairway to Heaven* over the speakers to get the correct levels.

The theatre still seemed to take second place to making mischief. Atkinson became one of those pupils who cleverly manages to juggle playfulness and academic achievement. He was an active member of the school, running the St Bees Film Society with Paddy Rickerby and their physics master for two years. In 1981, Atkinson told journalist Tony Bilbow how the club was run: 'no democracy whatsoever'. They decided what films the rest of the school could see and that was all there was to it. They had the keys to the projector room, so Atkinson and co would privately screen their favourite films many times during the three-day rental period. One particular favourite was *Monsieur Hulot's Holiday*, starring the gangly, lanky, perpetually pipe-smoking French physical comic Jacques Tati. The mercurial French actor played an accident-prone bachelor whose arrival at the seaside prompts a succession of calamities for those around him. There was very little dialogue in a typical Tati film – the narrative would be driven by his actions and the humour created by their consequences.

As the Film Society's projectionist, Atkinson was able to view his selections at his leisure. Having heard how good *Monsieur Hulot's Holiday* was, he watched it on the Saturday morning before the club screening. The friends then staged another private screening in the afternoon before the evening's school showing. Atkinson watched *Monsieur Hulot's Holiday* another four times on the Sunday, a total of seven times in all. By Monday morning, hollow-eyed, he knew every one of Tati's twitches and tics off by heart. He was particularly keen on the way Tati interacted with inanimate and even invisible objects. When he arrives at his holiday destination, for instance, he elaborately steps over a suitcase that is no longer by the door. The impressionable schoolboy loved succinct, simple yet intelligent moments like this.

Atkinson's other extra-curricular activities were less productive. Although he later saw the error of his ways and gave up tobacco in adulthood, as a teenager he was a typically furtive school smoker. Except that he had a habit of getting caught. Retribution was swift and severe – a £1-fine paid to the Marie Curie Cancer Memorial Fund – and in one week, legend has it, Atkinson was caught more times than anybody else.

Tough rituals were part of the public school way of life – get the dirty work over with now because when you are an adult you will be employing others to do it for you. One of the toughest tasks for Atkinson was the 24-hour exercise at summer camp when as a member of the cadet force he had to stand on the rainy Cumbrian moors in a trench on guard duty from 8pm to 2am. After one hour he was soaked through. After two he was standing in a foot of water. His only solace was a non-filter Park Drive cigarette, but he couldn't light that because his Swan Vesta matches were soaked through.

The last couple of years at St Bees saw a period of rebellion, but it was a nice, productive kind of rebellion. He was capable of great things but he had to be provoked to achieve them. His headmaster, Geoffrey Lees, bet Atkinson that he wouldn't get an English O-level, but this only provoked the pupil to pass with flying colours. The result was a mutual respect between them.

Anecdotes about his school days certainly suggest that Atkinson did have a tendency to be involved in tricks although not necessarily as the ringleader. There was one master with whom Rowan and his friends were particularly annoyed. According to later stories they got their revenge by teaching the teacher's toddler how to say 'fuck off'. It was not malicious, just an ingenious schoolboy prank, already revealing a sense of humour that was more about sophisticated cunning plans than rudimentary custard pies. To this day there is an urban myth at St Bees that this budding Guy Fawkes once tried to blow up the school pavilion. A fanciful legend but it means that his name lives on.

As an adult, Atkinson was unapologetic about the dark side of his schooldays because he didn't feel he had done anything wrong: 'I never meant any harm or offence to anyone – I was just trying to enjoy myself. Because, make no mistake, life is short.' A contemporary described him as being 'the one who is always kept behind after lessons and gets his revenge by writing scurrilous verse in Latin about the master who kept him in'.

Much of this bad behaviour was prompted by Atkinson's relationship with the housemaster of Foundation North, a strict teacher of the old school who wanted people to jump when he barked. Atkinson would later find these incidents and others increasingly amusing. Schooldays had taken on that inevitable rosy glow of nostalgia, and as an adult he said that gathering with old friends could 'make me laugh more than anything else in the world'. Memories of being forced to eat large plates of plain macaroni and unfluffy mashed potato suddenly seemed more hilarious than ever.

Yet despite the misdemeanours and the struggles with authority, there was one area where Atkinson seemed to feel really at home.

That experience in the lighting gantry had made him change direction and he started to perform in more school dramas. Two early roles stood out. He played the sinister head waiter Eisenring in *The Fire Raisers* by Max Frisch and Mephistopheles in Christopher Marlowe's *Doctor Faustus*. There was a reticence about being in the limelight that still lingers today, but when he did take part in school drama he always ended up as the star of the show and his contributions were eagerly anticipated.

Chris Robson was Atkinson's A-level physics master at St Bees and he endorses Dr Brian Crosby's assessment of Rowan Atkinson's academic potential as well as his social skills: 'In class he was very middle of the road. There was nothing outstanding about him. I didn't expect him to become a fantastic scientist. And he was a quiet lad, who walked his own path.' Robson remembers Atkinson's school drama career much more vividly: 'But when he walked onstage he was exceptional.' Even an incipient stammer vanished whenever the young Atkinson stepped onto the stage. It was the darker roles that seemed to suit him. In *Doctor Faustus*, he was Mephistopheles, the devil who made a pact with the doctor, giving him a decade of untold wishes in return for his soul. In *The Fire Raisers*, an allegory about the rise of fascism, he played an evil man who burnt people's houses down. A review from the 1970 school magazine singled out Atkinson's performance for particular praise: 'R. S. Atkinson found the ideal part in Eisenring, always in control of the situation from the moment he entered, smiling faintly as if at a secret joke.'

Nearly 30 years on, Chris Robson can still clearly remember Atkinson's Mephistopheles. 'There's no doubt about that, it was quite extraordinary. The final scene between Mephistopheles and Faustus, where Faustus is called back because he has had his ten years and now has to go to hell is terrifying. That was Rowan in his frightening mode. As a 14-year-old it was extraordinary.' According to the local magazine *Cumbrian Life*, the headmaster had remarked at the time: 'I have seen no better performance.' Atkinson was still only a junior and yet had been cast in the kind of major part a sixth former would have usually had.

Surprisingly, given his later achievements, there was little evidence of Atkinson's comic talents. But there was evidence of great stage presence. His skill at portraying evil incarnate was, says Robson, 'riveting'. In *The Fire Raisers*, Atkinson was particularly chilling, recalls Robson. 'Rowan came on and stood in the middle of the stage. The whole thing reeked of evil. There was a feeling that the whole place was going to go up in a blaze.' Richard McCaw also recalls the performance and noted the way Atkinson's personality changed in front of an audience: 'He was absolutely extraordinary as the arsonist. He took about half a minute to take his white gloves off. Absolutely mesmerizing. He was not a particularly noticeable character before he started acting, but onstage something changed.' According to Robson, Atkinson could encapsulate unquantifiable terror with the slightest gesture. 'He simply put his finger out across the stage and had a chalky white face and wiggled the very end of his finger and it was a moment of sheer horror. He was very good at that sort of thing. He didn't need to wear horns. That would have destroyed it, he just needed to move his little finger. There was a guy there who could transform a stage with his presence.'

Each summer play seemed to propel Atkinson further into the limelight; after *Doctor Faustus* and *The Fire Raisers*, the English master, Richard Elgood, took *We Bombed in New Haven* by Joseph Heller to the Edinburgh Festival Fringe. In this satire on militarism inspired by the Vietnam War, Atkinson played Captain Starkey. 'The most extraordinary thing was in *We Bombed in New Haven*,' remembers Richard McCaw. 'Rowan played the controller, a quiet, shy character who had to have this full-blown breakdown each night. I never realised he had that depth of tragedy and emotion in him.' The production went to Edinburgh's Lauriston Hall, but Atkinson's early impressions of the Festival didn't seem to be so much about the tradition of comedy as about the road layout. In a book about the Edinburgh Festival, *Sore Throats and Overdrafts* (Precedent, 1988), Atkinson told the author Michael Dale, who was Fringe Administrator from 1982 until Mhairi Mackenzie-Robinson took over in 1986, about his early memories: 'I remembered the traffic lights most: how long they took to change.' He seemed fascinated by the city's one-way systems, which meant that everything was 'extremely primitive'. He also recalled the Fringe reception where he saw people 'wandering around in white masks holding spoons in front of them trying to attract the media's attention'. This was the 70s, after all.

Despite his unassuming exterior in class, Atkinson clearly knew where his skills lay, and while he didn't channel his energies into comedy, his performing skills became widely known and teachers encouraged him. There was some comedy input too. As well as discovering Jacques Tati at school, at the age of 16 he also came across a P. G. Wodehouse book, *Uncle Fred in the Springtime*, and devoured it, developing a life-long fondness for the stylish, typically English writer.

By the time he left St Bees in 1972, Atkinson seemed to have got over his rebelliousness and had become a valuable member of the school, notching up achievements in numerous areas, including a stint as Captain of Shooting, although some memories of his military record seem to cast doubt on this. Alan Francis, his Cadet Corps Commander, recalled Atkinson's brief uniformed career in *Cumbrian Life* and claimed some responsibility for his future performances: 'He was a particularly inefficient Lance Corporal and some of his sketches were based on me. Let's say he was less than concentrated – not the military type. But a very pleasant shambles.'

Atkinson also become a valuable member of the choir. His singing was not great but his organizational skills and enthusiasm made him the right person for the job of choir secretary. But he would still be remembered simply for his acting talent. When he left with A-levels in pure and applied maths and physics, the masters were divided. Some thought that was the end of his performing life and he would now gain further qualifications before a career in the sciences. Others who had seen him onstage, such as Chris Robson, felt he would end up in the arts: 'When he left we thought, well he's probably going to end up on the stage.' It seemed the most natural progression for this most unnatural teenager. When he was about to leave the school, he finally received a glowing endorsement from his headmaster, Geoffrey Lees, who was used to sending his charges off towards careers in business and the city. In Atkinson's case, however, he revealed that he had been quietly impressed by the young man's comic skills, remarking that 'I have never recommended to anyone that they should take up a career in the entertainment industry, but it would seem silly for you, Atkinson, not at least to try.'

The teenager, on the other hand, seemed less committed than those who had seen him perform. Many years later he told *Woman's*

World about his lack of focus: 'I didn't know quite what I wanted to do when I left. But I certainly didn't have very high expectations of the future.' What he did know was that he would follow his brothers once again – this time to Newcastle University. But differences were emerging. Rodney had studied German and Norwegian; Rupert did metallurgy. Rowan won a place to study electrical engineering. However, there was a sign of his breaking away; he did briefly consider a drama course in Portsmouth, albeit concentrating on the technical side. He also thought that maybe his skills would be best suited to the job of cameraman. This interest in technical pursuits would stay with him. Even after graduating from Newcastle he would approach the BBC about vacation work as an engineer.

Beyond the school gates his interests had always veered towards the scientific. At home and on the farm he would spend hours tinkering with machinery and polishing tractors. He could barely wait until he was old enough to drive them. Eventually he got his first taste of speed behind the wheel, and while it might not have been up to Grand Prix standards, even 18mph can feel like 180mph when you are the person with your foot on the tractor's accelerator. Even before he was old enough to take his driving test he had learnt about motor mechanics by taking apart his mother's old Morris Minor, which she didn't want any more. It had done only 35,000 miles but the wheel kept sticking into the front wheel arch. Having fixed it, Atkinson would spend hours tootling around his family's private land in it. After a couple of years he even customized it by crow-barring the wings off. One by one he would pull the parts off until it was little more than a chassis, an engine and some seats. It was his way of turning something off the production line into something distinctively his – in a similar fashion he would later strip down comedy to its basic components when he created Mr Bean. He absolutely loved cars. One half-term his father took him down to London to the Motor Show as a treat. The young boy saw the latest Ferrari and maybe fell in love for the first time.

Atkinson finally passed his driving test on the third attempt. Each time he apparently failed for the same reason – not paying due care and attention to other road users. It was said that he had been treating other drivers as if they were escaped sheep.

In October 1972, he set off for Newcastle University to study for a

B.Sc. in electrical engineering. Once again, his performing ambitions appeared to have taken a back seat to his scientific pursuits. He would still take part in revues, but he didn't seem to be trying to do anything special with his very special talents. Instead he would just do old comedy routines at his hall of residence, Henderson Hall, remarking that there wasn't much point trying to come up with new material when there were 'the classics' to perform.

In the middle of his undergraduate years he returned to St Bees, not as the nascent star but as the aspiring boffin. Synthesizers were just emerging, and Rowan brought one along and gave a talk to the school's science society. 'Everybody ooh and aahed,' recalls Chris Robson, but it was at the scientific gizmo, not the visitor. 'I said to him, "I always thought you'd end up on the professional stage," and he said, "Well it hasn't worked out like that." It was as if he said, "OK, that's the sort of thing you do at school but you don't do it at university." It seemed as if he was knuckling down to a science career.'

Atkinson's creative energies went into his studies. When he graduated with an upper second in the summer of 1975 he was still only 20 years old. Rumour had it that in some papers he had gained the highest marks in his year. But for Rowan, the future remained uncertain. There was the prospect of running his father's farm in the long run, so maybe he ought to get some practical experience in the real world. Then there was the enticement of even further education after the further education of Newcastle University. It was a tough call and one that Rowan wasn't about to make with much ease.

Besides, there was a feeling of change in the air. Maybe farming was not the future. North-eastern industry would be decimated by economic decline. Things might have remained comfortable at home in Meadowfield Road, but away from the affluent suburbs, the fault lines of Britain were shifting. Both Atkinson and the place of his birth were about to undergo a seismic change. It was the mid-1970s. The country was in the economic doldrums, with strikes and working-to-rule dominating British industry and paving the way for Margaret Thatcher's election and subsequent revolution in 1979. Life would never be the same again.

2

The Face That Launched
a Thousand Quips

Instead of finding a job in preparation for taking over the running of his father's farm, Rowan Atkinson opted for a return to academia. It was a decision that dramatically altered the course of his career. He had spent the first 20 years of his life in the north. Now he made the move south. His excellent degree might not have helped him to get a job but it did win him a place at Queen's College, Oxford, where in the autumn of 1975 he embarked upon his research for an M.Sc. in electronic engineering.

Rowan Atkinson was not the first member of his family to study in the city of dreaming spires. His father had been an undergraduate there in the 1930s, when the *Brideshead Revisited* era of student decadence was at its height. This time round things were a little different. There were still plenty of Sloane Rangers and Hooray Henrys quaffing champagne, much as they had always done and always will do, but a typical night out for Atkinson was a cheap curry in one of Oxford's more modest Indian restaurants. Digs were a wire-festooned room in the college grounds and then later a ramshackle shared house on the Woodstock Road. Hardly the high life, although Atkinson was never desperately short of money.

It was the right place and the right time. Or rather, it was nearly the right place at nearly the right time. The pre-eminent seat of learning for aspiring comics was still Cambridge, which could boast John Cleese among its past alumni, and David Baddiel, Emma Thompson and Stephen Fry among its future stars. In the mid-1970s though, there was a move at Oxford to establish something similar to the Cambridge Footlights, which was nearly a hundred years old and well established as the great seed-bed for performing talent.

Many of the people involved in the Oxford Revue in the mid-1970s went on to become major players in British broadcasting, both in front and behind the scenes. Friendships and alliances were formed and still endure. If the Battle of Waterloo was won on the playing fields of Eton, then the battle for countless BAFTAs was won in the Oxford Playhouse bar in the 1970s. Geoffrey Perkins, for instance, was involved in the Revue, before becoming a minor television star as part of BBC2's ensemble sketch show *KYTV*. But when he moved into the production side he became more influential than ever. At the time of writing he is the BBC's Head of Comedy and the producer of Atkinson's *The Thin Blue Line*.

In fact, much of the core of British comedy's movers and shakers were part of the same circle back in the 70s. Jon Plowman, Perkins's senior number at the BBC, was at Oxford at that time. As was Kevin Lygo, who at the time of writing is the Head of Entertainment at Channel Four. Then there were other figures such as Angus Deayton, Phil Pope and Mel Smith. Post-*Python*, the balance of comedy power seemed to be swinging towards Oxford. But this is really only possible to see retrospectively. At the time, the Oxford Revue languished very much in the shadow of the Footlights. That was until Rowan Atkinson became involved.

It took a while to settle in at Oxford, but soon Atkinson landed on his feet. It is said that you spend your first year at university making friends and the next two years shaking them off. Having gone through that experience at Newcastle, Atkinson was fortunate and mature enough to meet like-minded people almost at the first attempt. Following that northern dry run he was now well equipped to get things right first time.

After a first term spent going to classical music and organ recitals, Rowan soon began to meet undergraduates with whom he would form lasting friendships. Until then he had been trying to be funny with old material; now he had the nucleus of a creative team that would stand him in great stead well into his professional career.

One of that team was Richard Curtis, a sandy-haired, bespectacled, alarmingly bright English student at Christ Church, who had previously been head of his house at Harrow. Curtis was unashamedly middle class but he had a rather colourful background. His father,

Tony, had Czechoslovakian roots and had anglicized his name to Curtis to avoid complications. But when Tony Curtis the film star rose to prominence, things became complicated again. The family had moved around, and the young Richard had lived in places as diverse as New Zealand, Manilla, Stockholm, Folkestone and Warrington. Harrow offered him some kind of stability and there he decided he wanted to be one of the Beatles. While waiting for a vacancy to be advertised, however, he did some acting; in the school production of *The Winter's Tale* he was a very good Hermione in a velvet dress. But, when his wig fell off during what should have been a moving death scene, he realized he wasn't cut out for a career onstage.

Still, maybe the Beatles would get back together and they would need a new member. Curtis was absolutely consumed by pop music; in the mid-1970s his passion was for Linda Ronstadt and Paul Simon. Inevitably he, like Atkinson, was well schooled in *Python* lore. His good looks actually seemed to count against him when it came to acting; when he wasn't being cast as a woman he was cast in bland roles. He decided the only way to appear onstage as someone he wanted to be was to write comedy material himself. He seemed able to do it instinctively, and teaming up with Rowan was the missing piece in the jigsaw.

Atkinson, for his part, needed a co-writer to push him in the right directions. It had been partly the lack of decent original writing that had curtailed his performances while studying at Newcastle. Things came to a head in the summer of 1975 when he performed at the Edinburgh Festival. He had just left Newcastle and was working with the Dundee University Theatre Group, playing Angelo in *Measure for Measure*. However, Atkinson had never been keen on performing Shakespeare; he even had little enthusiasm for the comic characters. In 1988 he told the *Newcastle Evening Chronicle* how hard the bard was: 'It takes hell of a lot of time and a lot of effort to get even the most willing audience to smile at someone like Touchstone (and I speak from bitter experience)'. But by now he was getting the hang of Edinburgh. He knew you had to work hard to make a trip pay, so he was also doing a lunch-time revue at the Roxburgh Reading Room. Only about 13 people turned up and by his own admission the show was 'diabolical', consisting largely of second-rate showbiz impressions of contemporary figures such as Denis Healey. It was patently clear that Rowan was in dire need of another creative talent who could focus his abilities. By 1976, Richard Curtis seemed to be the perfect foil.

Atkinson met Richard Curtis through a notice in a student newspaper asking for like-minded wits to get together and write sketches. They had sat together at a script-writing conference, but Atkinson did not seem inclined to say very much. In fact he was silent. Curtis thought he was so unobtrusive when they were gathered in a room that he likened him to a cushion. When it was Atkinson's turn to speak, however, it turned out that he had been doing some thinking. Curtis recalls Atkinson coming out with two perfectly formed visual sketches.

Underneath the quiet exterior there was clearly a need to perform. Atkinson later recalled that 'there was something inside me crying to get out.' Going to Oxford had had as much to do with getting noticed onstage as with electronic engineering. He was well aware that it was the place where talent scouts came, and if he wanted to be spotted it was the place to perform. He calculated, in suitably scientific fashion, that 50 per cent of his reason for going there was to see if he could try to get on in showbusiness. And yet he hadn't really done much comedy since his days as a grimacing pre-adolescent. It was only when he was 21, and was suddenly asked to do something funny for the Revue at the Oxford Playhouse, that he discovered his face.

While other students mounted their own plays and booked rehearsal rooms with frantic enthusiasm, Atkinson's big break was more modest, though incredibly swift. One afternoon Atkinson saw an advert pinned to a board asking for people to audition for a sketch show at the Oxford Playhouse that Easter. This was no road-to-Damascus moment; he simply thought he would have a go. But having landed a short spot he then realized he had to produce something to perform at short notice. It was a Wednesday and the performance was on the Sunday. He had never really written any comedy before. Instead of sweating over a typewriter, he came up with something in front of the mirror – pulling faces. It was a silent, slightly surreal character, recalling those funny expressions he used to pull in the school changing-rooms as an 11-year-old, before adolescent inhibitions took hold.

It was the first time he had done it for many years and he was quite amazed at the looks he could achieve.

In the north of England there are annual gurning competitions where locals stick their heads inside a horse's collar and pull ugly faces, but Atkinson was doing something completely different. Perhaps this was the reason his comedy at Newcastle had been so unoriginal – it wasn't just the lack of his own words, he hadn't yet found his own face. Now that he did it and got a laugh he realized why he hadn't done it for so long. It was the embarrassment factor; as he said many years later in *The Daily Telegraph*. 'I don't think it was a time when people who pulled faces were admired.' Not surprisingly, given his ambivalent feelings about this unique gift, he would spend as much of his career fleeing from his face as thriving on its extraordinary elasticity. It would be nearly a decade and a half before this face was christened Mr Bean, but the germ of the idea had been hatched.

He was soon making his name, however, as a solo performer in sketches. While Richard Curtis wrote his more verbal passages, Atkinson was developing his own mime work: 'In one piece he came onstage wearing a black skin-tight leotard, I think, with tights,' recalls a contemporary who saw an early show. 'He came slowly and shyly to the front of the stage, approached a member of the audience and was about to offer them something before seeming to become nervous and pulling back. He did this repeatedly and it was hilarious. If anybody else had done it, it wouldn't have been funny at all, but Rowan was clearly uniquely gifted.' Fellow student Doug Lucie was in the cast of the Oxford Revue that included this sketch and 20 years on still hasn't seen anything like it. 'It wasn't just the nature of Atkinson's performance though; it was also the fact that he was head and shoulders above everybody else in terms of scope and ambition.'

The Oxford Revue was still a fairly shaky proposition, remembers Lucie, but Atkinson revolutionized it: 'I hesitate to call it a show. It was a Sunday night revue thing and he already had a huge enormous reputation. I'd never met him before and on the night of the dress rehearsals out came this bloke in a pair of pyjamas (the leotard came later) with his hands all sort of gnarled, his hair, which was long and bushy at the time, all teased up like something out of the film *Eraserhead*. He had an envelope between his fingers and he went out onstage and just stood there for 15 minutes and didn't say a word of understandable English. He just offered the letter and gibbered. It was one of the most awesome things I've ever seen.'

To Lucie it wasn't just funny, it was also rather disturbing: 'It was frightening. The other thing is that we had been told he had a background in something to do with mental health so there was talk about whether he was mad or whether he had just been around mental patients. Later on he started doing other sketches that he has done since, such as shaving all over his face with the razor, and he started doing things with Helen Atkinson Wood (no relation) and Tim McInnerny. With the writing of Richard things really took off, but for me he never did anything better than that first sketch at the Oxford Playhouse.'

Richard Sparks was a few years ahead of Atkinson. He recalls how the Oxford Revue began to gather momentum in the run-up to Rowan's arrival. 'By the time Rowan came along it had been going a few years but was nowhere near as well established as the Footlights. In the early 70s it got a better profile, though the year I was in it, it was appalling. Then Angus Deayton, Phil Pope and some others came along and it got better again, but Rowan was always way above everybody else, even in terms of ambition. You already knew he was going to be bigger than everybody else because he clearly had so much talent.'

Atkinson's involvement pushed the Revue to hitherto unreached heights, confirms Doug Lucie: 'Rowan's first appearance was a beano sort of thing, a glorified party where everyone did their turn. We used to do a showcase once a term, then it splintered a bit with people setting up their own sort of groups. Prior to Rowan the Oxford Revue only really existed for Edinburgh; they might do a Sunday night here and there but after Rowan it was more regular, though it never acquired the same sort of kudos as the Cambridge Footlights.' Very quickly Rowan was outgrowing the Oxford scene, according to Lucie: 'Rowan eventually started to disassociate himself from it and be himself.'

By the time Atkinson came along, there was a framework for his unusual talents. At the same time he was perfectly content to straddle straight drama and comedy, appearing in various plays as well as sketch shows. However, whatever he was in, his approach was the same and it has not changed since: he would work out the mechanics of his part and once perfected, it would be the same in each performance. Even so, his mixture of drama and revue was particularly unusual at the time. Contemporaries such as Philip Franks, who found fame in television's *The Darling Buds of May*, acted in plays but steered clear of anything sketchy. Mel Smith hadn't shown any desire to make people laugh either. He ran the All Oxford Dramatic Society and directed straight plays.

Atkinson managed to do his own thing, never falling into line with what everyone else wanted to do or wanted him to do. The Geoffrey Perkins-era Revue had been a loosely satirical agglomeration, harking back to the anti-establishment japery of *Beyond the Fringe*. In stark contrast, Atkinson was simply a clown, doing material that had minimal topical content and very little political edge to it. It was a strangely apolitical interlude at the university.

Doug Lucie recalls that by the mid-1970s the brief spark of radicalism had been present in Oxford at the beginning of the decade had gone out again: 'Oxford became less political; then three years later the Tories got in and then three years after that everything was different again. Mel Smith was quite a firebrand at Oxford, but I remember a few years later having a row with him in a pub in Camden about politics and theatre and he said something like "I'm not in it for that." ' In some ways Atkinson was the same: the buck stopped at making people laugh.

Lucie recalls how political theatre in the shape of Howard Brenton and David Hare had a brief influence, but it was decidedly short-lived: 'The drama people had been very foppish, all scarves and jackets. It never lost that, but people like myself and Mel Smith tried to shake things up and succeeded a bit, but the atmosphere in the comedy area in particular was that these people weren't out to challenge everything. As far as I remember there was no political comment in anything the Revue ever did and that was my big argument with it. I don't think Rowan was ever very radical, and Richard Curtis was a big softy, although what he did, he did very well indeed. Light entertainment won the battle in the end and I retired gracefully.'

Yet only a handful of years earlier politics was a very important thing at Oxford. As one ex-student there at the time puts it: 'The late

60s didn't happen in Oxford until the 70s. You look at a photo from 1968 and the students are wearing boaters and have short hair. They were just there for three years to study and qualify for a job. By the mid-70s though everyone had long hair and the only students who weren't members of the Labour Party were even further to the left than the Labour Party.'

This may not have been strictly true. Atkinson was not the only inhabitant of Oxford who showed little inclination to be politically active. His near contemporary at Durham Chorister School, Tony Blair, was also at Oxford in the mid-70s, but he seemed to show little political inclination: 'He was too busy doing Rolling Stones impressions with his band at May balls', says a fellow undergraduate.

Atkinson had his own musical aspirations too. He played percussion in a band for whom punk seemed not to have happened. Instead, fronted by an American singer, they played naff hard rock. Doug Lucie recalls one particularly raucous local gig towards the end of 1976: 'They performed at David Profumo's 21st birthday party at the Randolph Hotel. There was a real frisson to the evening because his father, John Profumo, [the minister who had resigned over the scandal involving Russians and Christine Keeler in the 60s] was there. But most of all I remember the band trying to play while I sat at the front and heckled them for about an hour.'

There were a number of things about Atkinson that made him stand out. Without even trying he seemed to be at odds with people's expectations of what an Oxford star should be like. He had a strange angular relationship to Oxford University, and in particular, to the arts crowd, mainly classics and English students that he was starting to mix with and work with. He wasn't just from the north, he had never left the north until Oxford. Then again he was hardly a conventional Geordie, more a southern kind of northerner. He had been to a relatively minor public school and now found himself alongside Harrovians and Etonians; as a postgraduate he was slightly older than his new chums. In an ITV documentary, *The Story of Bean*, another *KYTV* star Helen Atkinson Wood recalls his being nervous of women. This didn't seem to be a problem though; indeed, the opposite sex seemed to find it endearing. But these characteristics still didn't necessarily single him out as anyone special. Holed up in his Woodstock Road digs with Richard Curtis he really needed to find an identity for himself, and if one wasn't going to emerge naturally he would have to invent one.

What made Atkinson stand out the most was that he, a scientist, had the temerity to aspire to be in the spotlight, rather than tinker with its wiring. One contemporary recalls that this went against the grain of Oxford expectations: 'There was usually a clear distinction between actors and writers and the techies. The former were arts students, while the latter were scientists and there wasn't really much crossover.' Doug Lucie recalls the social breakdown even more precisely: 'The performers and writers were arts students. The stage crew were lawyers and languages, and the technical people were scientists. Rowan was very much the exception.'

Atkinson wasn't just extraordinarily talented, he also had a different take on what comedy should be, as Doug Lucie illustrates: 'The others were all doing terribly middle-class stuff about doctors in waiting rooms, word-play stuff, typical Footlights fare. Then to have somebody doing something that wasn't wordy, that didn't have a single recognizable word in it, but also had a character, a stage persona that didn't rely on any of the normal kind of revue things, that was an absolute classic.'

Atkinson even had different ambitions says Lucie: 'Most people weren't even aiming at *Python* or *Beyond the Fringe*, but lower. More like "get an agent in Edinburgh, get some radio producers in to see us." A lot of people were influenced by radio and were maybe setting out to do very wordy things that were suited to radio. Another thing about Rowan was that visually he made it more exciting. *Python* was obviously an influence, but when I was working with Geoff Perkins his biggest influences were people like Clive Anderson and Jimmy Mulville, who had already gone on to BBC radio. But they were doing stand-up in the classic radio idiom.' Rowan's sights were clearly set on a visual medium.

Lucie got on well with Atkinson but did find him different from the other students. Both were outsiders – Atkinson a scientist from the north, Lucie a working-class lad brought up on a south-London council estate. He hadn't even gone to the theatre until he was 17, at which point he became hooked on writing for the stage, much in the same way that Atkinson became hooked on the machinery of comedy once he finally had access to a television in his adolescence. 'He was fairly academic and studious in manner, not like the rest of us,' counters Lucie, who was a bit bemused at times by Atkinson's almost don-like demeanour. 'In fact, he was so plug ordinary that people thought it must have been an act. He had a faintly Jonathan Miller-ish air about him but people thought it couldn't be for real.'

Generally though, Oxford was a golden period for all concerned. Atkinson soon moved out of halls into a house in the Woodstock Road. At times it seemed like open house, with everyone going to everybody else's parties. Different social groups would overlap, often living out of each other's pockets. Richard Curtis was usually there as well and became very close to Helen Fielding, who later wrote *Bridget Jones' Diary*. Lucie was a bit bemused by this scene: 'The women seemed to have a crush on a different student each week.'

Atkinson quickly established himself as a name to watch, appearing in numerous plays and ending up as the star of all of them, over-shadowing Curtis and others in their group. Atkinson's career seemed to be a virtual mirror-image of Emma Thompson's career at Cambridge. She had arrived there in the mid-1970s and had immediately been singled out. She was the principal boy in the college panto and was the obvious highlight of 'the Smokers' which were the comedic equivalent of football trials – if you did well there you had every chance of becoming a star of Footlights. But there were differences too. Thompson's mother was actress Phyllida Law; her father was Eric Thompson, the man behind *The Magic Roundabout*. In Cambridge arts terms this made her almost aristocracy. And Thompson had an air of confidence that suggested she knew she was going places. By contrast Atkinson seemed to exist only when the spotlight shone on him recalls fellow student performer Geraldine Bedell. 'As a person he was quite anonymous, but he was always the star of anything he appeared in'. Offstage here was this typically geeky science post-graduate, all bushy hair and jumpers, a huge contrast to the more dashing students with dramatic aspirations. Atkinson was emo-tionally clumsy even, but with the help of Curtis, his onstage per-sonality blossomed. This odd couple soon had a reputation as a team to watch. Ambitious young directors were eager to cast Atkinson in particular, despite his shambling and shambolic appearance, expect-ing him to win plaudits for their production.

Although he was becoming known as a comedian, Atkinson's reputation meant that he was also soon in demand as an actor. His most notable dramatic performance was in a production of *Magnificence*, a political piece by Howard Brenton at the Oxford Playhouse, put on by the Experimental Theatre Company, a group dedicated to staging controversial, invariably pretentious modern works. One of the cast remembers Atkinson very well: 'It was a rather agitprop-ish play about squatters, very 70s. There were three acts, and the first and third acts were very serious, set in this squat with all these terribly deserving and hypersensitive young people about to be evicted. The central act was set in a punt on the river and was simply a conversation between two dons, one of whom was Rowan (the other was played by Peter Nolan). The problem was that the whole thing was unbalanced by this absolutely coruscating second act, which was absolutely sidesplittingly funny, in the middle of this rather dour and gloomy play.'

It was, undoubtedly an important production, and one that might have made an impact without Atkinson's memorable contribution. This was the first time the play had been staged outside London and, in fact, the first time it had been staged anywhere since Max Stafford Clarke had directed it at the Royal Court in 1972. Its author, Howard Brenton, made a point of coming up to the Oxford Playhouse to see it.

Mia Soutariou, a young undergraduate at Wadham College, directed *Magnificence* and was responsible for casting Atkinson: 'What I remember most was seeing him for the first time at an Oxford University Drama Society Experimental Theatre Company Smoker, a one-off dinner with entertainment. I knew nothing about him and I just remember this guy doing a one-man rubbery-faced mime thing as part of the cabaret. And at that point it was just so original because people were still very stuck in the *Monty Python*-type of comedy. Then this man did this and we went "God who is that. My God, he brilliant." '

While the Oxford University Dramatic Society did the classics, the Experimental Theatre Company was more like the equivalent of the Fringe, doing a lot of new work. *Magnificence* was only its third play, but Atkinson's performance helped to put the ETC on the map. Soutariou had been so impressed by Atkinson's turn at the Smoker that he did not even have to audition for his role: 'The extraordinary thing was that we knew nothing about his past, he just burst onto the scene as this amazing fully fledged comic. He was only doing comedy at the time, but I had this brain wave, because of the characters in *Magnificence*. It was part naturalistic, part wild – these two characters who are very eccentric, one who is an elderly Oxford don on a punt in the river. It was the sort of part you think who the hell do you get to play that, because to get someone who can play old, eccentric and original is hard, and I thought Rowan was such a natural comedian he might be right. But he had never expressed an interest in straight drama, so first I had to find out if he would be prepared to be involved.' Soutariou tracked Atkinson down and was intrigued further: 'I went to his rooms, which were full of wires and equipment – by and large people who are actors tend not to be doing subjects like electronic engineering – that made him even more interesting. At first he seemed really reluctant, then he read it and went "Yes, I think I might be interested." '

Soutariou remembers Atkinson as very unlike most aspiring actors: 'He was not up-front, loud, arrogant or gregarious. More like Mr Quiet. I couldn't see a great burning desire to perform, but it was great he agreed because I couldn't think of anybody else that could play that part.' As rehearsals got under way it was clear to Soutariou that this was something new to Atkinson: 'It was a very different discipline, getting into a team thing. He was used to working on his own, so this was a departure. He brought a lot of physical originality to it, which is what it needed to play someone who is 80-something. He was able to do that with his physical aptitude, face and voice. He approached it as a comedy character.'

Doug Lucie recalls *Magnificence*, too, albeit for slightly different reasons: 'I thought, great, at last we've finally got someone here who has an amazing comic talent and who can also act, and who doesn't act like a student. I have always been totally disappointed that he hasn't done more of what I would call straight acting.' Atkinson's star quality shone through, as another contemporary recalls: 'It was just perfectly obvious that Rowan was an exceptional talent. In those days he was scruffy and unkempt and looked like the kind of electrical engineering student that he was. He seemed a bit hopeless. When not performing he was a slightly nerdy and bumbling, but onstage you wouldn't know it.'

Perhaps this was why Rowan needed to perform – to express himself in a way that he simply couldn't when he was being himself. Relaxing at college he was hardly the life and soul of the party. It would have been easy to overlook him if it hadn't been for his swiftly earned reputation as a performer. In a place and at a time when students were keen to shine, this postgraduate was not in any way smart or clever or quick-witted or outgoing, merely a brilliant actor.

The Oxford Playhouse soon became a focal point for Atkinson's performances. One of the attractions of the university was the potential of being able to mount comedy shows in a proper professional theatre rather than merely in a college hall. But it was his performances in the university revues rather than straight dramas that really created a buzz. Many of his sketches would become an integral part of his professional act and survive in almost identical form. One was a bizarre piece of silent mime, in which on a dark stage he chased a spotlight round and round, rather like a kitten chases a ball of wool. In the end though he had his revenge on the light – he produced a vacuum cleaner and sucked it up. The effect was cartoonish – more akin to East European animation than *Monty Python*. Another skit, a Shakespearean spoof in which he played different variants of medieval kings (mad king, king with physical defect, king with two physical defects, etc.), seemed like a dry run for early editions of *The Black Adder*. One song, *Do Bears?*, was a smouldering ballad built up around various rhetorical questions – the key line in question was 'Do I love you?' and just as you thought Atkinson was going to reply with 'Do bears shit in the woods?' he responded with 'Do bears sha … la la la la?' Timing, as ever, was everything.

Then there was the white-gloved concert pianist – all rubbery wrists, knocked knees and no piano – who would live on, and similarly the drummer without a drum kit. There were also mimes based around an orchestral conductor and heavy metal guitar solos, as Atkinson spoofed Australian rockers AC/DC. For a while Mia Soutariou played piano, following their collaboration on *Magnificence*. Even though Atkinson's comedy performances were a resounding triumph, he never seemed to be that bullish about his career, says Soutariou: 'He never came across as Mr Confident. He was quite internal, where Richard was chirpier and jollier.' Soutariou saw their partnership developing and knew that there was a special chemistry between them: 'Both are always good without the other, but my God they are bloody dynamite together. I remember doing *Do Bears?* with them, which Rowan did for a long time. I always find it funny when I hear it on Comic Relief and I remember, "Bloody hell I was doing it in Oxford." '

The remarkable thing is how fully formed Atkinson's work was at that time. Contemporaries can recall sketches at Oxford that later became a part of Mr Bean's internationally acclaimed repertoire. There was the scene in which an awkward man would try to put on his trunks on the beach, for instance. Other sketches devised by Atkinson and Curtis would also continue to pepper and punctuate his career. This stage in Atkinson's career did have its problems though. The main one was expectations that Atkinson would always be 'on'. Because he was so exceptional onstage people expected him to come out with great one-liners and conversation at parties. Contrary to Curtis's recollections of Atkinson doing a credible impression of a cushion, another undergraduate feels that he is remembered as silent simply because he didn't say anything memorable: 'It was not that he didn't speak; it was just the contrast. People must have expected him to be like Stephen Fry, brilliant and witty, and of course he is not that. He is just rather dull. Actively dull.'

Eventually, Howard Goodall joined Atkinson and Curtis and became a regular contributor. Goodall was an easy-going likeable music undergraduate who was also very witty and seemed to be the perfect foil, a combination of oddball and scholar. He had grown up in a musical family near Oxford, the second of three sons with a sister following later. When still young he was ill and at the age of eight his parents gave him a drum kit. They hoped the physicality of the instrument might help him develop into a tougher child, but a decade later he was still, by his own admission, weedy. He did have a gift for music, however, which emerged at an early age. He could sight-read when he had the drum kit and he was soon starting to write music, developing a keen interest in the kind of choral music that would later inspire the theme tune to *Mr Bean*. As Goodall grew older it soon became apparent that he would pursue a musical career. He earnt his place at public school through his musical abilities, mastered the organ but eventually moved to the Oxfordshire comprehensive school where his father was the headmaster.

By the time Goodall went up to Oxford he knew he wanted to be involved in performing in some way, and on his very first day went to the Fresher's Fair where he approached the Oxford Revue stall. Goodall wanted to write music for them. The person behind the desk was Rowan Atkinson, who said his friend Richard Curtis would come to see him. Goodall had fortuitously landed on his feet straight away and was invited to be the musical director for the Oxford Revue, which was due to be staged at the Oxford Playhouse in three weeks time. Talking on Radio 4's *Midweek* in 1998, Goodall recalled how pleasantly surprised he was by the nature of the immediate job offer that would last for more than 20 years: 'I thought they would want me to move the scenery.'

As an actor, Atkinson gained a reputation for meticulousness in his preparation for a role. Says a contemporary: 'It was noticeable that whenever he went onstage his performance was identical to the last time and the time before that. I remember particularly in *As You Like It*, which we did in Worcester Gardens. He was Touchstone and there was a scene where he had to walk on and walk round his cane. I remember being in a rehearsal with him and he must have done it 26 or 27 times. He walked round this bloody cane and just stood there while other people were waiting to get on. But that was the kind of attention to detail he had. It was absolutely minute preparation. One walk around a cane is much the same as another walk around a cane, but for him it really mattered which foot went first and the shape of his fingers on the piece of wood and the cocking of his eyebrow. He had to concentrate on every single muscle in his body to make it a precision performance.'

Some people expressed surprise that Curtis was prepared to take so much a back seat. Some even thought Curtis could have been more of a star. He was often just as scruffy as Atkinson, but he had an incredible charm that won him plenty of admirers. While Atkinson had few close relationships, countless females fell in love with Curtis.

For Richard Curtis things began to change. He became a regular full-time writer for Atkinson and his performances became less and less prominent, except as a straight man. This was a cause of some regret among contemporaries at the time. Fellow undergraduate Geraldine Bedell feels Richard could have been a star, and Doug Lucie agrees: 'I was always sad that Richard stopped doing more because he was terribly funny and had a loveable persona in revues. In fact, if it hadn't been for Rowan he would have been the star. A bit fluffy, but a star nonetheless.'

Rowan became increasingly dependent on Curtis's writing. It is a moot point how much Rowan could have achieved without Curtis. Maybe, given his acting in *Magnificence*, he could have achieved even more. 'It is hard to know how much he is dependent on Richard,' says Doug Lucie. 'Maybe they need each other. I'd love to see Rowan stretched by writers who have a different agenda; I'd love to see him do some Beckett. He has the capability to do some really really good acting.'

In 1976, Atkinson and Curtis decided to try their luck at the Edinburgh Fringe Festival, squeezing themselves and their equipment into Rowan's Volkswagen camper van and heading up the motorway. By now Atkinson was a bit of a veteran of the Fringe Festival. He wanted to get everything right, but there were some things he could not do anything about. Edinburgh had yet to become the media Mecca where television commissioning editors would snap up all the tickets and sign up the best acts for lengthy series before the applause had died down. It was only in the late 70s, with the advent of the Edinburgh Television Festival running in conjunction with the Fringe, that the London media would decamp *en masse* to the Athens of the north.

Nevertheless, 1976 would prove to be a crucial year. It was the point at which Atkinson thought seriously of becoming a professional performer. His performance in the Oxford Revue prior to Edinburgh had received a very good review in the *Oxford Mail*, which had suggested he was the 'next John Cleese'. Atkinson wondered what to do next and asked the advice of a zoology student, who said he should get an agent – agents may have been described as a primitive life form by some, but surely they weren't part of the zoology M.Sc. syllabus?

Atkinson decided to write to the agents of people he admired before he went to Edinburgh, enclosing his glowing plaudits in the *Oxford Mail* and asking them to come along to his show. As a fan of *Beyond the Fringe* and *Monty Python* he wrote to the stars' respective agents. Richard Armitage, who was in charge of the prestigious Noel Gay organization, flew up to see Atkinson and immediately took him under his wing; they worked together until Armitage died in 1987. Legend has it he was charmed by the fact that Atkinson's letter began

with 'Dear Sir or Madam', but it was the originality of the performance that really won him over.

Armitage later recalled that a couple of things about Atkinson stood out. When the other members of the cast went off at the end, Atkinson stayed on and the applause continued. And also that only once in the show did he speak in a normal voice. There was that strange, strangled nasal mumble, there was a whisper, but mostly there was simply silence. According to Armitage, 90 per cent of his act had been mime. How many English comedians could one say that about? Not that Atkinson was very keen on the idea of mime. He later told *Over 21* how he felt about the term: 'so worthy of drafty community halls'. In *Not the Nine O'Clock News*, Atkinson would cruelly send up the leotard-wearing practicians of this ancient art in a sketch in which he played a one-man radical schools theatre group called Alternative Car Park: 'My body is my tool.' This high-blown sincerity was accompanied by the kind of facial expressions and bodily contortions that only an idiot would attempt in public.

The show Armitage saw, by the Oxford Theatre Group at St Mary Street Hall, was significant because it was Atkinson's first real comedy show and the first time he had worked predominantly with Richard Curtis. By word of mouth Atkinson already had a reputation, and the show, unusually for a collegiate production, was a sellout. Atkinson's contributions certainly stood out; they were largely visual. Another person who was present was an up-and-coming BBC radio producer who specialized in comedy, John Lloyd. In 1997 he recalled having seen Atkinson 21 years earlier. He had been immediately impressed. When the curtain came down he quickly tried to find Atkinson: 'I was convinced he would be more famous than Chaplin,' Lloyd told the *Mirror*.

Also in the audience was fellow Oxford performer Richard Sparks, who was in his own show with a college friend called Peter Wilson, known affectionately as 'Wislon' – the *Private Eye* nickname for Harold Wilson. Sparks and Wilson were both exhibitioners who read English at Exeter College between 1970 and 1973, so were slightly senior to Atkinson. Sparks vividly recalls the impression the onstage Atkinson made: 'The first time I met Rowan was in 1976 when Peter and I did this two-man show that I used to do in my summer holidays. I was working for Welsh Television and would take a fortnight off and do shows for Richard DeMarco. The Oxford crowd came along to support us, so on the first night we had a packed house and I met this rather shy person at the end who said, "I don't know why we are bothering to do shows when there are people like you doing stuff like this," and I thought, what a nice modest young man. A few days later we went to see the Oxford Revue and there were these terrible dance routines, to *Alright Now* by Free. It was a really laboured show, then suddenly this lunatic came onstage with his hair sticking up all over the place. He had a tiny, torn piece of paper in his hand and he wouldn't say a single word. He just made strange noises and tried to give this piece of paper to people in the audience; half of them didn't know what to do, and Peter and I looked and our mouths fell open and I thought, Jeez, it's quite obvious we are seeing the real thing. In person he was very polite, sweet and nice, but put him onstage and the magic happened. My first reaction was, this is a modest young fellow, and then you see this genius.' Sparks could hardly take in the contrast between the person onstage and the person offstage. 'There isn't a person offstage; I think it's his evil twin brother Rick.'

Atkinson and his team had been able to turn the fact that there were so few decent acts up in Edinburgh to their advantage. Performing between the lazy dross that passed for satire and the druggy post-hippy performance art that was comedy's version of lumpen progressive rock, Atkinson's performance swept the board. With a high-powered agent representing him, it was only a matter of time before broadcasters became interested in Atkinson. One of the first to see him was Humphrey Barclay, London Weekend Television's head of comedy, who was himself a Cambridge Footlights veteran, albeit one who had escaped from the limelight and gone into the production side of television (Barclay had produced, among other things, *I'm Sorry I'll Read That Again*). Richard Sparks recalls taking him to see Atkinson: 'I drove Humphrey Barclay down to see Rowan at the Oxford Playhouse. He was very reluctant to go but I remember Humphrey sitting in the balcony, leaning forward saying, "I've got to go backstage and meet this guy." Something happened to Atkinson onstage that turned him from a nobody into a star.'

The end of Oxford was very much the end of one era and the beginning of another. Things would suddenly get more professional now. But the move from academia into showbusiness had still been a gradual one. In 1981, Atkinson told journalist Tony Bilbow on *Play It Again* that at Oxford performing had started off as a hobby while he had been doing his research and the ratio was ten per cent performing to 90 per cent study. By the time he reached his final year, however, he had already been commissioned to write for ITV.

Atkinson and Curtis seemed to be following a route well-trodden by other graduates of Oxford who glided through university into positions of power; but, while others seemed to be heading for Parliament or the professions or organizing the arts, Atkinson seemed to heading for stardom. Says Doug Lucie: 'Mel Smith was all set to run the RSC, he had already done stuff at the Young Vic. Geoffrey Perkins and Angus Deayton would end up at the BBC. Oxbridge is a greased path in that respect.' As the city's gilded youth decamped to London to take over the media, Lucie, the non-conformist, stayed in Oxford to escape from Oxford: 'Oxford moved to Camden Town.'

Atkinson's streak of success was looking less and less like a fluke and more like an embryonic career. The rest of the Atkinson family was beginning to realize that this performance thing was more than just a phase their son was going through. The farm would have to manage without him, but his mother, Ella, was still anxious about this showbusiness lark and worried that managers tended to be dubious predatory types with vulgar taste in clothes. Recalling the turning point in the early part of his career, the young comic later said: 'She thought it was full of bouncing cheques and homosexuals and people in nasty bowties, so I got a really well-dressed middle-class agent who looked like a bank manager and that reassured her a lot.'

3

Registering Fame

The Edinburgh Festival continued to play a huge part in Rowan Atkinson's rise, even after he had bagged an agent. One might have thought that he could have coasted his way into television with the help of the hugely influential Richard Armitage. An Oxford education had long been a dry run for a career in broadcasting, but in 1977, Atkinson headed back up to Scotland. This time though, he did things differently. After being the stand-out artist in a sort of semi-organized free-for-all, he now presented what was effectively a solo show. It wasn't supposed to be a solo show at all though, and its development suggests a determination and focus that hadn't yet been seen. Atkinson was working with an old friend from the Dundee University Theatre Group and between them they effectively became the Oxford Revue that year. As Atkinson told Michael Dale in *Sore Throats and Overdrafts*, they 'kind of took it over'. The double act didn't seem to work, with his partner doing unpalatable parodies of Brecht. Atkinson decided enough was enough and put his foot down: 'I wasn't really the stuff of popular entertainment. I'm someone who always preferred to entertain *for* people rather than *to* people. I thought it wasn't working, so I cancelled it for three nights and we rustled together a new revue.' While the audience would turn up only to be redirected to a nearby pub on the nights when there was no show, Atkinson prepared for what was basically his début one-man show. The process by which this début came about re-affirmed his perfectionist tendencies, preferring to scrap something rather than muddle through – but as the badly parodied Brecht would have said, the end justified the means. The new show was acclaimed and Atkinson was described by one critic as 'the funniest graduate clown since Jonathan Miller'.

When they tried it out at his old stomping ground, the Oxford Playhouse, there was a tremendous buzz. One review documented the excitement in the city as well as the action onstage. 'It is not many shows in Oxford that turn away audiences in droves and leave the street outside the Playhouse jammed at the end with customers so satisfied that they cannot drag themselves home.' One of the members of the audience who saw that Edinburgh run was BBC radio producer John Lloyd, who had already been converted to Atkinsonism in 1976. But Atkinson was a largely visual performer and Lloyd was still working in the aural medium. He was keen to put a show together for him, but it would be another two years before the circumstances conspired to allow Lloyd to put Atkinson on the screen, by which time lots of other producers, hungry for new talent, would also be after a piece of Rowan Atkinson.

Twenty years on it is hard to convey quite how quickly Rowan Atkinson became a star. But to put it into perspective it is worth comparing his career to his hero John Cleese. The *Python* linchpin went through the Footlights, graduated, did other bits of television and became a name in his own right with *Fawlty Towers* in the mid-1970s. In other words, it took John Cleese the best part of 15 years to become a household name. Rowan Atkinson was writing professionally while still at Oxford and within months of leaving was being feted for a showcase of his talents in Hampstead, and receiving offers from both the BBC and ITV. As if to compound the contrast, by 1979 he was appearing alongside John Cleese and assorted other Pythons in the Four Yorkshiremen sketch at *The Secret Policeman's Ball*. You don't need to be a rocket scientist – or an electronic engineer for that matter – to work out that Rowan Atkinson's rise was nothing short of meteoric.

Richard Curtis, meanwhile, was following in his slipstream, but catching up. As well as writing with Atkinson, Curtis was already contributing jokes to Radio 4's satire show *Weekending*, but it was not really the kind of comedy he wanted to do. They wanted gags that related to that week's news; Curtis just wanted to write about things he thought was funny, which might not have had any topical relevance whatsoever.

The success of the Edinburgh show in 1977 meant that it was only a matter of time before it transferred to London. One of Atkinson's fans was Michael Rudman, a former president of the Oxford University Dramatic Society. He had seen the show and wanted to bring it to the Hampstead Theatre. Hampstead Theatre was a small but well-respected fringe venue, with a capacity of little more than 170, that defied the airs and graces of its name by being a nondescript box-like building just off a major interchange in Swiss Cottage. Head in one direction and you hit the M1 and the north; head in the other and you hit London's West End – Atkinson was very much on the cusp of putting the former behind him and embracing the latter.

As the show was being put together, Michael Rudman decided to enlist the help of some other young comedy performers and writers who had more experience than Atkinson. Peter Wilson and Richard Sparks had seen the 1976 Oxford Revue show that had brought Atkinson into prominence; they had been doing their own two-man show at the time. Sparks remembers what happened: 'Mike Rudman called me in as a sort of senior citizen to oversee the writing and help Rowan, Richard Curtis and Howard Goodall, though we were not that much older. The previous generation was *Python*.' But the Oxford comedy scene did have a habit of extending its tentacles out and linking everybody. Not for nothing was there the phrase 'Oxford mafia', though it was admittedly more interested in mutual support than murder and extortion.

Sparks was not particularly surprised at hearing that Rudman wanted some fine-tuning – the show was obviously strong enough in places for him to consider bringing it to London, but there were moments that didn't scale the dizzy heights Atkinson would later achieve. There was still a terrible dance routine to Free's *Alright Now*, for instance, that had never really worked. Sparks and Wilson offered Rowan sketches from their own Edinburgh act, but it lacked that something special that would give the performance an identity. So many comedy shows in the London theatre could raise a laugh at the time but be completely forgotten about by the time the viewer had reached the bar next door. The team wanted to come up with something more memorable.

There was a question about the purpose of the show. Was it to be an ensemble production or a solo performance and vehicle for a would-be star? To Sparks it was quite clear that this was intended as a showcase for Atkinson, even though he, Wilson and Elspeth Parker, were also scheduled to perform in it. Sparks started writing more material for the show, and one morning, suffering from a hangover, he sat down and knocked off something that he felt was nothing special, 'just one of the things off the production line. I didn't know it would be a hit like that, there was no sense of the world shifting.' All it was was a list of odd names, read out by a tetchy schoolmaster, based on Sparks' own father, who had been a master at Cheltenham College for 20 years. 'It was dad. It's just a list of silly names and I thought the names were funny so I kept writing until I stopped.' The rest is history. As the register names became increasingly absurd and abstract they also became increasingly sinister: 'Aynsley ... Babcock ... Bland ... Carthorse ... Nibble ... come on, settle down ... Orifice ... Plectrum ...', all the way through the alphabet to 'Zob ... Absent'. *Monty Python* had liked to use silly names, but there was more going on here. John Cleese had occasionally used the trick of emphasizing the wrong words. Once, during a sketch in which he played a psychiatrist, he had said, 'This makes me very *irritated*,' putting on a strange voice at the end for no apparent reason. But there was more to the register than that. It wasn't just the student surrealism of the words, or even the perfect pauses in between each name, or the gown draped over those slight shoulders. It was the way Atkinson said the names. His full lips could make a short, tiny word like 'Nibble' resonate for ever, or they could make a long word like Witcherlywilliams-Wockett last only in a nanosecond. Any word with a 'b' or a 'p' in it came out sounding particularly comedic. And there was considerable menace in the vowels. At times the pauses seemed like as much a way of overcoming his stutter as raising a laugh, but the effect was pure comic genius. But there was also a subtlety to the routine that went unnoticed by many members of the audience. Before Atkinson had even spoken he had very gently rotated the pen in his hand – having realized that it was the wrong way round. It was a triumphant combination of a unique verbal skill and deft slight of hand welded to a face that one critic described as 'Peter Lorre in a panic'. In a nutshell, a truly memorable piece of comedy.

It was a hugely successful routine with everyone concerned. There have been stories that Atkinson based his delivery of the 'Schoolmaster' sketch on some of his old teachers – former headmaster at

Durham Chorister School, Canon John Grove, and the headmaster at St Bees, Geoffrey Lees, for instance – but Sparks disagrees, emphasizing again that his father was his only inspiration, although he is the first to acknowledge that the success of the sketch had as much to do with its delivery onstage as with the words written on the page.

When Sparks had first written the piece he had no idea how it would turn out. 'Because the show at Hampstead was conceived as a showcase for Rowan, I gave it to him and he looked at it and sort of grunted and then went away. I came back a day or two later and he was rehearsing it, and he did it completely in a way I hadn't thought of. For some reason I thought he would come onstage and hurl exercise books into the audience and shout the names out like a mad John Cleese would have done. Instead he did it really slowly. At first I thought this is going to die a death and then, I thought, he can't do it like this. Then I thought, actually by giving it the air between each name, by the time he got to the next silly name – and with a name like Sparks you've got to write silly names – he came up with it and it flew. It's one of those things where you watch a piece you've actually written and don't recognize a single word of it. It seemed so fresh and new. It seemed his. I didn't really have an idea how it would sound; I just wrote the words down. I thought it should be done fast ... then it would have been alright, but by doing it slowly it turned into a classic.'

Sparks doesn't think this sketch was typical of the show though. It seemed to have a viciousness that much of the act lacked. 'The Schoolmaster really worked for Rowan but I found a lot of his other stuff soft, the Schoolmaster was more edgy. I wished he had done more stuff where he took more of an in-your-face attitude to scare the audience, like Nicol Williamson did.' A few years later, Atkinson would toughen up for *Blackadder*, meeting the challenge of the post-punk comedy new wave, but it would be a short-lived toughening up. *Mr Bean*, which followed on from *Blackadder* would be called a lot of things, but no one would call it in-your-face comedy.

Sometimes fans did not realize who had written the Schoolmaster routine. One night, Sparks was in his local pub the Windsor Castle, in Notting Hill. He was doing the crossword quietly when he heard someone quoting his work to someone else: 'There was a girl and two men and I heard one of them say, "Oh put it away, Plectrum," so I looked up and laughed and they looked at me. When I said I wrote it, the girl said, "No you didn't, Richard Curtis did; he's a friend of mine." I said, "Look if you want to come back to my house round the corner I can show you the original manuscript." ' The trio looked at him as if either he were mad or this was one of the worst chat-up lines in the book: 'I went home and thought mmm.'

Despite this cavil, Sparks got on well with Atkinson, who could be relaxed and pleasant company offstage despite the myth of the gloomy introvert: 'You always expect someone should be like they are onstage when you meet them offstage, not shorter in real life. I wouldn't call him introverted offstage, just a perfectly normal bloke. It's just called finding a character, acting.'

At 7pm, on 13 July 1978, *Beyond a Joke* opened at the Hampstead Theatre. In adverts it was simply billed as 'A New Revue with Rowan Atkinson, Elspeth Walker and Peter Wilson'. The title sounded like a homage to that other classic college revue, *Beyond the Fringe*, but there would be plenty of originality here too. Sparks remembers that half the material at the Hampstead Theatre was still 'crap', but the roll-call was clearly a gem. Peter Wilson jokingly asked his friend why he hadn't given it to him, but if Sparks had given it to Wilson it would never have had the same impact. It was certainly above the general standard of the show. 'Me, Peter and Rowan came up with some dire stuff; we threw out stuff that had been done in Edinburgh and had to edit out stuff that was just bad writing.'

Another key sketch survived from the Edinburgh show. Atkinson did a number of mime sketches, but the most notable was the opening one where he woke up in the morning and started shaving. His electric razor did not end when it had circumnavigated his cheeks; it went over his forehead and down his nose, ending up on his tongue. Not a word was said throughout the scene, but it had the audience in fits of laughter.

Sketches that have now become classics were seen on the London stage for the first time during this run. Atkinson aired one of the all-time rude vicars. The dog-collared chap tells of the first time he was asked to clarify the Church's position on fellatio. Atkinson's vicar said he couldn't explain the position because he didn't know what fellatio was, and could the questioner show him: 'So she did, and now whenever a young woman asks me what the Church's position on fellatio is I say, I'd like to tell you, but I don't know what fellatio is.'

Vicars had often been easy prey for comics. Alan Bennett had first come to the public's attention in the *Beyond the Fringe* revue with the solo sketch entitled 'Take a Pew', in which he discussed the way that people were different, drawing repeatedly on the line 'My brother Esau is a hairy man, but I am a smooth man.' Bennett would then proceed to explain all aspects of modern life with recourse to this line, getting increasingly less convincing each time. Bennett's clergyman seemed to have difficulty talking in anything but aphorisms. At times he sounded like an Anglican Forrest Gump: 'Life is rather like opening a tin of sardines. We are all of us looking for the key.' Atkinson seemed to be drinking deep from this tradition of diffident, confused, dog-collared Englishmen. If you found his style amusing, it was another link back to *Beyond the Fringe*; but if you didn't find it funny, it seemed like another example of the paucity of wit among current middle-class comics.

This version was certainly different in line-up from the Oxford University Theatre group's version of *Beyond A Joke*, which had starred just Atkinson and future *Blackadder* actress Helen Atkinson Wood. That version had been written mainly by Atkinson and David Farrell, with additional material by Curtis and production manager Johnny Dias. Even Paddy Rickerby, Atkinson's old chum from the St Bees Film Society was involved back then, playing the clarinet and working on the lighting.

Things seemed much more professional now, though a lot of the best material had been performed before. Michael Rudman and David Aukin, who ran the Hampstead Theatre with him had even paid some commission money for the team to come up with new material. But after meetings in an Indian restaurant in Newbury and a spell writing in Devon, Atkinson, Peter Wilson and Richard Sparks decided to rely on established gags. The London showcase was too important an opportunity to risk sketches that had not been roadtested.

Some of the comedy did stray between the inspired and the insipid. As well as the face-shaving routine, Atkinson also brought a whole new meaning to 'instant coffee' in a way that would become one of his trademarks. Peter Wilson also recalls, among other highlights, a 'loony on the underground platform' and a politician's speech ('We must avoid pointlessnesslessness'). Other sketches were less typical of Atkinson. There was a Christmas musical put on by the trio, purporting to be staff of Barclays Bank, and a scene in which director Sir Peter Hall (Wilson) asked for an Arts Council grant to fund a girlie show.

The result seemed to pay off, for Atkinson, at least. Even the critics who did not like the material could not deny that a new talent had appeared on the London comedy scene. In *The Times* Irving Wardle confirmed that Atkinson 'has an extremely precise rhythmic sense that earns him laughs all the way through', though he also found the show adolescent and said he had preferred Wilson and Sparks' previous show, entitled *Hegel And Bagel*. In the *Observer* Robert Cushman also singled out the nascent star, but was more circumspect: '*Beyond A Joke* has a cast of three, most of it called Rowan Atkinson. Mr Atkinson has eyebrows, curly hair, a lower lip, and timing. These are all good things, but they are not in themselves hilarious.' There was no doubt that Atkinson was the centre of attention. In *Punch* Sheridan Morley even liked the format and sang Atkinson's praises: 'Revue is in fact alive and well and living in *Beyond A Joke*, a three-character Oxford graduate show conceived as a vehicle for Rowan Atkinson, who's an eccentric comedian pitched somewhere between Dustin Hoffman and Jonathan Miller.'

Not surprisingly, it was Atkinson's career which got the biggest boost. Peter Wilson's serious stage ambitions ended in Hampstead, though he still performed away from the limelight for a while. When Rowan Atkinson turned it down Wilson accepted the invitation to be the warm-up man for the late-night TV show *Saturday Night People* and then on another show, *A Question Of Sex*, but he left shortly after being asked to distract the studio audience from a cageful of copulating orangutans.

London's *Time Out*, wearing its agitprop heart on its sleeve, called it an 'Oxbridge revue containing a sub-Alf Garnet racist, a sub-Peter Sellers politician, a sub-Joyce Grenfell pianist, a sub-Alan Bennett schoolmaster and much else that's been done before, only better.' It wasn't taking the show to task for being dated – although it said it was that too – it was taking it to task for lacking 'direction and substance which gives comedy its guts'. The reviewer acknowledged that there had been plenty of laughter on the press night, but put that down to the auditorium being sprinkled with chums. Her conclusion at least spotted the potential of the show's star: 'Rowan Atkinson, who with the right material could be very funny indeed'. If the ticket sales were boosted by supportive pals, the team must have had a great number of pals indeed, since the show ran until early September. *Time Out* may have been harsh, but the problem was clearly quality-control, not the quality of Atkinson's performance.

Atkinson was 23 and yet he still looked very much the truculent schoolboy in his loose stripy tie and Wrangler jacket. He still seemed to have a bit of puppy fat on his cheeks and his hair looked as if it had only a passing acquaintance with a comb. Yet onstage he was transformed into a performer who was the consummate professional, someone who appeared to come alive under a spotlight.

Despite some sour reviews there was a buzz about the show. Some people went back to Hampstead Theatre every night if they could get a ticket. By now John Cleese had heard about Atkinson and was suitably impressed, reportedly remarking that 'I was very intrigued. He's very, very good.' Even when the gags were weak he felt that the performer was strong: 'He was making people laugh with some material I'd have paid money to avoid.' The Hampstead run confirmed that Atkinson was hot property and the race was now on to secure his talents. A number of broadcasters were keen to nurture this unique talent. Radio 3 was making overtures, but so was BBCTV and London Weekend Television. Humphrey Barclay, at LWT, had already talked to Atkinson and was a clear front-runner. He approached Rowan again, this time asking him to come up with some ideas for a programme for the mainstream channel.

As these deals were being hammered out, however, Atkinson nipped in and made his bona-fide television début on 19 February 1979 (he had appeared as a guest on a topical show *And Now The Good News* on BBC2 on 6 November 1978). It was with the BBC, but it was not the show that was expected. For fans who now consider Rowan Atkinson to have something of the children's entertainer about him, it may not come as such a shock to discover that the first show he starred in was *A Bundle of Bungles*, a one-off BBC children's programme. In what looked suspiciously like an unimaginative variant of *Play School* but without the soft toys, Atkinson led a trio of brightly coloured performers (well, two were brightly coloured, the third was a white-faced mime artist – the kind that Atkinson once joked usually performed in drafty community halls. Alongside Atkinson, were Nola Rae and Mikki Magorian). His character's name – say it out loud for full cringe potential – was 'Mr Ree'. Howard Goodall plonked away at a keyboard, original *Beyond A Joke* percussionist Bill Drysdale banged the drums and the whole affair was very embarrassing to see. In fact, it was just the kind of well-meaning but cheesy kids-show that six months later Atkinson would be mercilessly parodying on *Not the Nine O'Clock News*.

Yet there were a number of sketches within the show that had links with Atkinson's adult material. Decked out as a grand orchestral conductor, he led the 'band' (Goodall and Drysdale) through a classical version of *The Teddy Bears' Picnic* as he had done in *Beyond A Joke*, but typically upstaged them, prancing around the microphone stand, shimmying across the stage, and tugging on his baton as if it were a taut rope.

There was also a sketch in which he played probably the most hacked-off newspaper vendor in history. In his mac and scarf he moaned about how there were so many misprints in the 'Ee-Penning Tars'. As a result, the television schedules promised 'Charlie's Angles' ('they're sharp') and *Scratch of the Day*, at which point the trio embarked on a mass-scratching mime. In between these sketches, which Atkinson frequently performed with a decidedly pained expression, were East European cartoons. The whole affair had the feel of a low-budget production made by Communist Russia and did not really give him a chance to show the full extent of his verbal or physical dexterity. A fitness routine, in which he played Jim Slips, failed to extract any humour from the exercise, while he appeared to play the bowler-hatted Ronald the Rat with all the enthusiasm of a man being led to the gallows. The proceedings terminated with Atkinson tersely crying 'Wrap up', at which point a giant ribbon appeared and wrapped itself around the three performers. As a children's programme it might have worked, but it was hardly an avenue that Atkinson appeared to want to pursue when there were better, more attractive career opportunities around the corner.

The star of *A Bundle of Bungles* was soon forced to choose between adult shows for ITV and BBC. His big break came with *Rowan Atkinson Presents ...Canned Laughter* for Humphrey Barclay and LWT. Barclay described the tale at the time as 'simple and quite touching' and the humour as 'funny/sad, often visually humorous'. *Canned Laughter* -with Atkinson credited as the only writer – was recorded on 23 March 1979 and swiftly transmitted on 8 April. Its scheduling on a Sunday night at 10pm, unusually late for a comedy, was shrewd and ahead of its time. In the 80s that slot would become known as the alternative slot when appropriated by *Spitting Image* and *The New Statesman*. But in the 70s it was still a bit of a backwater, a slot where regional networks could opt out and show their own programmes. In fact Atkinson's adult debut was transmitted in the London area only, so Atkinson's parents were unable to see it.

While it contained some of his road-tested material, *Canned Laughter*, directed by Geoffrey Sax, was more than merely a showcase of Atkinson's stage talents. It actually featured him as three main characters. One character would recur throughout his career in different guises and with different names, but the others didn't really develop. Nevertheless, they did show that Atkinson's range went far beyond mere childish mimicry.

The action opened in a grim bedsit. Robert Box (Atkinson) is asleep, but woken abruptly by his radio alarm, which suddenly blurts out the bland dance music of the fictional Radio Suburbia. As this pre-Bean geek rises he goes through an interior monologue regarding the woman of his dreams, a colleague at the office. Should he, could he, ask 'her' out? Box ponders on what technique to use, giving Atkinson the chance to rummage through his facial rolodex. Happy? Sad? Quite seductive? Which in Box's book means arching eyebrows and sticking his tongue out lasciviously. The action soon shifts to the street where Atkinson's second character, Dave Perry, is strutting along to the soundtrack of the Electric Light Orchestra's *Mr Blue Sky*. Perry is a Geordie entertainer off to see his agent about his latest bid for stardom, though his sagging moustache, cowboy boots and pear-drop collars don't bode well – he seems like a man out of time even for 1979. It soon turns out that Dave Perry is some kind of comedian. In fact when he proffers a ten-shilling note to pay a 16-pence fare the disgruntled bus conductor says, 'What are you, some kind of comedian?'

Meanwhile back in the bedsit, Box is going through the already well-established classic Atkinson routine: shaving his face, his tongue and his forehead, the electric razor driving a path between his thick beetle eyebrows. When he suddenly realizes he is late for work he quickly downs some coffee – by spooning into his mouth the sugar and coffee, drinking some milk and then, in the ultimate *coup de théâtre*, swallowing the boiling water directly from the kettle and jumping up and down to mix it all together.

The third character is Mr Marshall, Box's malevolent boss, a Bond-type villain with a quick temper who has called a meeting in his office. At one point a colleague realizes he shouldn't be smoking in his presence and pops the cigarette in Box's pocket with disastrous consequences: when he finally asks Lorraine (Sue Holderness) out, his smoking jacket sets the fire alarms off.

Remarkably though, Lorraine is not put off by the gauche display and the finale finds them having dinner together in a quiet restaurant where Dave Perry has donned the obligatory frilly shirt and sparkly jacket and is the star turn. This plum booking reveals why he has never made it: his repertoire is a dim catalogue of tired and tasteless gags that soon has the diners looking the other way. Trying to be funny as an unfunny comedian is a tough nut to crack, but Atkinson has an impressively fair stab at it.

Meanwhile Robert Box is having problems of his own. The menu is in French, and Atkinson runs through a succession of trite pronunciation-related gags, culminating in his ordering 'Vat included'. Not surprisingly, the waiter looks at him as if he is either an idiot or an alien.

With the food dealt with and the floor show over, Lorraine and Robert decide to dance the night away, but it is clear the course of love is not going to run smoothly when Robert remarks: 'I used to dance at school but I gave up when we started using real women.' True to form, just as they are about to take to the floor the music switches from a gentle number to *King Rocker* by punk band Generation X. Box endeavours to perform with embarrassing consequences: he essays a strange mutant Morris Dance before having an altercation with a hat stand. Lorraine concludes, about half an hour after the rest of us, that he is an idiot. As the credits roll and with the aid of some primitive camera trickery, Box and Perry, two consummate losers, console each other while Mr Marshall looks on uncaringly. In one final note of post-modern irony, a loop of canned laughter replays itself over and over again. It's the only kind of laughter a comedian like Dave Perry would ever receive.

There was a suggestion that maybe Atkinson had been put on television too early in his career, but this seemed churlish. At 24 he had already been successful on the stage. So why shouldn't he now transfer his talents. There were verbal gags, physical gags and down-right farce, but it translated very effectively. The camera seemed to love the contorted expressions and, if anything, make them even more grotesque. In fact, this kind of facial humour was more suited to the intimacy of television than the sometimes impersonal theatres, where audiences may have missed the subtle nuances of a twitch here or a blink there.

Canned Laughter was memorable because it – and Atkinson – was so unquantifiable. It was a show that revealed the paradoxes of Atkinson. It wasn't slapstick and yet it was. It wasn't undergraduate humour and yet it was. Atkinson was an instant star and yet he also had huge potential. In the comedy world at least, this very English yet very exotic-looking chap seemed capable of every kind of joke, harking back to the Footlights and way beyond all the way back to music hall and the famed 'big boot dance' by the silent clown Little Tich.

Yet the biggest paradox of all was the fact that someone with such a distinctive face should get his next break on the radio. Atkinson's rocketing career was suddenly taking the scenic route to stardom via that bastion of classical music, Radio 3. It seemed something of a departure that a performer known for his visual work would get a broadcasting break on radio, but it revealed the breadth of Atkinson's talent. With the aid of Richard Curtis's sublimely silly scripts, Atkinson could be funny in any medium.

In the spring of 1979, Atkinson starred in *The Atkinson People*, penned with Richard Curtis. In three separate programmes, starting on Radio 3 on 24 April 1979, Atkinson embarked upon 'satirical and wry investigations into the lives of fictional great men'. The programmes were well received and were given a repeat airing that October, with an additional new programme turning the trilogy into a quartet.

By the 70s there was already a well-established tradition of Oxbridge alumni cutting their teeth on radio before graduating to television. In 1973, *I'm Sorry I'll Read That Again* had finally shut up shop as most of the contributors had found greater fame elsewhere. There was now a gap in the market for something clever and satirical. In 1974, Griffith Rhys Jones – a Footlights performer who had had a hit show called *Chox* also starring Clive Anderson and Douglas Adams – and John Lloyd came up with *Oh No It Isn't*, which translated the iconoclastic and silly humour of college Smokers for a wider audience. *The Atkinson People*, while less manic and broadcast on Radio 3, slotted very snugly into this tradition.

The four programmes, produced by the young ex-Cambridge Footlights BBC radio producer who now shortened his name to Griff Rhys Jones, consisted of spoof biographies, the kind of thing we have become used to through the work of Harry Enfield, who performed a similar trick with his television documentary, *Norbert Smith – A Life*, and Steve Coogan, who made unctuous slack-wearing sports reporter Alan Partridge just too realistic for comfort and created the corrosively monstrous middle-of-the-road smoocher Tony Ferrino. Peter Cook had done similar send-ups, but at the time the closest precedent was Eric Idle's pop pastiche, *The Rutles*, which had been transmitted in March 1978. That, of course, had an all-star cast and cameos from the likes of George Harrison and Mick Jagger. *The Atkinson People* had Rowan, some Oxford chums, Peter Wilson from *Beyond a Joke* and some stalwart members of BBC Radio's drama department.

In the first of the four programmes, broadcast on 24 April, Atkinson profiled thespian Sir Corin Basin. The *Radio Times* filled us in on this character: 'In the acting profession only a very few make it to the top of the tree: most are content to sit quietly on a lower branch; others climb higher, but fall and break their spines; and some, of course, are in a different forest altogether. But Sir Corin Basin is at the very top.' This sense of high-blown metaphor – in other words, lots of wordy, erudite waffle – set the tone for the rest of the run. The absence of any studio laughter, canned or real, added to the mock solemn tone.

The second edition spoofed renaissance figure Sir Benjamin Fletcher, whose lengthy career, nay careers, had taken in, among other achievements, 'cabinet minister ... Nobel prize winner ... farmer ... oceanographer ... and television personality'. Interviews with old chums revealed a less-complex figure than his lengthy curriculum vitae suggested: 'intelligent but never did a stroke of work', recalled one friend played by Atkinson, sporting a strong Glaswegian accent. He had, it was revealed, a great future: he was 'a turkey waiting to be stuffed'. At one point Fletcher became the agony uncle of the *New Statesman* – at the time an absurd idea, but now rather credible.

The programme also made use of spoof archive recordings. One, a speech at the Lord Mayor's Banquet at the Guildhall, was a variant of a routine that would crop up in Atkinson's live shows as an MP's address and featured the resonant line: 'She began by sinking into my arms and ended with her arms in the sink.'

The third edition, in what was taking on the appearance of one extended shaggy-dog story, looked at a great Gallic man, George Dupont. Was this French philosopher a great thinker or just someone whose name translated as George of the Bridge? Atkinson's main concern seemed to be how to make the word Dordogne sound as rich and fruity as possible. The lecture told how Dupont set out his philosophy in a series of controversial letters; 'Dear Sir, I am thinking,' then, after being asked about what, 'About it.' When he wrote to *The Times* 'I think that I am thinking,' he had reportedly thrown the whole process of thought itself into doubt. For some reason a northern sports reporter, Gerald Steele, had been despatched to the Dordogne to seek out Dupont. Information was hard to gather but Steele attempted to bribe the locals with onions. When that failed he tried a red hot poker up the behind and a punch in the face.

The final programme, broadcast, after a delay, on 2 November, homed in on Barry Good, 'The Pope of Pop'. Good was a cross between star-maker Larry Parnes and an even more cynical breed of Svengali that had emerged in the 70s with hides as thick as dinosaur skin and eyes focused as keenly on bank balances as on pop charts. He was not ashamed of the fortunes he was amassing. So what that a third of the world was going hungry – he was rather peckish himself at times. These shows broke away from the sketch format to confirm suspicions that Atkinson was capable of sustained characterizations. Here he created credible comic stereotypes with enough depth for 30 minutes; later he extended the principle to come up with larger-than-life characters that could last for a series and more.

Hilda Kriseman played parts in The George Dupont edition and Sir Corin Basin editions. She had come from a different background and was an established member of the BBC drama repertory company. In fact, Kriseman had been completely unaware of Atkinson up to this point. She thought he was a complete newcomer, so we can take her testimonial as honest and untainted by the fog of hype that was already surrounding the young performer: 'I do remember thinking how very talented Rowan Atkinson was, and telling him so, being quite unaware of who he was and his standing as a performer.' With praise like this, it was clear that Atkinson wouldn't remain in radio for much longer.

Only six months out of university, Rowan Atkinson had appeared in countless households even if he wasn't quite a household name. Yet although Humphrey Barclay reportedly offered him the chance of an LWT series he instead chose to take up an offer he had received from the BBC. John Lloyd, the radio producer who had seen his show was now finally developing his television sketch show, *Not the Nine O'Clock News*, and he wanted Rowan to be a part of it. Given the choice of his own starring vehicle and an ensemble comedy, Atkinson took the shrewder path of the ensemble show. Onstage it might be hilarious to see a clown fall flat on his face; offstage, in professional terms, it can be a disaster. One bad career move could ruin everything, so despite the offer of a solo series, Atkinson held back. As he reflected to Tony Bilbow in the Tyne-Tees programme *Play It Again* in 1981, there were huge risks with a solo venture: 'If you succeed, fine, but if you fail you really fail and it is hard to do anything for years after.' But perhaps, Atkinson was attracted by the prospect of working for the BBC as much as working for a team. According to an interview in the *Newcastle Journal* on 23 April 1980, he had turned down the chance of an ITV sketch show because, although ITV had more money to spend, the BBC gave performers more time to get things right. And that was something that was a priority for this perfectionist.

But there was still a risk involved. *Not the Nine O'Clock News* was a completely new venture. Its producer was new to television and a couple of months earlier had not even known that the series was happening. In early 1979, Lloyd had been up for three jobs, as a chat show host, a presenter of *That's Life* ('one of the boys at the back with the hair', he told the *Radio Times* in 1995), or as producer of a new sketch show. He chose the sketch show, but it was a steep learning curve. Then again, he couldn't have chosen a better year for a new show. It was a bad time for comedy in 1979: *Monty Python* was ten years old and the *Two Ronnies* ruled. *Not the Nine O'Clock News* seemed to be infected with a little bit of the punk spirit of the times, determined to kick over the traces and shatter false idols. In the process it was bound to be controversial. It would be only a matter of time before the letter writers were out in force. One letter in particular, sent to the *Radio Times*, seemed to highlight everything that was good about the show: 'Seldom has so much profanity, vulgarity and sheer lack of inventiveness filled my screen.' Anything that could prompt that sort of venom had to have something going for it.

Atkinson's career plan, opting for ensemble over solo work, certainly made sense. The very late 70s was part of a period in entertainment history, stretching back to the early 50s, when your first appearance on television from being onstage was as part of a troupe. Examples included *Monty Python* of course, but before that there had also been – containing many of the same performers – *At Last the 1948 Show* and *Do Not Adjust Your Set*. These shows were team efforts rather than the star vehicles that became the norm in the 80s and early 90s. It was very unusual in those days to promote stars and give them their own show. The people who commanded their own shows were the ones who had worked in music hall – Benny Hill, Dick Emery and Morecambe and Wise. The younger performers were put into teams, which meant there was less pressure. But more usefully for Atkinson, working as part of a team meant performer had to learn how to act, because in sketches they were not always playing the funny guy. In *Not the Nine O'Clock News*, Atkinson would play the funny lead, but also the straight guy or the bystander on the fringe. He had to learn to give other people lines and fit in with other performers. Ensemble sketch shows were incredibly useful tools for developing future stars – the Smith and Jones double act was a byproduct of *Not the Nine O'Clock News* in much the same way that *Two Ronnies* was a result of the apparent chemistry between these two comedians when they were part of the team on *The Frost Report* back in the 60s.

Probably the greatest confirmation that Atkinson made the right decision came a few years later when Emma Thompson, one of the next generation of Oxbridge alumni, was plucked out of the chorus line early in the mid-80s and given her own series. The critics had a field day, picking holes in a performer who simply was not ready for such close scrutiny. It is also worth noting that an Atkinson contemporary, Victoria Wood (who had a play running at London's Bush Theatre the same week that *Beyond a Joke* opened at the Hampstead Theatre), reportedly declined a place in the *Not the Nine O'Clock News* team in favour of pursuing a solo career, and it took her a considerable time to establish herself. What Atkinson opted for was not so much the easy route as the tried and tested traditional route. His ensuing success proved how shrewd he was even at that early age.

But things did not run as smoothly as this mechanic would have hoped. His *Not the Nine O'Clock News* début would be unceremoniously postponed. Although frustrating at the time, the delay to the launch of *Not the Nine O'Clock News* turned out to be positively advantageous. It would give the makers a vital breathing space in which to iron out creases in the show, which would conspire to make Rowan Atkinson stand out even more.

4

A Partly Political Broadcast

The original line-up of *Not the Nine O'Clock News*, put together in the spring of 1979, bore scant resemblance to the award-winning team that would eventually become household names. John Lloyd, the BBC radio producer who had recently done a stint on Roy Hudd's enduring comedy warhorse *The News Huddlines*, had moved into television and was looking to put together a team of comedians to bring satire back onto the screens for the first time since *That Was the Week That Was* in the early 60s. There was a theory that satire tended to be strong when there was a Conservative government; *That Was the Week That Was* had found its voice in the dog days of the Macmillan regime. In 1979, with the nation disillusioned with James Callaghan's Labour administration and a government that seemed to be constantly held to ransom by the unions, the mood in the air was for a swing back to the Conservatives.

The timing was certainly right, but was there the talent around to make a show like this work? If Lloyd had decided to make *Not the Nine O'Clock News* a couple of years later, he would have been able to cherry-pick the cream of the overtly political alternative comedy crop. Maybe Alexei Sayle or Rik Mayall would have been the linchpin in the ensemble. But in 1979 there weren't that many stand-up comedians apart from the Jim Davidson/Bernard Manning bowtied, frilly-shirted faction, who were happier singing the praises of the establishment and attacking embattled minorities than taking the mickey out of the majority. Instead Lloyd was forced to look to a mixture of actors and oddballs to make up his team.

For Atkinson it was the ideal set-up. As he had astutely observed, as part of a group he would shine if things were a success, and if things didn't work out as hoped, he wouldn't have to shoulder the entire blame himself. In many respects, *Not the Nine O'Clock News* was like a pepped-up version of the Oxford Revue. It wasn't exactly on the cutting edge of satire as some involved had hoped, and it could be smug and cosy at times, but it could also be very rude and very funny. Much of the success was down to the backroom team, and the combination of John Lloyd, who brought along his radio comedy experience, and co-producer Sean Hardie, who had a current affairs news background. It was a unique team-effort, taking comedy a step away from its traditional light-entertainment grounding.

Lloyd had been given a six-week slot on the proviso that he work with Hardie; between them they came up with a number of ideas and then promptly rejected them. At one point they were going to call it *Sacred Cows*, and each week dissect a modern-day trend. There was also an enthusiasm to do something that incorporated a visual element and wasn't just a television transfer of the radio programme *Weekending*. Lloyd tried to work out a way of incorporating the latex puppets made by the duo whose work finally ended up on *Spitting Image*.

Richard Sparks recalls visiting Lloyd in his flat when various ideas were still being floated: 'He said, "Look at these Fluck and Law puppets. I'm thinking of doing a show and calling it *United Nations TV*. I've got a couple of characters; the lead puppet is Perez De Quela. It's brilliant, but the problem is these puppets can't act." ' In the end he settled for the human puppet Atkinson, a man who could act but who was also as flexible as latex.

Atkinson's own philosophy of comedy seemed to strike the right note with Lloyd. In February 1979 he explained to the *Oxford Mail* how he believed it was possible to perform quality, credible work and also be hugely popular: 'I don't accept some people's attitude that if comedy is enjoyed by more than five people it can't be good.' At the same time, however, he did an impressive impression of an angry young man, suggesting that a number of the current comedians on television had got into a rut. The likes of the Two Ronnies, Dick Emery, Benny Hill and maybe even Morecambe and Wise were past their prime and things needed to be shaken up: 'They all roll back year after year and don't get any better. I can see why companies are pleased to pour money into new projects.' Fighting talk, indeed, from a young Turk who that month was still taking part in a revue at the Oxford Playhouse.

Only Atkinson would survive when the *Not the Nine O'Clock News* series made it really big. The unsung stars in that early line-up would have to find success elsewhere. John Gorman of comedy pop group The Scaffold and children's television show *Tiswas* was in the original line-up; lanky Chris Langham – almost as odd-looking as Atkinson, but not quite – made it as far as the first series before leaving to go on to greater things, working with the Muppets among others; he was almost the Pete Best of the group, but he has been so successful since that he could hardly regret his departure in retrospect. Veteran comic actor Willoughby Goddard, who had worked on and off with Charlie Drake for over 20 years, eventually cropped up as an archbishop in *The Black Adder*. Jonathan Hyde was also involved, but would ultimately find greater fame as a straight theatre actor. Then there was Christopher Godwin, another established stage actor, whose main comedy outings up to that point had been in sitcoms and plays by Alan Ayckbourn in Scarborough and at the Globe in London – 'I was very much an actor who played funny parts, while the others were mainly either stand-ups or people who worked in that genre. I remember thinking that this was a different discipline to the one I was used to. Very much more off the cuff.'

Godwin recalls working with Atkinson and his fleeting brush with comedy history that was dashed at the metaphorical eleventh hour. In reality it was more like the eighth hour: 'I was hired by John Lloyd, and we went ahead and filmed an episode. It was an attempt to renew a kind of comic political comment on television, but then a general election was called and a moratorium was put on anything that had a political content. We didn't know what was going to happen and then at about 8.30pm on the night of the recording, the *Not the Nine O'Clock News* team informed us that an election had been called and therefore there wasn't any point in our programme going out.' It was ironic that while *That Was the Week That Was* has been said to have played a part in bringing down the Conservative government in 1963, in 1979 it was the election of another Conservative government that nearly brought down *Not the Nine O'Clock News*.

The episode that was made was never screened in its original form, but Christopher Godwin recalls some of it did make it onto BBC2 after the elections. 'I saw some of the sketches go out when the series finally started. By that time though I was busy and I was not able to take part.' Chris Langham was surprised at the confusion surrounding the transmission delay; 'I can't quite understand how the BBC got itself into such a contentious position. They must have known an election was looming, but my memory of the period is bad because this was the 70s and I spent the time having too much of a good time.'

If the show had gone out as originally conceived, it would have made the links between Atkinson and John Cleese all the more explicit. Long before the age of post-modernism, the scheduled show was due to start with a sublime intertextual gag. *Not the Nine O'Clock News* was due to air on 2 April in the slot previously vacated by *Fawlty Towers*. This new sketch show, directed by Bob Spiers, started with John Cleese in Fawlty's character explaining that his sitcom was not ready so why didn't they fill the slot with 'a tatty revue'. There was more than a grain of truth to this remark: due to industrial action the final *Fawlty Towers* had yet to be completed, and was eventually transmitted later in the year.

Maybe Chris Langham's surprise at the last minute cancellation has a ring of truth about it. As he observed, the BBC knew an election was looming so why did they schedule it? It was actually listed in the *Radio Times* for two consecutive weeks but it went out in neither of them. There is a rather fetching media myth that maybe the transmission delay was the result of worries not just about the impending polls but also about the general content. Having made the programme, the powers that be may have been concerned not that it was controversial, but that it was just not funny enough.

This 'lost' *Not the Nine O'Clock News* episode was significantly different to the finished article. The rapid-repeat sketch style was the same and there were the same sort of satirical gags – such as an ad saying 'Come Home to a Real Fire, Buy a Cottage in Wales' that was eventually recycled – but the cast had been much larger the first time round. This was a show that, after *Python*'s freeform lunacy, was clearly trying to bring the punchline back. Atkinson explained the concept of the series to June Knox-Mawer on Radio 4's *Weekend Woman's Hour* in 1980: it was 'far less absurd ... we act quite well ... a sketch has got to be logical and real.' The original pilot and first show may have been too loose, and if it had been on ITV it may not have had a second shot. But the great thing about the BBC was that it was prepared to allow a series like to this to develop on the air rather than overdevelop beforehand and lose the spirit.

Not that there weren't some criticisms of the format from above. The delay gave Lloyd and Hardie a chance to go away and rethink things a little. The result was a tighter, more cohesive show that managed to nail down its targets rather than just flail around at anything in the hope of getting a few laughs. The cast, for example, was savagely trimmed back. In retrospect maybe the original *Not the Nine O'Clock News* wasn't exactly the political comedy that it had threatened to be. Its priority was clearly to be funny, with social comment as a fringe benefit. Christopher Godwin recalls that the original episode was pretty much made on the hoof. 'We only had a week's rehearsal and then we were lumped into this thing. We didn't know what the scripts were – they were giving us rewrites up until half an hour before recording.' Maybe it was no surprise that the programme had such an unstructured feel.

To some it might have seemed odd that Atkinson should have chosen to be part of this line-up. Despite his youth he had already been more successful in this field than the other members of the team. Maybe he should have taken advantage of his rising stock and gone solo, which is what a similar performer might do today. But he stayed, and the delay to the launch of *Not the Nine O'Clock News* worked to everyone's advantage. It gave John Lloyd and Sean Hardie a chance to take stock. Most of all, they took another look at the casting and decided it needed some honing. The result firmly swung the balance away from a comedy-acting direction and into an Oxbridge satire direction. John Lloyd had wanted a woman from the start but finding the right person had been the biggest challenge. He now went off on some very unlikely tangents. He had already approached Victoria Wood, who had sprung to fame on the ITV talent show *New Faces* but had yet to find a suitable television vehicle for her idiosyncratic comic songs, but she declined. Alison Steadman, who later went on to work regularly with (and marry and then separate from) Mike Leigh, was in the running for a while. In an attempt to prove that conventionally glamorous women could also be funny, he even considered Susan George, who was best known for her non-comedic role in the violent Sam Peckinpah movie *Straw Dogs* (though she had done some sitcom work, clocking up an appearance in ITV's *Doctor in the House*). Richard Sparks remembers Lloyd discussing his final choice, which, as is often the way in showbusiness, came about entirely by chance: 'He told me he had met this brilliant Australian woman, Pamela Stephenson, at a party.'

Smith and Jones were more likely contenders. Although Smith's background was originally in theatre, he had recently been doing a double act with Bob Goody; Jones had a background in radio production but Lloyd knew him well and knew he could do comedy (although for the first stage Jones was a subsidiary member, with Chris Langham retained from the aborted run as one of the core four). Besides, both Smith and Jones were from the Oxbridge performing pool – they *must* be talented. As Lloyd deliberated over the final line-up, the one constant element appeared to be Rowan Atkinson. It was almost as if *Not the Nine O'Clock News*, like *Beyond a Joke* and *Canned Laughter*, was a platform for his talents.

Eventually Lloyd opted for what, in retrospect, seems a pretty obvious format – a high-velocity sketch show taking a comic look at modern themes – a precursor of *The Fast Show* with fewer catch-phrases, fewer recurring characters and a more topical bent. The comedy was political but broad. Each week the team would get together to discuss what had irked them and would throw around ideas. The writers then went off, wrote furiously and the whole programme was made in one studio day the following Sunday. It was an extraordinarily tight schedule. There was little time for endless rehearsals; apart from the set-pieces shot on location it was very much comedy coming straight off the production line. When one routine was wrapped they would promptly move on to the next one. This quick turnover could create some problems. When the show started, the costume department had been worried about getting details of requirements far enough in advance. They hoped to get them the previous Sunday, but ended up getting them two days before shooting, on the Friday. But there was such a supportive atmosphere that everything seemed to fall into place.

Although it was often the political stabs that garnered public attention, there was plenty of material that wasn't that barbed. Sometimes it was the unexpected that received the most complaints. Footage would be shown of Iranians bowing down to Mecca *en masse* and a spoof BBC News voiceover would announce as a headline that in Iran the search was continuing for the Ayatollah's contact lens. Television programmes that took themselves too seriously were an obvious, but pertinent, target for mockery. When the first series finally started on 16 October 1979, the very first sketch would not be the Cleese/Fawlty one (that went out in the second week, the same week that the very last episode of *Fawlty Towers*, genuinely delayed by industrial action, was transmitted), but a spoof of the credits to John le Carré's award-winning spy drama *Tinker, Tailor, Soldier, Spy*. The Cold War credits looked similar: a Russian doll was opened up to reveal more Russian dolls. Except that in this version the final doll was opened to reveal a boiled egg.

In the summer of 1979, in the hiatus before *Not the Nine O'Clock News* started, there was an opportunity for Atkinson to attend to other outstanding business. He was invited to showcase some of his best material in front of the greatest comics around. *The Secret Policeman's Ball* at Her Majesty's Theatre in the Haymarket in London, directed by John Cleese and running over four nights from 27 June, was something of precursor of Comic Relief, gathering together benevolent, philanthropic showbusiness names in aid of a good cause. That summer the cause was Amnesty International, though most people who went to these shows were probably there to see the likes of Peter Cook, Victoria Wood, Billy Connolly, the *Beyond the Fringe* team and sundry Pythons. Human Rights came a little lower down the bill.

Atkinson may have been the new boy but his talents certainly justified his inclusion. Once again, it was the Schoolmaster sketch that earnt him the most rapturous applause. This was a routine now taking on classic status of dead-parrot-like proportions. Richard Sparks, who had penned the sketch on that hungover summer morning for the Hampstead Theatre show, remembers the event clearly. Until then his sketch had been a well-reviewed live favourite. Now, with sellout concerts (and a television transmission of the concert highlights on ITV on 22 December 1979, just as Atkinson was establishing himself on *Not the Nine O'Clock News*), the sketch would find a much wider audience. 'It was *The Secret Policeman's Ball* that launched the Schoolmaster sketch and the credit for that goes to John Cleese,' says Sparks. 'Rowan called me up, terribly excited, and said he'd just had a call from John Cleese asking him to do the Schoolmaster sketch. He asked me if that was alright and I said "sure".' The gangly star of the *Python* team had pushed Rowan's career up a few notches. 'Cleese was his mentor,' says Sparks.

Every member of the audience seemed to know the names on that notorious roll-call, but despite the odd interruption Atkinson's grim visage never cracked; in fact, when someone responded with the heckle 'here', he even ad libbed with a line that was threatening enough to silence any ex-public-schoolboy: 'I have a detention book.' It was not just those words. Atkinson's eyes darted around the room; his pen seemed poised like a deadly weapon. Eventually the audience could not contain itself any longer. By the time Atkinson bellowed 'Nibble, leave orifice alone' at the top of his voice, his was the only straight face in the house.

His classical pianist mime was also greeted by rapturous applause. As his hunched white-gloved figure played an invisible keyboard, Chopin's *Nocturne in C Sharp* rang out. As the song reached a crescendo, Atkinson would get overexcited; when the mood became melancholy he would become tearful. His upper lip would quiver, as if he was on the verge of suicidal despair. When it became too slow he would feign sleepiness. It was as if the music was dictating his very being. When he glanced at his watch and realized that time was moving on, he speeded up and rattled through the piece – at the point which, of course, it should have sounded like this. He had studied the piano for two years at school and regretted giving it up, but that short period of study had reaped benefits, inspiring one of the most enduring routines in his award-winning repertoire.

When he came on with John Cleese, Michael Palin and Terry Jones to do the Four Yorkshiremen sketch ('By God we 'ad it tough . . .') the response from the audience was a mixture of disbelief and awe. On the one hand, how could this upstart with the rubber face share stage-space with these comedy gods? It was like Donny Osmond duetting with The Beatles. Then again, dismay was soon replaced by admiration that Atkinson actually managed to pull it off, bluff Yorkshire accent, fake moustache and all, and fit in. If there was any comedy baton-passing to be done, it was done that night – this was the ultimate endorsement of Atkinson's talents. He seemed to be rapidly taking on the role of junior Python (in fact one internet website now – erroneously but understandably – claims that Atkinson was a late member of *Monty Python's Flying Circus*). He was really the only comic around that could assume that role. You couldn't imagine Billy Connolly, the former Clydeside welder, fitting in quite so neatly.

The connection didn't end there. In the Stake Your Claim sketch he played the straight quizmaster to Michael Palin's claimant who said he written plays that were over 300 years old, which, as Atkinson pointed out with ruthless logic, was where the claim falls down. His status was further rubber-stamped by the old guard when he appeared in a famous *Beyond the Fringe* sketch, The End of the World. Along with the likes of Peter Cook and Eleanor Bron, Atkinson squatted onstage with a v-neck pullover over his head, listening to their guru Peter Cook's every word and awaiting the apocalypse on the top of a mountain. It didn't come of course. All that came was a rapturous round of applause as Atkinson repeated over and over again in a sublimely strangled voice, 'Will this wind be so mighty as to lay low the mountains of the earth?' Eventually Peter Cook replied, quite simply, 'No'. That was why they had come up on the mountains – to evade the wind. When the end of the world does not come, everyone gets up to leave and Cook reminds them to come back tomorrow. Sooner or later they have got to get it right.

Atkinson was being groomed to follow in the steps of Cook and Cleese. Among all the relative newcomers who took part in the show he seemed to get the biggest breaks and the funniest lines. That Oxbridge Mafia, a bloodline coarsing through the veins of Peter Cook and John Cleese, was alive and well and onstage at Her Majesty's Theatre.

It seemed quite bizarre that, having conquered the West End of London and being on the brink of co-starring in a new television series, Atkinson should return to his old stamping ground, the Edinburgh Festival, in the summer of 1979. Maybe he realized this would be the last time he would be able to appear there as a relative unknown, This time though, things were different. Atkinson was a professional performer and he wasn't going to be performing in a back-street club where no one could see the stage; however, he nearly did.

Atkinson teamed up with three Oxford friends from the Woodstock Road days – Chris Naylor, who looked after the finances, designer

Will Bowen and Pierre Audi who worked on *Beyond A Joke*. They had the ingenious idea of setting up an audacious venue called the Wireworks in a huge, completely bare, disused factory behind the Festival Fringe office. Today the factory would be converted into desirable and chic loft residences. Then, at the height of the experimental theatre boom and the desire for unusual spaces, the more obvious thing to do was to put on a show there. Rowan donned his boiler suit and hard hat, grabbed his spanner and chipped in to help; nearly 50 tons of scaffolding had to be erected. It was a mind-numbing process, heaving gear in and out all day and rehearsing all night. If performers were told that rehearsal started at three, it usually meant three in the morning, not three in the afternoon.

Despite favourable word-of-mouth publicity, suggesting the show would be a big success, things didn't go quite to plan. The audience in the gallery, which jutted out, couldn't see the stage except from the front row, so there were only 18 seats that were useable. The other 150 seats, which they needed to fill to break even, were rendered redundant. The team tried to salvage things. They considered raising the stage to give more of the gallery a view, but then the people in the first six rows of the stalls wouldn't be able to see. Atkinson wasn't quite convinced that all the effort was worth it, but persevered with the shows anyway. In the future though, he would get things organized better, although he didn't blame the team. In the end though, this was Rowan's most enjoyable Edinburgh and his most successful, a spot of relative pre-fame calm before the storm.

Once again Atkinson's Schoolmaster took centre stage. By now he had done it so many times he was confident enough to know where it was safe to tinker about with it. As he walked on to lecture Form 4 and call out those names he was more restrained than usual, knowing that the gag was as much about the sound and the gradual build-up as it was about the actual names. 'You're a moron, Undermanager' wasn't just funny because it was abusive, it was funny because of the way Atkinson pronounced the word 'Moron'.

In another sketch, Senator Brea's Dead, Atkinson performed with Richard Curtis. They played a couple of whispering, gossiping mandarins, with Atkinson as an American unable to get to grips with the devastating news of the death of Senator Brea, not because of denial but because he is so dim. Curtis explains that he heard it from the horse's mouth, and Atkinson thinks he is referring to a real horse; they digress and start comparing the number of rinses needed with elderberry conditioner, which they both use. Once again, Atkinson's fleet of verbal foot wins the day when it turns out they both use it twice: 'I do two too,' he says excitedly. Another sketch, devised by Atkinson and Richard Curtis, also made its mark. Atkinson played a mute character who could not stop himself from dozing off. Atkinson later told the *Express on Sunday* that this marked the birth of Mr Bean.

The show was a critical success and won a Scotsman Fringe First, the huge copper plaque that in the pre-Perrier Award days was the highest accolade a comedy show could get in Edinburgh. It was a particularly strong year, too. Emma Thompson and Hugh Laurie from Cambridge were there, while Oxford contemporary Angus Deayton was a member of the spoof pop group the Heebegeebees, which was part of that year's Oxford Revue.

Today Atkinson's show might be eligible for a Perrier Award – though this is debatable because of a question mark over how much of the act was new and how much was from *Beyond a Joke* – but in the days before Perrier there was a bit of a fuss when the show took top honours because Fringe Firsts usually went to plays. But there was no way Atkinson could miss out on an award. If he wasn't known at the beginning, by the end of the Festival he was a fully fledged star. The Edinburgh Television Festival had started and the BBC bosses were flocking in like sheep to see the latest light-entertainment hope – of course, having pulled the plug on the initial run of *Not the Nine O'Clock News*, this was the only place they could see him. Atkinson's success seemed assured. He had consolidated his reputation with *The Secret Policeman's Ball* and built some rock-solid foundations with Edinburgh. Soon after that significant summer he started filming the BBC series he had chosen in preference to his own ITV show. Clearly he bore Auntie no malice, having failed to get a technical position there.

Interestingly enough, the final *Not the Nine O'Clock News* team seemed automatically to set up Atkinson as the solo male star because Smith and Jones formed such a natural team and Stephenson was the female star. Writer Dick Fiddy wrote some sketches and found Atkinson's contributions always useful: 'He was just superb. He worked in a different way then. That was part of being a group; it was much less intense.' The turnover of material was so rapid, being devised and recorded within the week of transmission, there was little time to get obsessed about one's performance. It was comedy against the clock and all the sharper for it.

Competition to get jokes in was fierce. Although there was a core team of regular writers, including Richard Curtis, John Lloyd and Sean Hardie operated an open-door policy so that anyone could submit material – as long as they didn't mind its being rejected out of hand. There were very few boundaries – the sketches had to be fast and, for reasons of realism, if they featured hospitals or trains they would have to look rundown and the staff would have to look harassed; they had to be contemporary rather than topical – but as long as the material was funny it stood a fighting chance. Among the aspiring new writers was an American actress called Ruby Wax, although sometimes her material took a bit of honing. Richard Sparks worked on the show for a while and recalls giving her some tips: 'She had this sketch about aeroplane passengers in a crash who were so hungry they ended up eating each other. I said you've got it the wrong way round. They were so hungry they started eating the airline food.'

As at Oxford, Atkinson's distinctive features – distinctive even among the most odd-looking comedy ensemble ever gathered together for a television series – singled him out as the star. One of his new characters, known simply as the Ranting Man, also became something of a national celebrity. Like Peter Cook's E. L. Wisty on speed cross-bred with Mary Whitehouse, Atkinson's invention would be lurking in the studio audience inside his mac and at an unexpected point in the show would stand up to protest at something that was annoying him. He was Disgusted of Tunbridge Wells gone mad, and there was, Atkinson conceded, some of himself in there too. The Ranting Man first appeared in the second show of the series, which came as some surprise to the commissionaire, who was there to make sure the audience didn't disrupt the recording by chattering or rustling sweet papers. Suddenly the commissionaire was confronted by someone standing up and shouting. Not recognizing Atkinson and not realizing this was part of the show, he intervened and tried to shut him up. Fortunately this just made the scene funnier and more realistic. The cameras kept rolling and the scene was screened, showing Atkinson putting the boot into bland programming such as *That's Life* (the show that Lloyd had nearly co-presented) and *Nationwide*, calling the latter, with some accuracy, 'bloody characterless commuter entertainment' that insisted on filling the screens with interviews with people who could impersonate trombones.

This proved to be a slightly ticklish matter when he appeared on the BBC early evening magazine *Nationwide* to promote some live shows. Atkinson, complete with punky, loose-hanging skinny tie, seemed to be attempting to hide behind his mop of hair as the clip was screened. Presenter Hugh Scully asked him if he really felt like that? Atkinson, the epitome of politeness, demurred and claimed that *Not the Nine O'Clock News* had been put together so frenetically that he didn't remember particular sketches. But he did concede that he may have caught an episode of *Nationwide* that had included these types of items and he had decided to let his character voice his complaints.

Of course, *Not the Nine O'Clock News* embodied a type of middle class punkiness. The team could hardly claim to be streetwise and probably thought the height of rebellion was repeated claims that Thatcherite MP Keith Joseph was dull. Their failure to embrace punk ideology was confirmed when they sent up punk rock with their own new-wave band, led by Mel Smith, performing *Gob on You*.

This was one of the first of many musical parodies that became the show's speciality. The way they approached the task broke away from the style of previous comics. They tried to make the song as real as possible and to get the look, whereas the 'Two Ronnies' for instance might have just donned a couple of wigs. (Their criticism of the older style of parody smacked of the disingenuousness of youth. The simple fact that Ronnie Corbett and Ronnie Barker were middle-aged gave them a distinct disadvantage when it came to sending up pop bands of the day. Ronnie Corbett's particularly flesh-creeping take on Boy George, complete with false dreadlocks, is still a haunting memory.) Meanwhile Howard Goodall, who did the bulk of the music alongside Philip Pope, Peter Brewis and Chris Judge Smith, would concentrate on aping the musical style of, say, Abba or Barry Manilow. It helped, of course, that the team was under 30 and loved music.

Neither Atkinson nor Richard Curtis was not afraid to try out new forms of comedy. While the show was supposed to have a toothsome satirical bite, Atkinson's routines tended towards the simply odd or classically funny, rather than the political. John Lloyd, with considerable insight, was open enough to their ideas to give them a chance. One sketch had a minimal script, just saying that Rowan was walking down a street looking at the camera and then he walked into a lamppost. Lloyd read the script and turned the page looking for the punchline but there wasn't any more to it. Nonetheless he was persuaded by Atkinson that it would work, and a small crew went off to film the sequence later that day. The result was hilarious, classic and wry. It was pure slapstick and also recalled the scene in Jacques Tati's film *Mon Oncle* in which a group of French schoolboys amuse themselves by trying to guess which passer-by will walk into a nearby lamppost when they are distracted. In the first clip Atkinson, grinning and waving camply at the camera as he walked, whacked himself in the head on a post. In the second clip, he smugly avoided the lamppost only to fall down a pavement cellar. If Buster Keaton hadn't already done that joke, or at least a variant, he certainly should have.

From word-of-mouth praise, the success of the series really began to take off by the sixth show. Monty Python's film *The Life of Brian* had opened in Britain that month and had been attacked by Christian groups. The Festival of Light condemned it as being 'a parody of the life of Our Lord Jesus Christ', showing him as an ignorant zealot. It was even banned in some areas. But, of course, the whole point of the film was the absurdity of following false prophets. The *Not the Nine O'Clock News* team took this to its logical conclusion and featured a sketch, written by Colin Bostock-Smith, in which Pamela Stephenson interviewed Mel Smith, who played film critic Alexander Walker, and Rowan, who played the cross-caressing film director, the Bishop of Wroxeter. The discussion was about the bishop's new controversial film *The General Synod's Life of Christ*, which, protestors argued, sent up followers of the much-revered comedy troupe with its ludicrous tale of the rise of a carpenter's son called Jesus Christ. Walker argued that this story of Christ was basically a blasphemous send-up of the Comic Messiah himself, John Cleese. Why, even the initials J. C. were the same. This turned out to be world turned upside down where the state religion was Pythonism. It was a cosy Oxbridge in-joke (you might have thought Cleese had even suggested it), but it was also a pointed and even political sketch about the nature of tolerance. Oh, and it was very funny too. After a faltering start, the team had made its mark.

Atkinson seemed to be making a habit out of playing vicars. Richard Curtis liked writing them because a sermon was a setting in which Atkinson would naturally be addressing a captive audience. It was also a very formal situation with a very formalized structure, and that too made it a rich seed-bed for comedy. Curtis was not the only writer who discovered this. Alistair Beaton wrote the Gay Christian sketch, which Atkinson performed. He was another typical tentative, repressed and awkward priest who tried to show tolerance to homosexuals, encouraging them to 'come out of the toilet, as the phrase has it'. He sounds sympathetic but in the end concludes that gay people are destined to have a hard time: 'God's like that. He hates poofs.'

The only element of the show that did not seem to gel was Chris Langham. He was let go at the end of the first series. Not surprisingly he was initially bitter about his ousting. More surprisingly, for a while he directed part of his resentment at Atkinson: 'Probably because he was the one that was getting so much press attention,' Langham recalls. He eventually accepted that in the end he only had himself to blame for his premature departure. But as the show grew in popularity, particularly after he had left, he had to find a way to cope with the events: 'I didn't read the papers for a year. I was a bit ashamed of myself.' For a while he blamed Atkinson, until later he found out that the young star had been very supportive of him: 'When I was dropped I was hurt and I nurtured a resentment of him. In fact it turned out that after I had left, Rowan actually went to John Lloyd to ask him personally to have me back.'

Atkinson, however, had become established as the real star of the show. Langham recalls one sketch that barely had a script but was still verbally hilarious: 'There was a sketch in which he walked through the audience just saying, 'bloody'. Everyone thought this was funny and outrageous in the late 70s, but it was also very funny because of the way Rowan said it. Through the controversy of the language, there was a naturally funny person too. And he seemed to get pleasure from it. He was a naturally gifted person and clearly not frightened to be laughed at, which is quite unusual among English comedians.'

The success of Atkinson made Langham realize what a fantastic chance he had blown. It had all been a great adventure to him and maybe he had not taken it as seriously as he should have. 'You don't think of things like that when you are young; you don't get into comedy and take out a pension fund.' Langham could see that Atkinson's way of working was unusual. 'Unlike America,' where Langham also worked extensively with the Muppets, 'the British way is to do things half-heartedly and then be a bit embarrassed when it works. There is a reticence among Light Entertainment to take the work too seriously. There is this love of the gentleman amateurs over here. We do ourselves a bit of a disservice; whereas in America there are endless retakes. Rowan can get a certain number of laughs just by pulling faces, but what makes it really work is the mental chemistry.'

As the 70s turned into the 80s it was a strange time for Atkinson. Apart from his *Not the Nine O'Clock News* colleagues and Curtis and Goodall, there seemed to be very few people on his wavelength. Atkinson was now known as someone who could be anarchic and unpredictable but also amazingly controlled. Physically he seemed able to get into positions no ordinary human body should have been capable of. He seemed to have more joints than was fair. Despite this remarkable facility for physical humour, however, he would still get nervous before a live performance, sitting silently for 45 minutes before going onstage.

Although there were some difficulties with fans when he was trying to go about his ordinary business in London, the extent of his fame only hit him when he went back to Stocksfield for Christmas at the end of 1979. Suddenly he found himself being congratulated by countless long-lost family friends appearing at cocktail parties. It finally dawned on him that he was really famous when he was recognized in the streets where he had grown up, quietly pottering away with anything mechanical he could lay his hands on. There was no turning back.

With Griff Rhys Jones promoted to full fourth member, things really clicked into gear with the second series of *Not the Nine O'Clock News*, which started on 31 March 1980. This was the series that would go on to win the Silver Rose at the Montreux Television Festival. Although they were a contrived group, as manufactured as the Spice Girls, there was an undeniable chemistry among the quartet.

Griff Rhys Jones was the lantern-jawed cynic who could also do a mean impression of Melvyn Bragg and Michael Parkinson; Mel Smith was the manic long-haired hippy; Stephenson revealed a genuine facility for mimicry; and Atkinson just kept doing what he had been doing in solo shows and on *Canned Laughter*. The series was irreverent and pacey, managing to combine the intelligence of *Monty Python* with accessibility.

It was a period when egos didn't get in the way and there was a general air that the team was doing something groundbreaking. Until then Atkinson had really specialized in silly monologues, but now the others encouraged him to stretch himself and he started to contribute more physical comedy.

The popularity of the show caused friction across the country. Hailed as the funniest comedy show in many years, it even had to be moved to 9.30pm at times because in those pre-video days there were so many household arguments between family members; some wanted to watch the real BBC *Nine O'clock News*, while others preferred this partly political broadcast on behalf of the Daft Party.

The show consolidated the team's fame, but also shored up Atkinson's working relationship with Richard Curtis as they came up with more sketches. Inspiration came from some strange areas. In one sketch, Rowan played the Under Secretary for Defence, giving out advice in the event of a nuclear war. (It should be remembered that nuclear war was an abiding national fear in the early 80s; CND was undergoing a renaissance and Communist Russia was seen as the greatest menace to global peace.) The advice was simply that men should make the most of their short time left and sow their wild oats. This idea had sprung from a conversation Richard Curtis had had with a friend who had told him that he had a 'four-minute pact' with a female colleague. If the four-minute warning went they had agreed to make the most of it and throw themselves into each other's arms.

But success was not straightforward for Atkinson. Television stardom meant that he was public property and he had mixed feelings about it. He had the kind of face that got noticed. Although perfectly relaxed with his friends, he was uncomfortable about the fame factor and its paradoxes. *Not the Nine O'Clock News* had fans chanting catchphrases and lines just as *Monty Python* had done a decade earlier and *The Fast Show* fans would do a decade later, but when sixth formers approached Atkinson and told him they were renowned in the school for their Atkinson impersonations he would swiftly beat a hasty retreat. Attention onstage was one thing, but attention off it was another. One evening he was in a pizza restaurant and someone leapt up and kept saying to him 'Is it Nine O'Clock yet?' The problem was that the public wouldn't let Atkinson lead an ordinary public life. On *Weekend Woman's Hour* in May 1980 he tried to put on a brave face about these intrusions, which got in the way of his life; nevertheless, he did admit that he was 'slightly irked' when a petrol pump attendant took it upon himself to announce rather surreally that, 'This is not a garage' while filling up Atkinson's car. He just wanted to sit in the pub and have a pint of Guinness, a bag of crisps and a sandwich, but it was getting increasingly difficult. Then again, his logical mind had computed the viewing figures and told him that he ought to be even more anxious if people didn't recognize him offscreen. Faced with the double-edged sword of celebrity Atkinson agreed to be interviewed by the press but found the experiences difficult. His stammer, which would disappear during performance, would sometimes return in the form of pauses when he was put under an intense spotlight by probing journalists eager to categorize him.

It seemed quite odd that this big star was still living something of a student life, albeit it in one of the posher corners of Kilburn. Having moved to London from Oxford, Atkinson was still sharing a house with his friend Bob Maxon-Brown, who had read law at Oxford. Atkinson's own studies came in handy too. It was an old house and when he had first moved in he had helped to rewire it in lieu of rent. Atkinson had the top room, but it was rapidly becoming cramped as he accumulated more possessions. His percussion kits were still stacked up in cases because there was little time to get them out – or little space to put them away, once assembled. Life was like a well-bred commune. Howard Goodall lived in the room below him. Doug Lucie was nearly right – Oxford had moved to Camden, or at least to nearby Kilburn. Richard Curtis, however, was putting down roots right in the heart of Camden Town. He was now living in a crowded townhouse at 15 Iver Street just beneath an old railway arch. It was a quaint little street with a colourful history. It had originally had a different name but after a gruesome murder the name had been changed so that it did not put people off living there. Some of the houses had been illegal drinking dens in the past, but the first tell-tale signs of 80s gentrification were starting to appear. At one point his house had been the smartest in the street, but the others were currently being bought up, skips were appearing outside and builders were making themselves cups of tea – a sure sign that work might be starting at some point. Curtis meanwhile tried to write in his basement while all around him things were changing.

Soon Atkinson's Kilburn lodgings became impractical, and he took out a modest mortgage and moved to the Kentish Town end of Camden. *The Guardian* visited his house and commented on its sparseness, noticing little more than ordered filing cabinets and a huge Laurel and Hardy photograph in which the silent comedians were moping around. The paper concluded that Atkinson was the definitive anal-retentive sad-eyed clown. It didn't allow for the fact that he had only just moved into the house and had been too busy to furnish it.

Later, however, the house would become cluttered with gadgets. The sitting room would accumulate expensive hi-fi systems and other equipment. Having studied electronics for six years, Atkinson did not completely squander his knowledge. In the evenings in preparation for his live shows he would help to put together sound-effects tapes. Technical matters had always been a riveting hobby when he had the time, which was becoming increasingly rare now. Back in 1976 he had attempted to construct his own electric organ, but by 1980 it was only half-finished and he sold it. Things were becoming more frenetic all the time and he needed some space. By the autumn of 1980, Atkinson was already considering moving out of London.

By now Atkinson was well aware that he had become a comedy star by a relatively rare route. He had never done what one would call stand-up comedy. Even in his live solo shows he didn't really tell what you could call jokes, or even stories. Like a one-man old-fashioned revue with an 80s anarchism, he simply created little characters and vignettes for the audience to chuckle at. When journalists would ask him to describe himself, he was keen to say 'character actor' or performer with a 'comic bias'. If you wanted to get on his wrong side, all you had to do was call him a 'comic'. In the *Daily*

Mirror he said he was already looking for ways of breaking out of the funny-face mould: 'I rather like the Woody Allen idea – he's a tragic character who plays it funny. I certainly see that as a sort of stage two in my career.' He even saw a future playing tragedy where other funny men had played the fool: 'Perhaps I have a slightly better chance of playing Hamlet than Ken Dodd,' he joked.

Even Atkinson's offstage pursuits set him apart from his peers. There was no celebrity golf, just truck driving. Having got into mechanics tinkering about with the equipment on his father's farm, he now liked lorries more than ever. He even did a send-up of his hobby in the third series of *Not the Nine O'Clock News* with a musical homage to the sexy Yorkie Man ads of the day with the innuendo-laden hook-line of 'I like truckin' and 'I like to truck.' The sketch caused outrage because a truck was seen to run over a hedgehog. Showing how quickly the writers could react to events, a spoof apology appeared the following week – but the gag continued. Using archive footage they made it look as if Princess Anne had also run over a hedgehog in her Land Rover.

Still a technician at heart, he told *The Observer* with great pride that he had helped build his Edinburgh Festival stage at Wireworks in 1979, but he was proudest of all of having passed his HGV Test; he could now drive modest-sized trucks on the open road himself, and he talked earnestly of the possibility of packing performance in and setting up a theatrical trucking agency. He felt there was nothing better than being out on the open road in the cab of a juggernaut all on one's own, although he was also partial to fast cars and still only in his mid-20s was already awaiting delivery of his first Aston Martin. There was a primitive kind of job satisfaction in getting into a large vehicle and conveying goods from A to B. One could say that performing was also conveying something from A to B – passing his comic insights on to an audience in return for laughs and appreciation – but Atkinson didn't see it like that. Performing was too abstract by comparison, and the road on which those laughs were transported could be a tortuous and depressing one. Driving was simpler, with less scope for failure – traffic jams and breakdowns permitting. Even washing cars gave him an inordinate amount of pleasure. A shiny car was a job well done and gave him a great sense of achievement. 'I've always been a bit of a loner and lorry driving is a loner's dream,' he told the *Daily Mail*. 'I love the sense of power and responsibility. I suppose it reveals a suppressed megalomania.' Standing onstage was far more fraught. In 1981 he told Tony Bilbow: 'If it works, all you can feel is relief; I've rarely felt real elation, more thank God that worked.' Comedy was a precarious business and Atkinson behaved as if every great joke might be his last. It seemed that there was too much responsibility in putting on a solo show for there ever to be much enjoyment in it. And yet, to continue the motoring metaphor, performing was very much what he was driven to do.

Atkinson spent the time between the second and third series of *Not the Nine O'Clock News* taking his well-honed show on the road for four months. It was something he seemed compelled to do, even though at times he felt it was the loneliest job in the world. He was also doing something unique. He was not being himself, or being a stand-up comic telling jokes, he was occupying a halfway house between stand-up and acting. Fortunately though, people seemed to appreciate what he was doing. Apart from the occasional matinée where the elderly might have been sheltering from the cold in the cheap seats, he seemed to go down very well. He rarely got heckled; a dozy silence was the worst response when he had appeared live a couple of years earlier.

This time round he harked back to his Oxford Revue act, but combined the set-pieces with some skits from *Not the Nine O'Clock News*. It was immortalized on his first album release, *Rowan Atkinson Live in Belfast*, recorded at the Grand Opera House in its week of reopening at the end of the tour. Atkinson started the show with a moment of sublime self-parody. As the man in seat C23, a live incarnation of his television ranter, he complained out loud about modern architecture, the shooting of J.R. in *Dallas* ('give me a gun and I'll shoot the bloody lot of them') and shouted that he wanted opera, not this 'rubber-faced twat'. It was the way he had already been described by a thousand critics and now he was turning it back on them by mocking himself.

As the audience settled down, Atkinson made his way onstage to present a speech from a member of the great and good, Sir Marcus Browning MP, which revisited the talk of Sir Benjamin Fletcher in *The Atkinson People*, his 'directionless blather' that harked back to an Alan Bennett sketch in *Beyond the Fringe*. Browning was either sozzled or had a speech impediment rather like Roy 'Woy' Jenkins, or both, confessing that this was the worst economic crisis since 1380 and lusting after the Lady Mayoress. His political affiliations were not spelt out, but he certainly seemed more Tory than Labour.

As Atkinson hit his stride he embarked upon his by then well-established Father of the Bride routine. Richard Curtis had recently found himself being invited to more and more weddings and each time the same archetypes seemed to crop up. Without consciously studying these characters, he did register some of the more comic aspects of their personalities for future use. Nipping behind a curtain at the back of the stage when costume changes were required, Atkinson initially assumed the persona of a trendy vicar at a wedding, talking of 'God the laughter giver' and 'Christ the comedian'. He then took on the role of the best man presenting his wedding speech. Unfortunately he is not only horribly hungover, he has lost the speech and starts jibbering and stuttering. In the end it is all he can do to wish the happy couple a ripping time and hope that the dress survives. Putting icing on the cake, Atkinson then assumed the role of the father of the bride, who is unhappy about his daughter's choice of husband and unhappy about the cost. Having suggested that she is getting hitched to the kind of man you would emigrate to avoid, he concludes by toasting the caterers and the pigeon who left its mark on the groom's limousine outside the church. Perhaps the only remark that did not hit the right note was describing the son as an 'utter spastic', even though it was not such an unacceptable term of abuse in the early 80s.

Atkinson followed this up with his now established musical number *Do Bears?* Sporting aviator sunglasses, large lapels and a gold lamé jacket, he listed those rhetorical questions – 'Is the Pope Catholic? Is Luxembourg small', before concluding, somewhat coyly, 'Do bears sh...alalalala?'. Senator Brea's Dead, his two-hander with Richard Curtis, was also revived. Then he once again donned horns and played The Suavest Devil in town – 'but you can call me Toby.' Various demographics were damned, from bank mangers to looters to everyone who saw *The Life of Brian* – a new reference just to put a topical spin on an old show. When there had been a furore about the *Python* film, some bright spark had pointed out that if God exists he would be omniscient so ought to be able to deal with a little English film. Apparently they were wrong: 'He can't take a joke after all.' Of all of his material, the Devil sketch had the most straightforward one-line jokes in it ('Sodomites – over there against the wall'). For once the writing had been more of a free-for-all, with anyone chipping in gags they thought were appropriate.

There were more echoes of *Python* in Impatient Man in Queue behind Student, in which Atkinson did his best Cleese/Fawlty exasperation to date as a commuter held up in line and finding everything about the person in front annoying – even the fact that a student has a Barclaycard.

It seemed that at his best, Atkinson had the potential to outshine the Pythons. His material was strong and varied and he was confident enough to try anything. He even did the old routine about the secret of great comedy, where the answer, 'timing', is delivered at precisely the wrong time. The joke was deconstructed to the extent that in anyone else's hands it might have ceased to be funny, but here it made a fitting climax to the show. Particularly as Atkinson had indeed discovered the secret of great comedy.

There was a hero's welcome by the time the tour hit Oxford. During his three nights at the Oxford Playhouse the audience was laughing so loudly it was hard to hear what was being said onstage; however, since much of the act was essentially visual anyway, it was not too much of a problem. Atkinson was at the peak of his powers. Chris Gray in the *Oxford Mail* praised his timing: 'At its best in his role as an American diplomat answering non-stop calls on three telephones, trying simultaneously to bargain with world leaders, tell knock-knock jokes to his children and order a take-away pizza'.

This was Atkinson's most successful year to date, when he combined live performance with two runs of *Not the Nine O'Clock News*. But Atkinson also developed a rather useful sideline as a star for hire, appearing in cameos on other people's shows. But whenever he did it, he always appeared as Rowan Atkinson, and anyone who had Atkinson as a guest risked being upstaged.

In April he was an unlikely guest on *Lena*, the mainstream variety show hosted by the child-star Lena Zavaroni. It must have been the first time Atkinson had ever been introduced by someone even younger than himself, and he dutifully performed his classical pianist piece, donning his tuxedo and white gloves and miming to a Beethoven sonata, dozing off in the slow bits, weeping in the sad passages and finally shutting his fingers in the imaginary lid.

But by the summer of 1980 he appeared to be carving out a niche for himself as a character comic who could nip into other people's shows without compromising his own style. Often when he appeared on someone's show, his sketches would not include the host of the show. He was becoming very adept at what were effectively star cameos.

One of his appearances was in *The Innes Book of Records*, the music-based show fronted by Neil Innes, the former Bonzo Dog Doodah Band musician who had frequently worked with the *Monty Python* team, particularly Eric Idle (Innes wrote the music for Idle's pop spoof *The Rutles*). Innes's show tended to dispense with the usual broken comedy format, instead presenting itself like a record – instead of sketches there were tracks, maybe a punk pastiche or a brass band take-off. Innes had a quirky sense of humour, but also a very gentle one, a million miles away from the topical humour that the *Not the Nine O'Clock News* team was capable of. In this context, however, Atkinson's main contribution to the 30 June edition seemed decidedly perverse, but it did reveal his extremely fortunate ability to fit into all sorts of comedy categories. 'Hallo, today I'd like to talk to you on the subject of organs,' he said in that strangled voice, part E.L. Wisty, part John Major-before-anyone-had-heard-of-John-Major, that he often pulled out when he wanted to be particularly annoying. Likewise, he sported a rather irritating tweedy jacket and stood in front of a huge church organ, making it clear that, obviously, there was nothing of a sexual nature in his use of the word 'organ'. The innuendo was not lost on the audience, particularly when he continued to talk excitedly about his fondness for organs – the musical variety – because there were no small ones: 'only big ones'. The pipes, on the other hand, came in all sorts of sizes: 'I've seen pipes so small you can't see them.' It was a sketch that could have appeared on any show. Innes didn't feature in it, and it was only notionally connected to music. It ended as abruptly as it began, cutting to a couple in a boat listening to a wind-up gramophone, which introduced the next skit from Innes.

As the *Innes Book of Records* was being transmitted on BBC2, Atkinson filmed his appearances in *Peter Cook & Co.*, an LWT one-off special executively produced by his early television champion Humphrey Barclay. Peter Cook had never quite punched his weight as a solo performer and in the 70s had appeared content to swan from chat show to chat show being witty and urbane. This would-be star vehicle lined up a host of comedy stars, ranging from John Cleese to Beryl Reid, to the point where Cook was virtually overshadowed.

Despite writing much of the show, which was transmitted on 14 September, Cook didn't even appear in a railway carriage sketch in which Atkinson, sporting a mac and reedy voice sat opposite bowler-hatted city gent Terry Jones. 'Hello. Are you gay?' asked Atkinson in that distinctive nerd voice that he had recently used on the *Innes Book of Records*. Jones said 'no' and hid behind his *Financial Times* but Atkinson persisted. The punchline was the fact that the carriage turned out to be 'GNS' – gay non-smoking. In another Cook-less sketch, Atkinson played David, a sinister Lostwithiel shopkeeper who engages a customer, Mrs Crawford (Paula Wilcox), in conversation. As the chatter carries on it becomes more and more sinister: 'If you've got a big family it involves a lot of other things . . .' and he persuades her to purchase an extra large steak for her husband.

It seemed as if Cook thought Atkinson's only talent was playing strange, creepy men, either that or straight sidekicks, which rather missed the point. One of Cook's lesser moments was as expert Professor Heinreich Globnick, an off-the-peg Germanic boffin, 'numero uno in the ant racket', interviewed by Atkinson about his fascination with insects. Atkinson, in his camel-coloured suit, was effectively little more than his 'feed', prompting Pythonesque witticisms from Cook along the lines of 'They are a shambles' and 'They can't operate heavy machinery after a bottle of vodka.' The outcome, ironically, was that the show was more of a showcase for Rowan's skills and for Cook's limitations. There was no disputing that Cook was immensely talented, but maybe it was a rarified kind of talent. It was easy to see which of these Oxbridge alumni had the greatest potential for mainstream stardom as a solo performer.

There was only one blot on the landscape in 1980 and that was at the scene of some of Atkinson's early triumphs. That summer he took his show back to the Edinburgh Festival to appear at the Children's Music Theatre in George Square. Two series of *Not the Nine O'Clock News* seemed to have turned him from newcomer into old guard, and the young journalists who covered the comedy at the Festival wanted to knock him down a few pegs now that he had moved on to a television career. Television success meant that a backlash in Edinburgh was almost inevitable. Success meant that young critics eager to make a name for themselves were gunning for Atkinson.

Maybe the press in Scotland had reason to be cynical. Because of his demanding workload, Atkinson didn't put on an all-new show reworking some of the previous year's Fringe First winner and the show he had taken round Britain. Furthermore, the new venue seemed to lack the charm of Wireworks. The best thing he could say about it was that it was 'one of the cleanest venues I've ever played in'.

Perhaps it was no surprise if Atkinson now seemed a little jaded with Edinburgh. He could fill a London theatre, hold together a national programme that was fast becoming a national institution. Maybe Edinburgh seemed a little parochial. There was also the problem of being a famous face out in public for virtually the first time, as he told Michael Dale: 'Perhaps it was when I was just trying to come to terms with the whole idea of heads turning in the street and what have you. I experienced it in Edinburgh, which was somewhere I'd known and liked so much as an unknown. I had that feeling of the world being my oyster and not having to pay any price yet. Then suddenly I felt as though the price was starting to be paid as the real fame hit me. It's very odd. It's a bit like going back to Newcastle-upon-Tyne now, to the places of my youth, which I knew so well when I was just another face.' Atkinson didn't like the feeling and shied away from the whole Edinburgh experience. He had experienced the Festival from both ends, struggling as a student and returning as the conquering hero. If his recent appearances had been for commercial reasons, his early appearances had been about trying to find a role for himself. He had soon moved on from acting, but it was his appearances in those early plays at Edinburgh, such as *We Bombed in New Haven* in 1973, that had pointed him towards the stage and made it seem like a serious prospect. Atkinson told Michael Dale: 'That play which no one remembers was probably the thing that gave me a taste and the inspiration to do what I now do ... I remember what a tremendous, genuinely good and inspirational thing it was to go to the Edinburgh Festival, just as a schoolboy.'

By 1980, Edinburgh was on the cusp of great change. In 1981 the Cambridge Footlights team, which included the formidable Emma Thompson, Stephen Fry and Hugh Laurie, would win the inaugural Perrier Award, but from that point on the new wave of non-Oxbridge comedians would take over and hold sway. Innocent college productions hoping to get talent-spotted would be lost in the background.

Despite invitations to appear, Atkinson didn't return to the prestigious Festival until 1986, by which time he would be back in favour with the youthful cynics thanks to the cynicism of *Blackadder*. His relationship with the Festival did continue however. He joined the Festival board, attending meetings between 1981 and 1983. Part of the reason for this was his abiding love of the city. The meetings gave him an excuse to visit three or four times a year and he nearly bought a house there. But a more important reason for his continued involvement may have been an element of guilt about his own success and his changing attitude towards the Fringe. He had known what it was like to be at the bottom of the pile, playing to a handful of tourists, and then he had returned because it was a sound business decision; now he wanted to help others break through too. His meetings with Edinburgh solicitors and accountants may not have achieved much, but it was at least a generous gesture for a man whose spare time was fast becoming an endangered species.

If proof were needed that *Not the Nine O'Clock News* series was a roaring success, the merchandizing spin-offs spoke volumes. The first album sold half a million copies. Further albums would match that success, and Christmas books would also top the best seller lists. The *Not!* book in 1980 straddled a very shrewd line between the type of topical public-school satire seen in *Private Eye* and the punchy single-joke cartoons that would contribute to the 1980s success of the magazine *Viz*. (An official-looking map of the capital, responding to an early 80s worry that the River Thames might flood, asked the simple question: 'What would you do if London flooded? Underneath, in equally official-looking type, came the answer: 'Drown'.) It was a shameless spin-off of the television series, of course, but the fact that it still worked on the page was a testament to the fact that the writing, at its best, was funny in any medium. The only television-based gag that fell flat was Rowan Atkinson's Ranting Man. In a spoof *Radio Times* letters page, his vocal opinions of *Nationwide* were credited to one Eric Swannage of Liverpool, but they rather lost their satirical bite on the journey from the stage to the page.

The success of the two 1980 series would prompt the team to take stock. Running straight into another series might have kept them in the limelight, but it might also have made them stale. It was decided to put *Not the Nine O'Clock News* on hold for a while so that when the team reconvened it would feel fresh again.

5

Success in Stages

It was an indication of Rowan Atkinson's rapid rise that when he appeared at London's Globe Theatre, starting a 12-week run on 19 February 1981, he used material that had its roots in his original Hampstead Theatre revue. By now though, his popularity, thanks to *Not the Nine O'Clock News*, was such that his show could run for three months and had sold out by the time the first rave reviews appeared. It transpired that producer Michael Codron had been trying to get him to mount a show for some time, but his television success had meant that there simply hadn't been any free time available for a theatrical run. Even though its eponymous star was still in his mid-20s, *Rowan Atkinson in Revue* had the air of a greatest hits compilation about it, with a few new additions to please an already large and loyal following.

There was something hugely symbolic about the way the show started. Atkinson came on as a dim-as-a-20-watt-bulb stagehand, innocently pushing a broom. It was a restrained, subtle start, which was representative of a more thoughtful, if not necessarily mature, mood. When the stagehand couldn't find a dustpan, he swept dust into his shoe. A few moments later, a befuddled expression appeared on his face. He was wondering why his shoe was suddenly so uncomfortable.

When the putative star of the show broke his leg in three places, however, the stagehand/Atkinson had to take his place. On the one hand, this was the Hollywood rags-to-riches myth made flesh, with the understudy grabbing his big break, but it also seemed to have an allegorical echo. It seemed to be saying something about Atkinson's own ambivalence about performing. This was the man who had expected to be a lighting technician up in the gallery. Instead, thanks to a natural, unique talent that couldn't be suppressed, however hard middle-class England tried to button it up, he was always destined to be the main attraction.

The humour was the kind of irreverent timeless flummery that people had come to expect from the star. In a selection of characters, caricatures sometimes, bordering on almost live cartoons, the themes seemed to be that of one man's battle to fit into the way the world did things – unfortunately this man would always do them differently. He was the perpetual square peg attempting to lodge itself into the round hole.

His speciality was poking fun at recognizable figures. He did it with the Schoolmaster sketch and continued this theme with his Father of the Bride speech in which he played those three stereotypes – the trendy vicar; the forgetful, hungover best man; and the grumpy father. As the not-so-proud parent he talked about his new in-laws as a 'compost heap' and his new son-in-law as the 'greatest weed growing out of it'.

A combination of putty face, nasal voice and, as *The Sunday Telegraph* put it in those far-off pre-politically correct days, 'funny body ... almost spastic', seemed to whip the crowd into hysterics. With the aid of Mel Smith's fluid direction, Atkinson was able to cram a lot into a show that ran for nearly two hours. He took a rare break from the stage to allow Howard Goodall to sing *I hate the French* ('I'll be buggered if I'll go to gay Paris' – this was, remember, the pre-political correctness early 80s). Richard Curtis played the straight man for what would turn out to be the last time. In one enduring sketch that was also used in *Not the Nine O'Clock News*, Curtis read the week's news while Atkinson provided comic sign language for the hard of hearing. Margaret Thatcher was summed up succinctly in the combined gesture of shaking hands followed promptly by a knee in the groin.

Back in front of a live audience, Atkinson relished the opportunity to make a mockery of organized religion as Toby the debonair devil. Unlike his Mephistopheles of the mind in *Doctor Faustus*, this one had all the get-up, including horns and a smoking jacket. With a tone that mixed vindictiveness and spite with a sense of natural justice, murderers, looters, pillagers, thieves and lawyers were all corralled by their horned host into the same group.

Atkinson's humour focused on feeling uncomfortable about one's body and the embarrassment of being English and middle class and partially naked in a public place. In one well-established sequence, he combined all of these elements, playing a man on a beach trying to put on swimming trunks without removing his trousers. It looked like a magic trick, done with trick pants perhaps, but while it must have been a strain, it was certainly genuine. With a few minor changes it would reappear, nearly a decade later, in the very first *Mr Bean*. Mr Bean would eventually also perform a variant of the sketch in which Atkinson is in church, listening to a sermon and trying to avoid both sneezing and snoozing. When he does finally sneeze, in the absence of a hankie, he has to blow his nose on the lining of his jacket. This pivotal sneeze added another dimension to Mr Bean, who though still nameless, had probably been floating around Atkinson's mind ever since he first pulled a face in the changing rooms at the Chorister School. This character had certainly been in mind when Atkinson devised his face-shaving routine. Both Atkinson and Curtis put Mr Bean's origins down to the falling asleep scene at Edinburgh in 1979, but by the time of the 1981 show it was becoming fully formed. It was a historic moment. Even the sneeze itself, when not directly associated with Mr Bean, would become an unlikely motif throughout Atkinson's career.

Vicars were also clearly becoming a part of his staple routine. The 1981 show included a return sermon from the rather rude vicar, still giving advice on the Church's position on fellatio after he had been shown what fellatio was. The germ of Blackadder may also have been there in his master class in which he rattled through the different ways of playing medieval kings. Another sketch still surviving from his Oxford days, was the concert pianist, *sans* piano, playing the invisible keyboard with seemingly elastic hands, while his face conveyed a range of emotions from arrogance and overconfidence to boredom and rapture. His characterizations were so sharp he hardly required costumes; he simply needed to pucker his lips, bend his pipe-cleaner body with its larger-than-life head and turn into somebody else of a different age or class. For an act about the awkwardness of the human form, onstage at least, he seemed remarkably at ease with his own form. Not surprisingly, *The Times* said he was 'in a league of his own as an entertainer,' and the celebrities in the audience ranged from Auberon Waugh to David Bowie.

The show wasn't without its tensions. Goodall and Curtis – as well as Atkinson himself – had to adjust to the fact that Rowan was becoming such a big star. While Atkinson was being acclaimed as the youngest person ever to have a solo show in the West End, the critics tended to overlook the fact that Curtis and Goodall were intimately involved as well. And not just the critics. When David Bowie went backstage to meet the team after the show, he saw Richard Curtis who 50 minutes earlier had been performing onstage and asked him what he did. Atkinson and Curtis were certainly not a double act in the Morecambe and Wise vein, but this was certainly not a solo show either. Perhaps the best description for it was 'A One and a Half Man Show'. Curtis explained his role on *Weekend Woman's Hour*: 'My job is to look as ordinary as possible all of the time.'

This notion of the invisible sideman would keep cropping up. When Angus Deayton appeared with Atkinson a few years later, he later recalled how he drew Rowan's attention to the fact that the only name on the poster was Atkinson. According to a joking Deayton in the 1997 ITV documentary *The Story of Bean*, the star's only response was that the lettering should have been green, not yellow.

Onstage though, the newly voted Royal Variety Club Showbiz Personality of the Year still had his feet on the ground, mixing his best old material with characters from television – his Ranting Man made an inevitable live appearance to complain about the state of the show midway through the set. It wasn't exactly the cutting edge of satire; Pope, Swift and *That Was the Week That Was* didn't need to worry about their reputations, but it was tremendously funny in a jolly-silly middle-class schoolboy anti-establishment sort of way. It was more social satire than political satire. A sketch about trying to get served in the post office when you are stuck behind a student wasn't about the run-down state of British post offices or the problems of being a cash-strapped student; it was simply about trying to make oneself heard in a public place. If Atkinson was making a pertinent point it was about the problems of communication. Despite being a deceptive six feet tall, he was excellent at playing the little man up against faceless bureaucracy: Norman Wisdom with an M.Sc.

Accents and impressions abounded. There was even a revival of the Barry Manilow impression he had essayed on *Not the Nine O'Clock News* in December 1980 – though with the size of Rowan's own nose the words 'glasshouses' and 'throwing stones' spring to mind. The funny thing was that when the sketch had first been performed he had received complaints from disgruntled Manilow fans. Luckily many also turned out to be Atkinson fans so he was able to placate them.

But despite the take-offs this was no Mike Yarwood manqué. Unlike Yarwood there was no cheesy 'and this is me finale'. In fact, you ended up not really seeing the real Atkinson all evening. Once onstage, the quiet science graduate was gone, only to return to take a modest bow when the curtain fell. It was even hard to know what the unprepossessing Atkinson really sounded like.

The 1981 show was a triumph, a challenge met. On television he had the benefit of edits, retakes and camera tricks. Live he only had brief breaks when Goodall and Curtis stood in before he had to be back onstage in another sketch. He had to rely, as in the old days, on the elasticity of his own face rather than make-up. That he pulled it off was confirmation that here was a great star. It may have seemed arrogant to appear solo, particularly to those new fans who only knew him from the ensemble success of *Not the Nine O'Clock News*, but beneath a reticent exterior beat the heart of a consummate, obsessive professional performer determined to get things right.

The reviews echoed the frantic ticket sales – they were certainly kinder than the Edinburgh critics the previous summer. Some notices carped at the over-familiarity of some of the material, but the consensus was that this was the homecoming of a star. In *The Daily Express*, Ian Christie put it simply: 'Rowan Atkinson is both witty and original, a combination that is hard to beat.' In *The Observer*, Robert Cushman was suitably impressed: 'If there is a funnier act around than this one I would like it brought to me. Now.' With reviews like that it was no surprise that at the end of the year Atkinson was voted Comedy Performer of the Year by the Society of West End Theatres. Give or take the odd dash of Edinburgh cynicism, he seemed able to win over any audience he cared to. Or at least almost all. When the show returned to Newcastle later in the year, the local critics did find fault among the comic gems. David Isaacs in the *Newcastle Journal* was unhappy about the foul language, which he considered to be a comedy cop-out: 'The four-letter word punchline may earn a laugh cheaply – but it is not the hallmark of the established comic.' In the *Newcastle Evening Chronicle*, Phil Penfold also had his concerns over the juvenile nature of some of the material, condemning Atkinson's Man Changing on the Beach sketch as unoriginal and his Actor Explaining How He Develops a Character routine as 'mundane'. But the man in church, without a handkerchief and dying to sneeze was, he said, 'a classic of its genre'.

Just before the live shows opened in London, Atkinson had appeared on Michael Parkinson's BBC1 chat show, alongside actress Sarah Miles, her dog Gladys and light entertainer Des O'Connor. Instead of coming down the famous Parkinson stairs, Atkinson interrupted his host's fawning introduction from the audience in the guise of his Ranting Man. As this protester came onto the stage he quite serenely removed the mac and suddenly transformed himself into the polite, retiring Atkinson.

Atkinson's rise had been so fast it had even taken him by surprise to a certain extent and he was still prepared to give away some of his secrets on *Parkinson*. He demonstrated an array of faces to show how he had picked up ideas from sitting opposite man on a train. He also revealed that the secret of acting drunk is to act sober: a drunk person never acts drunk; he tries, but fails, to act sober. Atkinson demonstrated this brilliantly by speaking a bit louder than normal and exaggerating every gesture. His inspiration for many of his sketches came from the unexpected things people said. In the post office he had once heard the man in front of him tap on the glass and ask for 'three O-levels please'.

Awards seemed to be raining down. A month after being voted BBC TV Personality of the Year, the BAFTAs voted *Not the Nine O'Clock News* the Best Light Entertainment Programme, and Rowan Atkinson scooped best Light Entertainment Performance. It may have been a team effort, but with his idiosyncratic style it was proving impossible not to single him out. (Around this time Blondie was one of the biggest pop groups in the country, with Debbie Harry garnering all of the attention because of her distinctive looks. The record company responded with an advertising campaign that announced that 'Blondie Is a Band'. Atkinson must have known how Debbie Harry felt.)

On the brink of the big time, Hampstead, 1978. © Universal Pictorial Press Agency

Hampstead, 1978: Sha la la la la – crooning to colleague Elspeth Parker. © UPPA

The Barclays Bank Christmas Show, 1978. Left to right: Atkinson, Peter Wilson, Elspeth Parker. © UPPA.

Not quite the *Not The Nine O'Clock News* team: left to right: Billy Connolly, Griff Rhys Jones, Atkinson, Mel Smith. © Rex Features

Record-breaking: the famous *NTNON* line-up. Left to right: Atkinson, Pamela Stephenson, Mel Smith, Griff Rhys Jones. © UPPA

Success by stages,
November 1980.
© UPPA.

'Oh, I just can't wait
to be king!' How to
be a medieval
monarch, The Globe
Theatre, 1981. ©
UPPA.

Man and mentor: Atkinson
and John Cleese. © Kobal
Collection.

The Black Adder, Mark I,
1983. © Scope Features

The Nerd with Tony Steadman,
London, 1984. © UPPA.

Early days at Durham School: Rowan Atkinson, top row right, Tony Blair, middle row left. © Tom Buist

The Black Adder, Mark II, 1985. Plotting with Tony Robinson as Baldrick. © Scope Features

West End Boys: Angus Deayton and Atkinson in London, 1986. © UPPA.

Another day, another dog collar. London, 1986. © UPPA.

Will the real Rowan Atkinson please stand up? London, 1987. © UPPA

Those dancing nuns. Atkinson as Ron Anderson with sidekick Dexter (Jeff Goldblum) in *The Tall Guy*, 1987. © Kobal

His character comedy was garnering comparisons with the great Peter Sellers, and he did admit to a fondness for Inspector Clouseau, prompting rumours that he might take over the role of the accident-prone French detective following the death of Peter Sellers on 24 July 1980. And he revealed to *The Guardian* in February 1981 that he was already getting 'Broadway-ish offers'. He wasn't quite sure whether to pursue them yet though, because he still felt uncomfortable about the cult of celebrity. Some honours, however flattering, were simply unwanted. In April 1981 he was voted President of the Young Liberals. This was despite the fact that he had never expressed any allegiance to the party. Atkinson beat the party MP Alan Beith by 83 votes to 76 at the group's Easter Conference, which didn't say much for the junior branch of the party's attitude to its own Westminster representatives but said a lot about the popularity of Rowan Atkinson and *Not the Nine O'Clock News*. Atkinson promptly declined the offer, preferring not to be drawn on his political affiliations. There were, however, some non-party issues that he was linked to. In December 1980 he was billed to appear alongside Mel Smith in a special benefit concert at Oxford Polytechnic in aid of Campaign Atom, an Oxford-based nuclear protest group that was against the siting of cruise missiles in the UK. As for an American tour, he confided to *Guardian* readers that in the long run it certainly was not out of the question, but it did have its drawbacks: 'Maybe next year or the year after. The idea interests me, but what frightens me is the celebrity buzz. Over there they tend to pester you a lot.'

Rowan Atkinson was doing his best to do an impression of an unlikely celebrity. Even fans who were media-literate enough to realize he would not be a laugh a minute kept expecting him at least to resemble his stage persona. When people met Atkinson for the first time they were surprised that the putty-faced performer could look so gloomy in repose. After all, he was still only in his mid-20s. So young, in fact, that in one *Not the Nine O'Clock News* sketch he could convincingly play a 12-year-old chess prodigy from Stocksfield, Northumberland. But not all comedians look comical. You only had to think back to that huge Laurel and Hardy picture, one of the few objects that had graced his new home, in which the two Hollywood legends look particularly downcast. There were further resonances. The non-smiling Stan Laurel – whose father had worked for Atkinson's grandfather – also made it bigger than he could have ever imagined after trying his luck in America. Grinning cheesy end-of-the-pier stand-up comedians didn't loom large in Atkinson's mind. Even the Pythons and the Footlights people were too cerebral to smile inanely on cue. John Cleese might have been one of the funniest men in England, but he still looked like a civil servant. Peter Cook had been expected to go into the foreign office until his comedy career took off, and in repose he still often looked as if would be more comfortable shuffling papers in an office off a corridor in Whitehall. But there was no pleasing some people with the way Atkinson looked. Even his mother would call him after a television appearance and say that he looked too thin.

Atkinson compared himself to Barry Humphries in the way he would hide behind characters, but he certainly didn't see himself as a latter-day Mike Yarwood, trotting out impressions in two-minute sketches for a living. He told journalist Sheridan Morley that he saw himself as the English Jack Lemmon, 'not that anyone else does as yet'.

Atkinson was clearly getting itchy, looking for new challenges where he could nurture ideas. In interviews he talked intriguingly of writing a sitcom with Richard Curtis along the lines of *Fawlty Towers*-meets-*Starsky and Hutch*. He revealed to the *Daily Mail* that while he didn't want to analyse his comedy too much, he wasn't actually that happy about his television performances: 'I'm just not at my best on TV, working around the clock for sketches which last two minutes at the most; all that whizz, bang, crash stuff. I much prefer the stage where I can stretch myself and really develop my act.' He felt his current television show's sell-by date was approaching and wanted to quit while he was ahead.

Success, it seemed, had come too fast, almost too easily. Paradoxically, the ease with which he achieved it was what made him insecure. He couldn't see that it had been easy because he was so gifted; all he could see were the disadvantages and potential pitfalls. He was already gaining a reputation as a perfectionist, but this attention to detail was partly because having risen so fast he didn't want to fall on his face. 'The rate of my success has frightened me,' he said in November 1980. 'I was inundated with offers to do all kinds of jobs, from opening supermarkets to oddball commercials which would have driven me mad.' Worst of all though were the fans who got too close: 'They tend to scream at me across restaurants: "Give us a funny face, Rowan," which I truly hate.'

This odd way of making a living was very quickly making him part of the showbusiness establishment. On 17 November 1980 he had appeared in front of the Queen at the Royal Variety Performance at the London Palladium, marking the Queen Mother's eightieth birthday. He had enjoyed meeting Prince Charles, who had said he was a fan of *Not the Nine O'Clock News*, except that it was annoying because he never seemed to be in on a Monday night. But some of the showbiz protocol had come as a shock to Atkinson. When he was planning to go on, the band asked him what play-on music he wanted. Not having come from a variety background he did not realize what they meant. In his revues he had been used to just walking onstage.

By the summer of 1981, Rowan Atkinson had comfortably eased himself into position as Britain's funniest man. His stage work had been acclaimed, his television work had made him famous and quite wealthy. He also had fans in high places. When Prince Charles married Lady Diana Spencer in July they received a telegram wishing them 'All love, fun and laughter from the cast and company of the Rowan Atkinson Revue'. Many people might have sent the couple their best wishes, but few would have received this prompt reply: 'Enormous thanks for your wonderful message which is heartily reciprocated. Charles and Diana.' Ironically the *Not the Nine O'Clock News* team had a different cheekier tribute; John Lloyd and Sean Hardie put together a book, *Not the Royal Wedding*. On the front cover Griff Rhys Jones and Pamela Stephenson were dressed in Lady Diana's outfit, while Mel Smith stood next to Prince Charles. On the back cover Atkinson's head appeared to have been superimposed onto Prince Charles's body in the classic pose where he had his hand on Lady Diana's shoulder as she showed off her engagement ring.

For Atkinson though, watching the royal wedding was a prelude to more heavy work. No sooner had the couple set off on their honeymoon than Atkinson set off from north London for Edinburgh. He was not performing this year though. With his HGV licence under his belt, he had hired a 40-foot trailer and was helping some friends transport their sets to the Festival. He had another important task to perform at the end of the Festival. A new competition had been set up to decide on the Fringe's best comedy show, and Atkinson was asked to go onstage at St Mary's Street Hall to award the inaugural Perrier Award to the winners, the Cambridge Footlights, which included soon-to-be regular colleagues Hugh Laurie and Stephen Fry as well as Emma Thompson and Tony Slattery. Unfortunately his reputation for comedy went before him. No one knew much about this new-fangled Perrier Award and the venue didn't have a curtain to signal the end of the show, so the audience thought the presentation was another sketch or some kind of art-school Brechtian parody of an awards ceremony. Alistair Moffat, the Fringe administrator, had to step in to insist that the show had actually stopped. Atkinson-the-man had become so overshadowed by Atkinson-the-clown that often, to his frustration, it was hard for comedy fans to know where one ended and the other began.

While he was up in Scotland, BBC2 screened another recent attempt to twin the world of comedy with the world of charity. *Fundamental Frolics*, which took place at the Apollo Theatre in Victoria, marked a turning point in the evolution of comedy. For the first time a new breed of comics were starting to break through. The Comedy Store club in Soho, opened in May 1979, provided a platform for a new wave of comics who did not want to go through the usual apprenticeship of working-men's clubs and holiday camps. Inspired in part by the club of the same name in Los Angeles, the new acts welded a punkish iconoclastic sensibility to their stand-up humour. Many of the acts owed more to radical theatre than to Butlins. Street credibility seemed to be essential at the time, although it would soon emerge that most of the contributors had degrees – usually in drama – and more than a few had a public-school background. Atkinson himself had been down there back in 1979, not to perform but to check out the competition. By 1981 there had still not been much television exposure for these new acts. BBC2 had showcased the main performers – Rik Mayall, Nigel Planer, Adrian Edmondson, Keith Allen and Peter Richardson – in two shows entitled *Boom Boom ... Out Go the Lights*, but the alternative-comedy movement, as it had become known, was still a long way from major recognition.

With *Fundamental Frolics* however, things began to change, and Rowan Atkinson would soon emerge as the perfect bridge between the old wave and the new wave. Richard Sparks, Atkinson's old collaborator from *Beyond a Joke*, was involved in putting together *Fundamental Frolics*, and as he helped to assemble the line-up it soon became apparent that this benefit had plenty of comics to pick from and didn't need to concentrate on the usual philanthropic suspects who had been the backbone of the Amnesty galas in the late 70s. Sparks recalls asking Michael Palin if he would take part in this new fund-raiser: 'He said he had done loads and now there were plenty of young comics who could do it.'

By now, Atkinson was already well established enough to subvert and rework some of his early material. For *Fundamental Frolics* he trundled out his Schoolmaster again, only this time it was different. In keeping with modern changes in education, the school had now become co-educational. 'Undermanager had had a sex change,' recalls Sparks.

The line-up that appeared on the edited television version was the perfect cross-section of comedy at this historic turning point. Atkinson was there as part of the re-united *Not the Nine O'Clock News* news team and – showing that there were clearly no hard feelings about his ousting – Chris Langham was there too. Neil Innes was a link back to *Monty Python* via his work with Eric Idle in the *Rutles*. But Sparks had also approached the leading lights of the new wave: 'I went to Rik Mayall. And Alexei Sayle, who had been at art school with my wife and was terrified of her. He had been this bearded shy person who used to giggle, then a few years later he became this lunatic. Rik was supposed to do a five-minute solo spot but he went on with Ade Edmondson and did 20 minutes instead. They were very good.'

Atkinson would slowly start to shake off the Oxbridge shadow of John Cleese and Peter Cook and begin to assume the mantle of mentor in his own right, supporting the careers of these new red-brick comics.

Atkinson seemed to be able to balance a private life with an increasingly successful public career. In September he headlined a show at the Oxford Apollo to raise money for the Oxford Ice Skating Trust, an organization campaigning to build a skating rink in the city. In recent years John Curry and Robin Cousins had been world champions, and at the turn of the decade, with English soccer and cricket in the doldrums, it looked as if ice skating was the only sport the nation excelled at. As a result there was something of a minor skating boom.

Atkinson was also booked to appear at a much more significant fund-raiser for those that did not necessarily consider the triple axle to be the height of aesthetic achievement. Once again he was one of the turns at *The Secret Policeman's Other Ball*, which took place at the Theatre Royal Drury Lane from 9 September to 12 September 1981. Only this time he was one of the star turns. The cause was the same – it was another fund-raiser for Amnesty International – but the money-raising tactics were slightly different. Whereas the 1979 show had been made with television, this one, directed by Ronald Eyre and assisted by John Cleese, was staged and filmed for a cinematic release and then a future release on the nascent video market as well as another album release. There was a twofold philosophy behind avoiding television transmission. Not only did it mean that the performers had more freedom to perform material that would not be considered suitable for broadcast, it could also raise more funds via film distribution and video sales than it might through a single showing on television. And after all, it could always be edited down for a television screening after all other markets had been exhausted.

The money raised over the four sold-out nights was impressive by theatrical standards of the day. According to the introduction on the album, released through Island Records, ticket receipts for each night came to £17,560, even though Cleese jokingly chastised the skinflints who had bought the cheapest £3.50 tickets: 'People are being tortured to death and you cough up the price of a prawn cocktail.' Atkinson chipped in by adding that it was the people who bought the second cheapest seats that really got his goat – and they were probably Social Democrats too. This was a friendly but ironic dig indeed – the man standing next to him, John Cleese, turned out to be an early SDP supporter.

As with Atkinson's own show, there were flashes of jingoism running through this event that if performed today would make the right-on members of the audience shuffle uncomfortably in their seats. Atkinson's satirical lecture on road safety announced that the death toll in Germany from car-related accidents was higher than in France and a cheer went up – it was as if giving money to stop human rights abuses in the Third World made it acceptable to laughing at innocent dead Europeans or call the Spanish 'dagos'. The advice provided was that these figures were not high enough, and when the British were travelling abroad they should travel on the British side to cause more accidents.

Atkinson also played the straight man to John Cleese's obsessive bee expert Reginald Prawnbaum – presumably a distant relation of Peter Cook's ant-fixated Heinreich Globnik. Except that this time the interview could not run smoothly because every time Prawnbaum said certain words Atkinson would respond with various nervous tics. He said 'sshh' when Prawnbaum said 'hive', squawked when he said 'life', and ran around the chair when Prawnbaum said 'interviewer'. In the end he fell off the stage into darkness and was shot by Prawnbaum just for good measure.

There hadn't been a television version of *Not the Nine O'Clock News* since December 1980, but three-quarters of the team reunited for their Divorce Service sketch, in which Atkinson donned another surplice to end the marriage of Griff Rhys Jones and Pamela Stephenson so that she could run off with Frank Hodgkiss from accounts, played – in the absence of Mel Smith – by John Fortune. Fortune – one of the original 60s Oxbridge Mafia – also popped up as one of the team members alongside Griff Rhys Jones in a comedy variant of the antiquated television quiz *Top of the Form*. John Cleese read the questions, and Atkinson, despite his formidable track record as schoolmasters, donned a grey blazer and tie and joined the boys' team (the girls' team was played unconvincingly by Graham Chapman, John Bird and Tim Brooke-Taylor in pigtails). With the questions and answers all muddled up, the punchline came when Cleese asked who shuffled his cards just before the programme started.

Having done his classical pianist routine in the last Amnesty gala, this time Atkinson wheeled out his eccentric classical conductor, who was just a little bit too enthusiastic about Beethoven's *Fifth Symphony*. As the music picked up he started waving his baton round like the sails of a windmill so frantically that he flicked the pages on his lectern and lost his place. Managing to regroup, he directs the (unseen) orchestra as if he is directing traffic and eventually marches around the stage high-stepping, in the manner of a Junior John Cleese, to rapturous applause.

Autumn of 1981 found Atkinson touring the show that had done so well in London. The sold-out signs soon went up everywhere, as tickets, including those for three nights at Newcastle's Theatre Royal, were soon snapped up. Atkinson arrived to find a city that had changed dramatically since he had studied there. Shopping centres and one-way systems seemed to dominate the city centre. Trying to get to Eldon Square, where he used to go on his way to lecture, did not require a map; it required a post-graduate degree in urban geography. One thing had not changed though: there was still a warm welcome for the city's local hero. The only people who were not bowled over were the critics, who felt that Atkinson was not living up to his full potential.

The fourth series of *Not the Nine O'Clock News*, which started, after more than a one-year break on 1 February 1982, confirmed that Atkinson was certainly not an endangered species. There was now a confidence to the writing and performing that gave some of the sketches a real edge. In one sketch Atkinson made an early appearance as a policeman, but one who was very different to the kind, gentle traditional officer he would play in *The Thin Blue Line*. As Constable Savage (a name that seemed to describe the character's nature), Atkinson was being interviewed by his superior about why he kept bringing unfounded charges against the same man – 2,354 charges, including Living in a Residential Area during the Hours of Darkness and Grievous Bodily Odour. When the man's name was revealed to be Mr Kodogo it was clear that the target was not an indiscriminate one. It may not have changed police behaviour but the sketch was at least publicly addressing the prejudices of some officers long before this became public knowledge. This was the strange thing about *Not the Nine O'Clock News*; just as you were convinced it was something written by a group of giggling overgrown public schoolboys with a collective penis fixation, it came up with something that had the ability to shock. Although political comedy would expand in the 80s with the likes of Ben Elton at the forefront of the anti-Thatcher agenda, there was plenty in this BBC2 show that would stand the test of time. It was no surprise that the performers and most of the backroom team would continue to thrive as others caught up with their style.

If the Policeman sketch touched on a taboo, most of the material in the fourth and final series still relied on more innocent totems of the day – Mini Metros, space invaders, cash-point machines – and Sir Keith Joseph. In a mocked-up interview with the minister, Atkinson, yawned, put on his pyjamas and aged into an old man while Joseph droned on. The cult of the pop video was sent up when the quartet hammed it up as new romantics singing *Nice video, shame about the song*, with Atkinson looking uncomfortably fetching in eye-liner and Gestapo regalia.

Nevertheless, the fourth series did seem a little tired, compared to previous high-water marks. The spark that had lit up the third series had diminished, but Atkinson could still come up with some delicious laughs. Following reports that it was good to talk to your plants, he played a character who could be heard to shout through the window 'Grow, you bastards'. There was another nice knock at those who grasped at celebrity when he played a vicar who berated his congregation for only turning up because they thought the *Songs of Praise* cameras were going to be in their church. And then there was *Hey Wow*, the spoof children's programme in which Atkinson in a leotard came on as radical one-man mime troupe Alternative Car Park. While Atkinson pulled funny shapes (and, no doubt, thought of those drafty community halls), Griff Rhys Jones played the tolerant, trendy presenter, who gradually became less tolerant as the group watching Atkinson became increasingly restless.

The best sketches, though, were moments that would also find their way into Atkinson's live shows. As the Alien Zak he warned the earth of a great crisis ahead, but just as he was about to go into detail the machinery that translated his voice into English started to play up and he began to spout gobbledygook. In another priceless Curtis moment, What a Load of Willies, he played a French architecture expert interviewed by Stephenson as Janet Street-Porter. What starts out as a serious discussion soon collapses into an argument when it turns out that this expert sees something sexual in every building in London. St Pauls, for instance, is a 'huge titty', and Nelson's Column, inevitably, speaks for itself.

It was decided that the series would wind down, but in order to finish on a high note there were live shows in Oxford and London's Drury Lane Theatre in April, directed by the man who made the original *Not the Nine O'Clock News* pilot, Geoff Posner. At the time the BBC – in those days not the quickest off the mark when it came to merchandising – had yet to realize the full potential of the video market and did not release any of the shows on video. There was, however, one final album, *The Memory Kinda Lingers*, released in October 1982; it had two sides gathered from television material, and two sides from the live show. The sleeve illustration typified the way that the team liked to poke fun at the pretensions of suburban normality. The picture featured an average middle-class nuclear family gathered around a dinner table. Father was cutting the roast, but instead of beef or lamb it was a hedgehog. If you looked closely you could spot a family portrait hanging on the wall. Except it wasn't the family, it was Atkinson, Jones, Smith and Stephenson. Even the fact that the family lived in a mock Tudor home seemed ironic – the album was all about mocking.

There might have been fears that Atkinson, as the most visually orientated performer in the quartet, might have been at the greatest disadvantage on vinyl, but instead the album confirmed the facility for verbal gymnastics he had first demonstrated on *The Atkinson People*. In Holiday Habits for instance, written by Richard Curtis, he assumed a Belgian accent to explain Low Country etiquette. If anyone travelling there had taken his advice seriously they would have been in for a shock, as he informed listeners that burping after a meal was a compliment and breaking wind even more of a compliment.

Atkinson also performed in sketches that were not written by Curtis. Brain Death by Mick Deasey was an unusually morbid moment. He donned a thick working-class Geordie accent to portray a union official complaining to the management about the dismissal of a worker who had been found dead at his machine. The rep believed that the dismissal was in breach of regulations because rigor mortis had not set in – although this was only because the corpse was tied to a radiator in the print room. Some sketches did lose something without the added visuals. Hey Wow did not quite work without seeing the pipe-cleaner-thin Atkinson kitted out in a clingy one-piece leotard as he announced 'I am a mime. My body is my tool.'

Sometimes it seemed as if the album of greatest hits had been put together to cause maximum offence. Richard Curtis's Polish Show was a Hollywood-style awards ceremony for Pole of the Year full of clumsy mispronunciations. And when not being irreverent, Curtis tended to revert to simple silliness. On the live part of the double album, *Not in Front of the Audience*, Atkinson's sex-obsessed French critic returned. This time he claimed that the theatre was an enormous vulva: 'Every night pricks come in and out and twice on Saturday.' Where *Do Bears*? had derived its humour from not actually saying the word 'shit'; *The Memory Kinda Lingers* attempted to shoehorn as much rude-sounding innuendo onto BBC2 as possible. Despite irate complainers who kept the *Radio Times* letters page and BBC1's *Points of View* busy, the team now had the confidence and the general public support to feel able to push back boundaries of taste on a regular basis.

Recording the live show was an opportunity for the group to leave their mark in a pre-video age when television seemed transient. It was performed in the same theatre that *Monty Python* had recorded their immortal album in the mid-70s, so they had a lot to live up to. Not surprisingly the album homed in on a combination of priceless sketches and ones that were unforgettable because they were so tasteless. Curtis's Alien had a swift reprise: it was the kind of piece Atkinson was born to present. He had even been called an alien at school and now he was one – Zak: 'I come from another planet where there is no death, no gravity and a different-shaped gearstick on the Mini Metro.' Some targets were easy subjects for humour, but the team also managed to eke out original laughs where it was least expected. A visit from the Pope was presented as a rock tour, complete with sound check and merchandising – Papal Pimple Cream was a big seller. If religion was an obvious subject, British Rail was even more obvious, but there was an example of the first Catholicism/ transport crossover gag when it was suggested that the Pope's first UK miracle would be ringing British Rail enquiries and getting an answer.

With *Not the Nine O'Clock News* consigned to history because of an amicable agreement and what Atkinson jokingly called 'proximity fatigue', he needed some new projects. His sitcom idea was still bubbling away, but he seemed to be regretting comparing it to *Fawlty Towers*. It was a lot to live up to, and now he and Richard Curtis were rethinking it so that they could come up with a situation that would not have any reference to a certain hotelier in Torquay.

The John Cleese connection that had developed over the last five years had resulted in some intriguing films that would never be seen by most Atkinson fans. Back in 1972, Cleese had been involved in the setting up of Video Arts, a company that made instructional films for industry. By the end of the decade it was a lucrative business with blue-chip clients such as General Motors and Hilton Hotels. Cleese made sure that the short films, which often gave advice on management techniques (something Basil Fawlty could have done with), had the highest production values and the best casts. Among those that had acted in them were James Bolam and Penelope Keith, as well as various Oxbridge pals. Cleese had invited Atkinson to become involved after *Beyond a Joke*. Atkinson came onboard and had the chance of not just acting in the films but also writing scripts.

Between tours and television, Atkinson managed to find time to be involved in a number of other projects. While he had been performing at Newcastle's Theatre Royal in the autumn of 1981, he showed that he had not lost touch with his Newcastle roots and appeared alongside Peter Elson in *University: A Day in the Life of a Student*. The fee was minimal and the exposure was not much greater, but it was a cause that Atkinson wanted to support. The film was a promotional tool to attract prospective students to his old university. It gave a flavour of the courses and activities. Even this modest enterprise picked up a prize; in December it topped the Best Video Recording and Best Visuals Categories at the Educational Television Association's annual awards.

Atkinson also appeared in a short film written by Richard Curtis. In *Dead on Time*, which offered advice on time management and was directed by Lyndall Hobbs, Atkinson starred alongside Nigel Hawthorne, Peter Bull, Leslie Ash and Greta Scacchi, playing a man who discovers he only has half an hour to live and tries to cram the next 45 years of his life into those 30 minutes. And he was increasingly involved in John Cleese's Video Arts projects. Atkinson co-starred with marble-mouthed sitcom stalwart Geoffrey Palmer in *Mr Kershaw's Dream System*, made in 1982, and also co-wrote the script with Antony Jay. The 23-minute film was made for British Telecom to show businesses the benefits of using BT's 'Monarch' call-connect telephone system. In 1984 he wrote and co-starred in *Oh What the Hell*, made for Sun Alliance Insurance. This time round it was Atkinson who was the eminence grise, as Rik Mayall came onboard to demonstrate safety-awareness routines, cutting between hell and office/factory situations. These films worked on the principle that the best way to get a message across was through humour. Cleese had always excelled at stuffy, quietly mad management types and this mantle seemed to be passing to Atkinson.

The beginning of 1983 found Atkinson joining his comedy elders for yet another good cause. On 23 January, he appeared in another fundraiser, *An Evening at Court* at the Theatre Royal, directed by Humphrey Barclay. Once again Atkinson straddled the comedy generations. Alongside John Cleese, David Frost and The Goodies, a young female double act was on the bill. Dawn French and Jennifer Saunders were now making inroads into the big time in the same way that Atkinson had five years earlier. Still less than 30, he increasingly found himself in a uniquely paternal position as a whole raft of newcomers would emerge and invigorate British comedy. As his own power increased, he offered more career opportunities to the comics coming along after him.

Atkinson was also quietly developing a burgeoning film career, although so far he had little more to show for it than a first-class flight to the Bahamas, a nice holiday there and a small cameo in Sean Connery's one-off comeback Bond movie, *Never Say Never Again*. Atkinson played the bumptious Mr Nigel Small-Fawcett, the British Embassy representative in Nassau who keeps interrupting Bond when he is preoccupied with business, or more usually with a beautiful Bond girl. The part was slight, but that was not surprising given that it only came about late in the day. The film had already been cast, but it was an indication that Atkinson's growing stature that room was found for him and writers Dick Clement and Ian La Frenais were asked to come up with some scenes for him. It all happened very quickly in November 1982. The role was confirmed and the next day Atkinson was on a plane to Nassau to film it.

It was odd if Atkinson had been brought in for comic effect since Sean Connery seemed to be doing that perfectly adequately already, if in typically corny style. The film starts with 007 being sent to a health farm to get back into shape. At his medical he is by the bed when a nurse at a counter asks him to fill a beaker with a urine sample: 'From here?' deadpans Bond.

Atkinson's three scenes were clearly for light relief, rather than narrative drive. In the first scene he briefs Bond and asks him not to do too much killing because it will damage the tourist trade. Bond is supposed to be undercover, but Small-Fawcett makes a bad start by shouting his name across the quay. Later he interrupts Bond when he is in bed with a woman to brief him further and to invite him snorkelling, which is not what Bond has in mind at this point. Finally, Bond is with Kim Basinger when he hears an intruder in the bushes and throws him into the swimming pool fully clothed. It turns out to be Small-Fawcett again, bearing a message for Bond to come back to the secret service for the sake of global security.

Interestingly the lock-jawed mandarin is the only character Atkinson has ever played who he openly admitted is based on someone in his past – a contemporary at Oxford who had a little Hitler moustache. Everyone else Atkinson has ever played has been either completely fictional or inspired by someone else deeply buried within his unconscious – or, of course, inspired by his own personality. Yet ironically, Small-Fawcett was one of the first times he had professionally performed something comic that wasn't written by himself, Curtis, Goodall or one of the *Not the Nine O'Clock News* team. It was not, in the end, a particularly rewarding experience. He got to travel first class and enjoyed the luxuries that come with a movie role, but the part was not to his satisfaction. He later said: 'There aren't many things I look back on with dismay. But that was one. There was something so clichéd about it. I was hoping to have done a character rather than a caricature.'

Following the end of *Not the Nine O'Clock News*, Atkinson seemed to take some time to find his focus again. Work was plentiful but it was not really taking him in any particular direction. As fun as it might have been to be in a Bond film, it was hardly his life's ambition. When discussing his work he was asked by chat show host Terry Wogan if he had ever wanted to be James Bond. He replied that he would quite like to be a villain who said 'not so fast, Mr Bond', but the only fictional character he had ever really hankered after was Dr Who. He thought, however, that a future step might be doing a detective-style comedy on the lines of *Minder* or *The Professionals*.

Atkinson was the most unusual British comedy star to come along in decades, but for a while it looked as if he might be conforming to type and falling into the stardom trap of becoming more interested in what money could buy than what work one could do to bring the money in. It was already well known that he was a car fanatic, so news that he had bought a Range Rover was hardly cause to hold the front page. But reports that he was looking for a Scottish castle to buy did sound very unlike the sensible, scientific north-London boy. It seemed a drastic way of escaping from people in the street asking him to pull a funny face.

In the event the castle didn't materialize, although he did reportedly put in a bid for a small one. Instead, he settled for a Grade II listed eighteenth-century rectory in the village of Waterperry in Oxfordshire. It was ideal: a short tootle down the M40 to the BBC in west London, its own tennis courts and plenty of room to park his ever-growing fleet of classic cars. Atkinson confessed that he liked nothing better than to spend his afternoons mowing the lawns. Maybe the sense of history that came with the house played its part when he and Richard Curtis finally came up with the idea for a sitcom that could never be compared to *Fawlty Towers* because it was set at a completely different era. In fact, numerous different eras.

6

The History Man

The BBC had been encouraging Curtis and Atkinson to come up with a sitcom even before the end of *Not the Nine O'Clock News*. They had been working on this intermittently for ages, but it had undergone a number of rethinks since the early *Fawlty Towers* meets *Starsky and Hutch* pitch. At one point it was going to be a detective story about bicycle thieves set in Camden Town, with the hero an incompetent assistant in a lawyer's office, but after a couple of weeks they gave up on that concept. Every time they thought they were getting somewhere, Curtis would become demoralized, overwhelmed by the thought that they had not matched the brilliance of *Fawlty Towers*.

Both comics wanted to do something different. It wasn't just the fact that *Fawlty Towers* comparisons would be invidious. They wanted to be freed from the whole *Terry and June* style of middle-class sofa-based domestic comedies dominating the BBC at the time. In 1998, Richard Curtis told the magazine *Cult TV* that they decided to 'do a sitcom where stuff happened. It was in an age when most sitcoms had tiny *Vicar of Dibley*-type plots and small domestic things happened. We thought it would be great if people actually died.' Carnage seemed more appealing than cars breaking down. Then one day, while throwing ideas about, they began talking about the *Hitler Diaries*, the hoax papers that, embarrassingly, had been published in *The Sunday Times* in 1981. These documents, purporting to reveal the Fuhrer's innermost thoughts, had shed a whole new light on recent German history. Historians had confirmed that they were genuine only for it to be finally concluded that they were false after all.

This gave Atkinson and Curtis the idea of positing an alternative history of England, one where the shadow of Basil Fawlty wouldn't loom so large. This would be a place where if you did something wrong you did not get hit on the head with a frying pan and blamed for being from Barcelona; this was a place where a dispute could result in a red-hot poker up your bottom. Once the initial premise had been established, it opened up all sorts of options that had not been done in sitcoms before. It also marked a direct contrast after the strictly contemporary comedy of *Not the Nine O'Clock News*. The thought of not having to make jokes about Keith Joseph was enough to inspire anyone. And it slotted neatly into the refreshing anarchic mood that the alternative-comedy brigade was championing in shows such as *The Young Ones*. They called their new series *The Black Adder*.

The *Hitler Diaries* element was woven into the fictional scripts, which revealed that Henry VII had come to the throne 13 years later than history reports that he did. Apparently Richard III, who was really rather nice, did not murder the Princes in the Tower, and one of them, Richard, Duke of York, became Richard IV. It was actually Henry VII who was the evil tyrant, and when he came to the throne he put the Gregorian calendar back 13 years, in the process destroying any trace of the previous reign. That was, until a lost document, telling the story of Richard's son Edmund surfaced. This series set out to retell the story of those missing years. Atkinson would play Edmund, Richard IV's tight-wearing accident-prone nincompoop of a son.

At one point the plan had been to set the first series in Elizabethan times, but there was a feeling that maybe that era was too soft. The idea was to set it at a time when people were mean: 'Humour is about human suffering and hurt. In any humorous situation someone is always having something terrible done to them or rude said about them,' explained the star.

While *The Black Adder* certainly achieved its ambition in steering clear of the shadow of *Fawlty Towers*, it still had its notable comic precedents. Naturally there was *Monty Python and The Holy Grail*, which had opted for a slightly earlier, grimier period. And Morecambe and Wise had frequently performed the historical dramas that Ernie wrote. But the most obvious antecedent was *Up Pompeii!*, the Roman Empire-based comedy built around the malleable camel-like features of Frankie Howerd, that started in 1969. Though even that owed a debt to the musical *A Funny Thing Happened on the Way to the Forum* – Howerd had appeared in the London production as far back as 1963.

Following the success of *Up Pompeii!*, its makers saw the potential for repositioning the same character in different historical periods. The theory seemed to be that if the toga was replaced by costumes from a different period, people would not notice that the shows were almost identical. Two movies moved Frankie Howerd on to the Crusades (*Up the Chastity Belt*) and, in a foreshadowing of *Blackadder IV*, into the First World War (*Up the Front*). On television, Howerd's attempts to repeat that early success fared less well. ITV revived *Up Pompeii!* in 1991 as *Further Up Pompeii*, but it was a shadow of its former self. There was also the easily forgotten 1973 variant, *Whoops Baghdad*, with Howerd as Ali Oopla, sporting 'new costumes but the same old jokes'. The only thing of note here was that it was produced by John Howard Davies, who would be the BBC's head of comedy when *Not the Nine O'Clock News* was devised and would later be a champion of Atkinson behind the scenes at Thames Television during the emergence of *Mr Bean*.

Look beyond the shared lack of trousers, however, and there were some distinctive differences between *Up Pompeii!* and *The Black Adder*. From the start Curtis and Atkinson avoided addressing the audience. They called their project a situation tragedy and approached their work as if they were making a serious costume drama. Similarly, they were not going to trade on daft anachronisms, referring to modern events for a cheap laugh. Nevertheless, there was never any serious intent to get the historical accuracy absolutely right. In fact, over the years, enough anachronisms would be planted to keep any pedantic fans busy.

Atkinson appeared on BBC1's *Wogan* on 16 April 1983, introduced as the man with 'a face like a gerbil with lockjaw'. He had not intended to talk about *The Black Adder*, not wanting to give too much away at this stage, but his savage haircut necessary for the part (comically incongruous in conjunction with a sober grey suit) had not yet grown back, and it seemed that no sooner had Terry Wogan mentioned it than, partly out of nerves, Atkinson had started to talk about the new sitcom that had taken up much of his life over the previous 12 months. Part of the attraction of *The Black Adder* was the chance to get away from being known as 'a face puller' – his mother did not like it, but she did have a good sense of humour. He thought he had probably inherited his comic timing from her. Atkinson explained that for some reason old people did not like his faces. Once, when he was doing a matinée performance of *Beyond a Joke*, there were a lot of senior citizens in the audience and he clearly heard one of the say to her friend: 'You know it can't do his face any good.' And yet, like a beauty queen, his face had been his fortune.

With the ground rules of the series in place, the team seemed ready to commence. But things were still not going to be that simple. The story of the making of this historical comedy is one of the most curious episodes in British sitcom history. In many ways it was a landmark series, not just in terms of the sheer verve and brilliance but in terms of how it nearly didn't come about. The fact that it became so enduring despite shaky beginnings is an object-lesson for sitcom makers and critics – never write something off too early.

The funny thing is that legend has it that the relative failure of the first series was reputedly down to the success of the pilot episode that was never actually transmitted. Geoff Posner, who had made the early *Not the Nine O'Clock News* edition that never went out, was brought in to produce the dry run in 1982, but left afterwards, handing the reigns over to the other *Not the Nine O'Clock News* alumnus, John Lloyd.

While the pilot script ended up forming the basis of the second episode in the first series, 'Born to Be King', there were significant differences between the pilot and the first series. Not the least is the fact that initially Rowan Atkinson's character was a schemer rather than the idiot he was in the completed first series. The scheme returned for the second run onwards.

The other difference was in the casting of the pilot, which was delivered to the BBC in 1982, not long after the end of *Not the Nine O'Clock News*. Bellowing thespian Brian Blessed had yet to make Richard IV his own – instead the part of the king and the Black Adder's father was played by John Savident, an experienced actor who had appeared in a number of sitcoms including *Yes, Minister* (he played Sir Frederick, otherwise known as Jumbo) and more recently as Coronation Street's butcher Fred Elliot. Baldrick was also not quite the finished article. Instead of Tony Robinson, Philip Fox, who later went on to play Sidney Clough in the ITV sitcom *Watching*, played the royal servant. And Robert Bathurst, a former Footlights performer who seemed to have a gift for playing upper-crust clots, played Edmund's brother Prince Harry of Wales – this role was eventually taken over by Robert East. There was also a different opening sequence – initially an animated book revealed the title, followed by a scene of the king's castle burning down.

The BBC was so pleased with the initial pilot that a year later, after Atkinson and Curtis had decamped to France to concentrate on writing the series, they lavished a generous budget on the first six parts. Atkinson showed equal commitment to his part as snivelling, runtish Edmund, Duke of Edinburgh, who takes on the sobriquet of the Black Adder soon after accidentally decapitating Richard III (Peter Cook) following the Battle of Bosworth in August 1485. Where other actors might have opted for a wig or a hat, he had a severe pudding-basin haircut, which he then had to sport throughout filming. It was a sign of devotion to authenticity that any method actor would have been proud of.

When it came to thinking up the nickname for their star, Curtis and Atkinson cast around for ideas. But they didn't particularly want a name that was a silly or clever pun; they were keen to come up with something dark that smacked of an old Hollywood swash-buckler, maybe something that Errol Flynn had starred in. Well, you could not come up with something darker than black for starters. Danny Kaye had played the Black Fox in one of his historical romps. This creation was certainly as slithery as a snake (presumably the reptilian reference was a completely accidental nod to *Monty Python*). One urban myth is that Richard Curtis once saw the name of Black-adder on an old board inside a college boating hut on Oxford's River Cherwell. But, whatever the source *The Black Adder* was born.

The historical conceit may not have been wholly original, but it was still an inspired idea for a sitcom. In a way it was sending up all the great BBC costume dramas of the early 70s about Elizabeth I and Henry VIII. The medieval period was not only a rich source of silly costumes and severe haircuts; it was also a time when life was cheap, and comedy, by contrast, was a way of coping with that.

The dialogue, meanwhile, was riddled with the kind of Shake-spearean parodies that had been the stock in trade of Oxbridge sketch shows for decades. Peter Cook – whose rendition of Richard owed much to the Laurence Olivier version – had been a member of Cambridge's The Pembroke Players, who had toured Germany with their reinterpretations of Shakespeare. (*The Merchant of Venice* had sailed rather close to the wind with its anti-semitic storyline less than 15 years after the end of the Second World War.) Cook would continue to dip in and out of Shakespeare throughout his career. In the early 60s the bard had even made it into a routine at Peter Cook's bastion of the satire boom, The Establishment Club, in an update of an old college piece entitled 'So That's the Way You Like It'. Jonathan Miller had contributed coy pastiches of the bard's verse which, nearly 40 years on, haven't aged very well – 'Oh Saucy Worcester, dost thou lie so still?' There were also various nods in the direction of the bard where the action was concerned: in the very first episode, 'The Foretelling', the dead Richard III returns as a ghostly apparition, much in the way Banquo appeared before his killer Macbeth and Hamlet's father haunts the great Dane.

The Black Adder, directed by Martin Shardlow, took period comedy to even giddier heights. Transmitted on BBC1, starting on 15 June 1983 (precisely 11 days before the five-hundredth anniversary of Richard II's accession to the English throne), it moved Atkinson further into the mainstream. The comedy worked on two levels. The literate could appreciate the pun and wordplay; the less literate could just laugh at the muddy pratfalls. It should have been a great success, but in the world of television things that sound great on paper invariably have a nasty habit of coming a cropper once the cameras roll.

The intention was that the humour would emerge from the very fact that it was being taken so seriously. Curtis believed that this would lend the series a healthy absurdity. Instead of filming in a BBC studio as is the norm for a sitcom, the cast travelled up to the Northumbrian coast and filmed in Alnwick Castle in February 1983. It was a beautiful spot, which was later used for some of the outdoor scenes in the 1999 film *Elizabeth* to stand in for Mary of Guise's Scottish stronghold. The castle was the home of the twelfth Duke of Northumberland and his wife, but they had to become used to film crews temporarily taking over and moved into other parts of the spacious castle while filming was taking place. After filming *The Black Adder*, the castle was used for *Robin, Prince of Thieves*.

The trouble was that this no-expense-spared quest for authenticity seemed to override the quest for comedy. Atkinson, for his part, had riding lessons to master the art of horsemanship (although when the final version appeared, his main equine task appeared to be falling off his steed). The location shoot involved a crew of up to 30, plus numerous horses, dogs and even pigeons, just for effect. Furthermore, the horses, around a dozen, required handlers who also did not come cheap.

The wintry outdoor shoot was blighted by snowdrifts in the Capability Brown-designed gardens, and things didn't get any easier indoors either. It didn't help that the sets were so large, often taking in vast medieval halls. A decision was taken that instead of an audience they would have an empty studio, which meant they could have lots of smoke, blood and special effects. But what they could not have was genuine laughter and live feedback. The team had thought this might help to create a dramatic yet ultimately comic effect, but instead it seemed to slow down the narrative when it needed to be driven along. As the star said, 'The action got in the way of the humour.' The best sitcoms – *Dad's Army, Steptoe and Son, Hancock* – always seemed to be about tight groups of people in small spaces; this first series couldn't have been in a larger space if it had been filmed at Wembley Stadium.

Viewing figures failed to break records. Even Atkinson's haircut, a symbol of his commitment to the part, came in for a critical panning from the public. The actor told the *Daily Star* that he would go into shops and people would say, 'Poor thing, he's just been let out of the Belgian army.'

By the time of the second episode, the series still had not really settled down. It seemed odd that having established Richard IV as king in episode one, he promptly disappeared to the Crusades in episode two, 'Born to Be King'. Edmund thinks this has given him the chance to grab some real power from his brother Harry, who, much to Edmund's annoyance, has been made regent in his father's absence. But instead he soon finds out that he has to organize the 'frolics', the celebrations to mark his father's return. Struggling to come up with some Morris dancers, eunuchs and bearded ladies at short notice, Edmund curses his sibling: 'Why is Harry such a bastard?' 'If only he were, my Lord,' says Baldrick, 'then you would be regent now.' Edmund acts on Baldrick's advice and attempts to prove that his brother is illegitimate, only to find out that if anyone is in a position they are not entitled to, it is probably him.

Life was notoriously nasty, brutish and short in medieval times, and *The Black Adder* took advantage of this. The third episode, 'The Archbishop', revealed the nature of the violent property battle raging between the Church and the Crown. When wealthy landowners died, they could choose who inherited their land; if it went to the Church however, the Archbishop of Canterbury tended to die in mysterious circumstances soon after. When another vacancy for archbishop comes along, Edmund hopes that Harry will be appointed. Instead Edmund the reluctant becomes the new Archbishop of Canterbury, putting his life in danger. Only a quick change into a nun's outfit and a display of swordsmanship that would have impressed Errol Flynn saves the day.

Each episode had a plot in its own right, but also picked up threads from previous ones. Throughout the six-part series the rivalry raged between the two brothers as they vied for their father's favours. In 'The Queen of Spain's Beard', Edmund finally thinks he is going to win his father's favours by marrying the Spanish princess, the Infanta, and forming a diplomatic alliance. But when he sees her he has second thoughts. She is played by Miriam Margolyes and is not the great beauty he had been led to expect. Furthermore she cannot speak English, though her interpreter, Don Speekingleesh (Jim Broadbent), can. In choosing this name, Curtis and Atkinson demonstrated they weren't ashamed to use end-of-the-pier gags when naming peers. Edmund manages to extricate himself and marry the beautiful Princess Leia of Hungary, who likes to be read to at bedtime. After all, she is only ten.

If the Princess Leia character was a small nod to the Carrie Fisher role in *Star Wars*, the fifth instalment, 'Witchsmeller Pursuivant', was a bigger nod to the cult film staring Vincent Price, *Witchfinder General*. Frank Finlay plays the Witchsmeller, the man who treks across the length and breadth of the land hunting down servants of Satan. Unfortunately he decides that Edmund is 'The Great Grumbledook'. Things look bad. After a brief trial in which he is convicted of conspiring with animals and propagating a poodle, Edmund is about to be burnt at the stake. But, just as the flames start to lick his heels, a doll, given to him by his mother, catches fire and the Witchsmeller fries instead. Edmund is saved, and his mother twitches her nose in the manner of Samantha in the American sitcom *Bewitched*. There clearly was witchcraft in the family after all.

The Black Adder only really worked when Edmund was the butt of the plot, so when it came to the final episode, 'The Black Seal', things had to end very dramatically for him to achieve the fullest comic effect. His father the king, who has never really been able to remember Edmund's name, strips him of all of his titles, apart from Warden of the Privy, and gives them to his kinfolk as St Juniper's Day presents. Cast out, Edmund seeks revenge. In a homage to *The Magnificent Seven* – but on a BBC budget – he rounds up the six most evil men in the land to help him seize the throne. But the Black Adder himself is captured by the Hawk, who is even more evil. Having been mutilated and nearly tickled to death, it is left to Baldrick and Percy to save the day. Unfortunately they poison the court's vat of wine. Everyone drinks it and dies, making a sequel look very unlikely.

The sitcom had mixed reviews, but Atkinson himself was among those who was not satisfied with it. For years he could not bear to watch it. As a young man, he had sat in the lighting gantry and wanted to be onstage. Now it was as if he wanted to be back in the gantry again. *The Black Adder* was not a complete failure though. Patrick Allen's resonant scene-setting introductions each week obviously made an impression on Vic Reeves and Bob Mortimer, who, nearly a decade later, hired him to do a virtually identical job on their BBC2 series *The Smell of Reeves and Mortimer*. Another positive outcome of *The Black Adder* series was that it firmed up the links between Atkinson, Curtis and the new band of comics beginning to emerge. Rik Mayall, riding high as the star of the *Young Ones*, which started in late 1982, had an eyeball-rolling anonymous cameo as Mad Gerald. And Atkinson's Oxbridge connections were not overlooked. Fellow Oxonian Angus Deayton cropped up as a Jumping Jew of Jerusalem, one of the acts booked to entertain the royal court. Carolyn Colquohoun, one of Atkinson's female friends from Oxford, played the nun, Sister Sara, and Tim McInnerney made his mark as Percy, Duke of Northumberland.

Watching the series again, it does seem to have had an unfairly bad press. Perhaps it suffered from the classic sitcom syndrome of needing time to bed in. The structure wasn't hugely different from the later, more successful series, apart from outdoor shots of Atkinson riding a horse or feebly attempting to round up some sheep. Even the crudeness could be explained away as good, honest Chaucerian vulgarity. Perhaps the drubbing can be explained by the fact that its star had been so successful to date that a backlash was due around that time. The cruelty of the era was being paralleled by the cruelty of the press.

Atkinson had his own theory about the negative critical response. In retrospect he thought that maybe Prince Edmund may have been 'a little too despicable. Heroes of the classically successful British comedy series tend to have won a high degree of sympathy and affection from the British public, like Frank Spencer and even Alf Garnett. Basil Fawlty certainly did. To run a small business and hate your customers is very British.' The *Radio Times* had described Edmund as 'the scummiest toerag in the great basket of human history', which probably explained why the public did not immediately warm to him. In 1986, Atkinson admitted to the *Evening Standard* that he was not very happy about the first series for another reason: 'I think we went to a level of rudeness which surprised even me. I don't mind rude humour as long as it is funny, but there is nothing worse than a rude joke that doesn't work.' He may have been thinking at the time about his penis-shaped codpiece, but there were plenty of other examples of medieval rudery to choose from.

The Black Adder was Atkinson's first high-profile critical failure, although by chance Atkinson was performing and promoting the programme in Australia by the time the series ended and missed some of the flak in Britain. Not even an International Emmy in the Popular Arts Category in America in November – the television equivalent of an Oscar – could sweeten the pill. It wasn't a complete disaster, but after high expectations it was a huge disappointment. The team of Atkinson, Curtis and Goodall were relieved, however, to be told there would be a second series, though the budget this time round would be less than half the cost of the first series. They realized that with some nipping, tucking and rethinking, a second series would put things right. With everyone apart from sidekicks Baldrick (Tony Robinson) and Lord Percy (Tim McInnerney) dying at the end of the series after being poisoned, the creators would have to come up with a new scenario to justify bringing the same cast back.

In the break between series, Atkinson was much in demand as a live performer. On 9 November 1984 he appeared in front of Princess Diana at the Royal Variety Performance at Victoria Palace, alongside a rainbow coalition of comics that extended from Barry Humphries to Ronnie Corbett. But a more significant event that autumn took place further away from the limelight when Atkinson returned to the stage for a nascent project that, unknown to him, would play a crucial part in the future direction of his career. An article in *The Sunday Times* by Stephen Pile had complained that arts festivals always take place in glamorous places such as Edinburgh. To counter this, Charity Projects, a well-meaning fund-raising organization, had become involved in an event in the preposterous-sounding Nether Wallop, a microscopic village in Hampshire. Despite, or maybe because of, the bizarrely comic location – the very concept attracted comedy's quirkier bedfellows – a remarkable bill was lined up to appear in the 400-capacity marquee, a bill with as much credibility and celebrity as the early *The Secret Policeman's Ball* benefits. Peter Cook and Mel Smith did a turn as lesbian synchronized swimmers, complete with rubber hats; Atkinson revived some of his own classic routines. It was an event that helped to fire the imagination of Richard Curtis, who, having seen that comedians would be happy to turn out for a good cause, would be instrumental in kick-starting Comic Relief. Charity's gain, however, would be Atkinson's loss; Curtis's diversification (as well as his move into film and other sitcoms) would mean that ultimately he would have less time to work with Atkinson.

Since those live shows at the Globe, television had taken up much of Atkinson's professional time. Now the elastic star looked for different ways of stretching himself. He chose to go back into the theatre, but this time it wasn't a one-man show but a full-length play by someone from a very different background, and it was a little-known play at that. He was taking quite a substantial risk as the eponymous nerd in the comedy by American playwright Larry Shue. Atkinson seemed to think he could pull it off because he felt there was a nerd in him. Or at least there had been when he was nine years old. To play the part of a friend of a friend who turns up and wrecks other people's lives, he delved back into that peculiar adolescent mix of niceness and nastiness that most children have.

Nerd was a word that originated in America, but it was an immediately recognizable universal archetype. On Russell Harty's chat show, Atkinson recalled how one of the production team, Harry Dixon, told of his experience of being visited by a nerd who had turned up on his doorstep, taking advantage of Dixon's hospitality, causing great inconvenience and thinking of no one but himself. At four o'clock in the middle of the night the phone had rung and the operator said, 'This is your call to India'.

After warm-ups in the provinces, *The Nerd*, directed by Michael Ockrent, opened at the Aldwych Theatre on 3 October 1984. In *The Financial Times*, Michael Coveney made the point that Atkinson's stage career was a case of love-it-or-loathe-it: 'I reckon you will find *The Nerd* either very funny indeed or not funny at all.' Coveney was, however, a fan and championed Atkinson's portrayal of Rick, a tedious chalk inspector from the Midwest who turns up at the house of Willum, an architect – whose life he saved in Vietnam – and remains there for a week. It is people's worst nightmare: their life being saved by someone they don't like. And in the great tradition of drama, it just happens to be the most important week in Willum's life, a make-or-break seven days for both his professional and personal life.

Atkinson had the character off-pat by now, though maybe his television work had made him a little too concerned with minor details. The overgrown schoolboy scruffiness was perfect for the stage, but the cracked half-framed glasses came complete with sticking plaster to hold them together. It was the kind of observation that was certainly valid, but whether anyone could spot the join beyond the first six rows of the stalls was another matter.

Like that other awkward character still germinating in his mind, Rick was a complete monster. In fact, he enters the mid-American suburban house as a green monster, as if at a fancy-dress party. Unfortunately it is five days after Halloween and he simply causes a child present to faint. Everything he says is a *faux pas*, everything he drops is a clanger. He congratulates the others on their costumes when they are in civvies, he bores people to tears; he walks out of the toilet with half a loo roll sticking out of his trousers (in a later scene, prefiguring a famous Mr Bean sketch he appears with his shirt front poking through his flies). He is unaware of everything he does. He is so lacking in self-consciousness that he starts sniffing his socks and armpits during the crowded party scene.

By the time the play resumes after the interval, Rick has set up home in the living room, complete with washing line. A sock inevitably drips on some of Willum's vital designs for a new hotel, causing the ink to run. By the end of the play the other guests are determined to see off the nerd. But whatever they do, he is firmly ensconced in Willum's flat.

The critics, though, were harder on Larry Shue's script than Rowan Atkinson's performance. In the *Express on Sunday*, Clive Hirschhorn said: 'His highly individual brand of humour comes to the rescue of this trite little farce.' Francis King in *The Sunday Telegraph* pointed out that at a running time of 140 minutes, it was about 100 minutes too long, but did observe that the role might have been created for Atkinson.

King was closer than it seemed. Many of the visual gags had been devised by Atkinson and director Michael Ockrent and had not been in the original Shue script, in which the character had been written to encapsulate all the people he had ever met who he did not like. It did seem very much a continuation of Atkinson's previous roles – and also a pointer to his future role as Mr Bean. Critic Ros Asquith described Atkinson's Rick as having the face of an 'apoplectic tortoise ... and an uncanny ability to look slimy and scaly at the same time', and the same could certainly be said for the equally dysfunctional Mr Bean. Michael Billington in *The Guardian* also noted the nascent behaviour of Mr Bean: 'Mr Atkinson, looking like a gargoyle untimely wrenched from the side of Rheims Cathedral, reminds one that a lot of comedy is based on social disruption.' In *Punch* Sheridan Morley was particularly vituperative. While he called Rowan Atkinson a 'great comedian' and compared him to Danny Kaye, he had nothing positive to say about the play or the writer, whom he called 'one of the most mirthless writers since Strindberg'. It was a credit to Atkinson's talent and pulling power that audiences came to *The Nerd*. Morley concluded this was 'the worst comedy to have hit London in a very long time'. Not exactly the kind of thing producers would want to see plastered on adverts outside their show.

Atkinson seemed frighteningly capable of carrying off this portrayal of thick-skinned crassness even where the momentum of the drama dipped in the second half. Although the reviews were critical of Shue, Atkinson's career prospects got off almost scot-free. Maybe you could fault his choice of play, but you couldn't fault the 100 per cent comic performance he contributed to it. All he needed to do now was to harness this character that was another manifestation of something that had been bubbling up in him since his youth and find a more suitable vehicle for it. Of course, the difference between Rick and Bean was that Rick spoke. John Barber in *The Daily Telegraph* described the voice as a mix of crashed gear and chalk squeaking on slate. Maybe it would be better to cut it out altogether. In the programme notes, Larry Shue actually suggested that there was no such thing as an English nerd. Mr Bean, the nerd's silent cousin, would soon prove him wrong.

With its Vietnam veteran subtext, *The Nerd* had a darker theme at heart and maybe one that British audiences could not relate to very easily. Not that this was much comfort when the bad reviews came in. Atkinson had forced himself into the public arena to promote the show but it had not been the success that was hoped for. When *The Nerd* went on a national tour in March 1985 the title role was taken on by folkie-comedian Jasper Carrott.

As busy as he was with the present, Atkinson also seemed to be making plans for the future and looking at a non-verbal approach to complement the very verbal Black Adder. He talked to *Midweek* magazine about a tour of the Far East now that he had conquered most of the English-speaking world: 'Prague. Peking. Moscow. Tokyo. A totally visual show and a six-city tour of the eastern bloc. Being a star in Russia is a terribly exciting idea – so extraordinary. Charlie Chaplin was probably the last person to do it.'

It was an intriguing idea that seemed to have been germinating since he had been on holiday in Venice. While shopping he had seen a postcard stand; the racks were filled with pictures of artists such as George Michael, Phil Collins and Duran Duran. Atkinson, always thinking, even on a day off, had pondered over this phenomenon. English pop stars were famous all over the world. Why weren't there any English comedians with the same level of global celebrity? Music, of course, was an international language, but English comedy was rooted to the English vernacular. To succeed he had to come up with a largely visual variety of humour. Then again, it struck him, that was what he had been doing ever since his Oxford days. Yet he was not the kind of performer who got great joy from a successful show.

On the one hand he wanted to conquer the world, on the other he still had to conquer his own insecurities. He explained that after a show there was never much elation just relief. 'I always feel thank God that's worked: and now there's the problem of doing it again.'

Perhaps he would find like minds for his visual comedy in Eastern Europe. His comedy had been compared to cartoonish Czecho-slovakian humour in the past. Those speechless cartoons by the German animator Mordillo had punctuated his television debut in *A Bundle of Bungles* and they seemed to complement perfectly his own speechless material. Of course, he had yet to conquer *all* of the English-speaking world. America in particular had yet to witness the live Rowan Atkinson.

The Nerd was very different to his previous professional stage appearances. His shows at the Globe had been a series of well-worked sketches; this was a play and a relatively untested one. But Atkinson had always said he was an actor not a comedian, so it was a challenge he had to take on. It was, he said in *The Observer*, all about 'trying to get into a character and make it sing'. Because this wasn't a solo show, the nerves didn't jangle quite as much, but even this seemed problematic. Nerves were a good thing because they pumped adrenaline through the body and could power a performance.

In the *News of the World*, his outlook sounded particularly bleak: 'Being funny is agony. The longer I spend in the business the more depressed and uncertain I get. I worry about everything. Honestly. Every single thing. If an audience laughs, then I worry in case it's only half of them laughing.'

When Atkinson reluctantly appeared on television as himself, you could see this pain in his body language. He had appeared on Russell Harty's chat show in September 1984. He was smartly dressed, his curly black hair flattened down into a hirsute doormat, but Harty's line of questioning did little to put Atkinson at his ease. Unlike chat-show host Michael Parkinson, who had been able to coax him out of his shell through a mixture of flattery and intelligence, Harty had a habit of cutting straight to the chase. Facing Atkinson on the sofa he put the inevitable question to him: 'God had a good day when he gave you your face, didn't he?' Harty proceeded to address the problem of whether there was any pressure on feeling that one had to be funny even when 'off-duty'. Atkinson dismissed the question as if he had been asked it a thousand times already that week, with a convoluted answer that suggested that Harty needn't have bothered putting the question in the first place: 'Not so much any more because it's almost quite a well-known cliché now and it's a talent that most comic performers of my ilk don't have.' This was in marked contrast to his entrance onto the show when he had marched resolutely out of the audience, down the steps and onto the stage as a variant of his Ranting Man who was now purporting to be Rowan Atkinson's agent. Whereas a veteran comedian like the late Eric Morecambe was always funny, Atkinson seemed almost proud to be a straight man offstage – after all, wasn't he providing more than enough laughs onstage?

There were moments, however, when things looked brighter. In January 1985 he was visited by his fan Prince Charles; both men had things in common, including being Aston Martin owners – Atkinson was awaiting delivery of a Vantage Zagato, the second of only 50 made. It was such a rare car that in the summer Atkinson allowed Aston Martin to display it at the Motor Show. Its value rocketed over the next few years; Atkinson paid a reported £87,000 for it and in 1990 it was estimated to be worth £300,000.

Both Atkinson and Prince Charles had a destiny to live up to. Charles would have more than his fair share of difficulties with his role as heir to the throne. By comparison, Atkinson's difficulties – two disappointing roles on the trot – were relatively minor. Besides, they were both laying the groundwork for future successes. But a perfectionist like Atkinson had to resolve his difficulties.

On 6 January 1985, Rowan Atkinson had celebrated his thirtieth birthday. It had been a year of changes, a year of shedding the skins of the past and facing the future. In 1984 his father, Eric, had died. By then, the idea of Rowan taking over Hole Row Farm had long been abandoned. Eric had sold the farm at the beginning of that year. In April he had been to see his son in *Never Say Never Again* at the Empire Theatre in Consett, part of the cinema chain that Rowan's grandfather had run all those years ago. Eric and Ella travelled from their home in Bridgehill to sample their son's latest career move only a few weeks before the death of Eric.

The north was changing almost as fast as Atkinson. The 400-acre farm had been sold and turned into the Royal Derwent Hotel. Despite the restructuring and radical alterations, there was one nice story about something that remained the same. Behind the radiator on the wall of what is now the bar but was once part of the original building, it is still possible to make out the initials 'R. A'. The star was long gone but he had left his mark on the north-east. Of course, even if the story is a true story, the initials might have belonged to either of his brothers.

Following Rowan's own birthday, he was invited to join in with the celebration of Bob Hope's birthday, a West End variety gala in which the legendary entertainer shared the royal box with the Duke of Edinburgh. Onstage, film star Brooke Shields presented the acts in teased hair and a succession of increasingly lurid frocks. In many respects the evening was a tribute to British comedy – Hope, of course, had been born in Eltham, south London. Chevy Chase came on and made a speech about Chaplin, Laurel and Hope – three great Brits who had made it in Hollywood – before introducing Rowan Atkinson. Could he be another great transatlantic clown? For the evening Atkinson revived his *Not the Nine O'Clock News* alien, Zak, who came from the place where there was no death, no gravity and, this time, taking into account developments in the motor industry, 'a different-shaped gear-stick on the Honda Civic.' His slicked-back hair, green tin-foil suit and silver gloves may have looked like the costume was put together on a shoestring budget, but his gift for verbal sounds – and non-verbal sounds, coming out with gibberish when the alien's translation machine failed – was priceless. Zak also had some new, valuable advice for earthlings: 'Beware the one who calls himself Princess Di and cannot be trusted.'

Before his historical sitcom could return, however, some shortcomings had to be ironed out. There was a feeling that the writing had been a problem. Atkinson and Curtis had never written together on something as long as *The Black Adder* series, and it could be a tortuous process at times. Comic stalemates would be reached when they couldn't come up with a punchline to a joke. After saying something like 'He is about as funny as ...' there would then be lengthy pauses while Atkinson attempted to come up with suitable similes. If the series was going to continue, the writing approach clearly needed a revamp. On *Wogan*, Atkinson was keen to emphasize that his new incarnation of Black Adder was superior to the original one. Calling it 'significantly improved', he admitted that he was not a great fan of the first series. It had had some great moments but they had been too few and far between. This time round the jokes would hopefully fly thick and fast.

The main change for *Blackadder II – The Historic Second Series*, screened from 9 January to 20 February 1986, was to set the action a century on in the court of Queen Elizabeth I (Miranda Richardson) so that the cast could play the descendants of the original ensemble. But since the Black Adder died without issue, it was not exactly clear how these descendants were related – presumably his great-great-grandfather was *not* the Black Adder. It was said that this new Edmund was the bastard great-great-grandson, if that made any sense. From this point on, as with the *Carry On* films, there would now be a sense of continuity to the character that each actor played, although there was one immediate change – Lord Edmund Blackadder was the schemer and Baldrick the slow-witted dreamer rather than the other way round. Pretension also played a part in his charm armoury. Blackadder thinks he is a great swordsman and seducer, when in fact his main tasks around the palace are straightening the royal pictures and herding sheep. At one point he would be made chief executioner but he barely avoided losing his head himself.

The other change was the replacement of Atkinson, and occasional contributor William Shakespeare, on the writing team with Ben Elton, the ambitious, fiery young alternative comic had made his name as a co-writer on *The Young Ones*. The first Black Adder was incredibly stupid, so there was not much room for verbal gymnastics, but this time round he was sharp enough to get his tongue round those complex insults that Elton excelled at. Stars always get the credit for the performances in sitcoms, but Atkinson also deserves credit for taking a backseat and putting the writing in the hands of a new team as strong as Richard Curtis and Ben Elton.

There was no denying that Atkinson realized how crucial the second series was. On the evening of transmission he told *Time Out*: 'My future credibility with the BBC probably rests with the success or failure of this series.' He had learnt a number of lessons after the first series, which he now viewed as part of 'a growing-up process'.

Growing up also involved coming to terms with being a celebrity and being public property. One of his most embarrassing experiences had been when he had been coming back from Bristol one night in his Aston Martin. Feeling tired, he stopped at a crowded service station and was queuing up for a pot of tea and a Danish pastry and trying to avoid being recognized by attempting to 'retract my head into my body like a tortoise'. Unfortunately when he got to the till he realized that he had left his wallet in the car. The checkout woman was convinced this was all an elaborate Jeremy Beadle-style practical joke and was looking round for hidden cameras. Eventually Atkinson put back the cake and cuppa and fled. Another time he was in a hamburger bar and when he went to the counter he could hear the staff arguing over whether it was 'him' or not. They did not seem to care that he could hear their debate.

In many respects the *Blackadder* cycle picked up where *The Young Ones* left off, becoming that rare beast, a hugely successful cult. Before you could say pox, flummery and gadzooks, the critics had done a volte-face and were praising it. Everything seemed to fall neatly into place. The BBC's decision to recommission seemed like an act of great foresight. Even the theme tune fitted neatly into the production, with Curtis and Elton letting Howard Goodall have a look at the scripts in the pub so that he could jot down ideas for lyrics on a beermat and later incorporate the individual storylines into each episode's closing song. For Goodall, one of the advantages of knowing Rowan and Richard for so long was that he had an instinct for the kind of thing they would want to hear. Goodall did not aim to write funny songs just because it was a funny programme. He had seen Rowan taking rehearsals extremely seriously and, despite getting ideas in the pub, he would go back to his piano later and apply the same kind of artistic rigour to the musical aspect of the production.

Another advance in the new series was in Atkinson's performance. It meshed perfectly with the lines, but he also had the measure of his character, making it larger-than-life and yet still within the bounds of credibility – what Richard Curtis called 'exuberant naturalism'. There was a spark to it that ignited the entire programme. A little idea could go a long way when Atkinson took it under his wing. There was now great optimism in the *Blackadder* camp. The second series had not even been transmitted and there was already talk of another series taking things up to the First World War and focusing on the antics of the German air ace Baron von Blackadder. And maybe one day, Atkinson conjectured on *Wogan*, setting events in the future and following the adventures of Staradder.

But the change that made all the difference was the addition of Ben Elton to the team. And yet this was something that came about largely by chance. After the first series Richard Curtis happened to bump into Elton and they started to chat casually about *The Black Adder*. Curtis was always open to suggestions, and Elton said they should have done it with a studio audience – as a stand-up comedian as well as a writer, Elton knew how important spontaneous response could be. Curtis decided to take Elton's advice and get an audience in. He also got Elton in as a co-writer. As Elton recalled in *Cult TV*: 'Let's get into the studio and have two wooden, cardboard sets, because the money's in Rowan's face.' Dialogue was then developed to go with that face.

The second series nearly didn't happen though. Just before it went ahead the team received a bolt from the blue from new BBC boss Michael Grade. He had been looking over the accounts and had decided that in the first series there were 'not enough laughs per pound'. The joke doing the rounds at the BBC at the time was that the first series looked like a million dollars but cost a million pounds. Grade wanted to axe the programme immediately. According to Richard Curtis, speaking on Radio 4's *Desert Island Discs* in 1999, a letter was even sent out by the BBC saying they did not want any more. When Curtis, Elton and Atkinson heard about this, two scripts were quickly finished off and they sent them round to Grade begging him to read them. He did, he laughed, he recommissioned the show, and the rest, if you'll excuse the pun, is history.

There was the proviso however; the budget had to be tighter. This time round there were just three sets and six main characters, costing two-thirds of the original series. The script was more interested in verbal interplay, going for Bilko-style one-liners. Instead of a continuous plot, each episode was a self-contained comedy, revolving around the imbeciles in Queen Elizabeth's court and the cynical Blackadder's perpetual attempts to get one over on them.

The second series cut back on the scenery – the Virgin Queen's court, for instance, was about the size of a suburban lounge – and was inspired when it came to casting. The biggest revelation was Miranda Richardson, who at that time was not really known for her comedy –

her most famous role to date was Ruth Ellis, the last woman to be hanged in Britain, in *Dance with a Stranger*, which had been released in the previous year. It was a role in marked contrast to the Virgin Queen, but her way of relaxing off-camera during the making of that serious film had offered more than a hint of her comic potential. To stay sane between shoots, Richardson developed a habit of play-acting on set and sometimes took on the character of, what James Saynor in *The Observer* called, 'a psychopathic, Benenden-style schoolgirl throwing facetious, screechy-growly tantrums to entertain her co-workers'. It was here that the seeds were sown for Queenie. Talking to James Rampton in *The Independent* in 1998, Richardson reflected on how the second *Blackadder* series worked so well: 'The scripts were very detailed and arcane. It was the combination of, if you like, Ben the yobbo and Richard the scholar. The same elements are in *Monty Python*. It was scholarly, wide-ranging and mentally adept as well as wild and woolly. That sort of anarchy is very English.'

Richardson relished her role as the young Queen. Still only in her mid-20s herself, she let rip playing a woman who had inherited a huge amount of power at an extremely early age. The way Curtis and Elton wrote the role – which seemed to have a grain of truth – was that she had problems relating to men; this explained why those who did not lose their hearts to her had a habit of losing their heads.

Richardson was brilliant as the squeaking Virgin Queen who would lisp 'off with his head' at the drop of a hat. There was also the rising Stephen Fry as Lord Melchett, one of her toadying sidekicks, and Patsy Byrne as her ever-present Nursie. And then there was Tim McInnerney, back as Lord Percy, a man so dull he would 'bore the leggings off a village idiot'.

With *Blackadder II* there was a physical departure for Atkinson. In the first series he had been preoccupied with pulling his face into a permanent sneer. Now he grew a beard and looked rather dashing in his Elizabethan ruff and tights. There was something of the Errol Flynn about him. Not a lot, but something. The change to his appearance was particularly appealing to him. As he said in the *News of the World*: 'All people want from me are my bloody silly faces. And if there's one thing I hate about myself, it's my face.'

The new writing team of Curtis and Elton worked perfectly; Curtis's Harrovian sensibility meshed like a well-oiled machine with

Elton's combination of north-London wit, Manchester drama studies irreverence and punk-inspired cheek. Curtis and Elton had another thing in common. They were both intensely passionate about music. In fact, they had to do their collaborations separately because they knew that if they worked together in the same room they would spend all their time arguing about the relative merits of Madonna and Madness. When they did meet up, Elton would ask Richard, whose face was anonymous, to go out to the shops and buy him Kylie Minogue videos because he was too embarrassed to be seen to be buying them himself.

At this point, Elton was gigging regularly and Curtis was based in a cottage in the country, so they would communicate via computer disc, writing drafts and then rewriting and posting back each other's drafts. They had one strict writing rule – if the other one edited out a joke because they did not think it was funny, they were never allowed to reinstate it, however funny the writer thought it was. After all, as in real life, you couldn't keep telling a joke expecting someone to laugh if they didn't find it funny the first time round. It was this rigour that kept the standard so high over the next three series.

Elton and Atkinson also had shared interests, which made them a perfect team. They both, for instance, loved the writing of P.G. Wodehouse; consequently, there was more than a touch of Wodehouse's masterful use of the foibles of the English language in the work they did together.

Ben Elton was, in many ways, a complete mirror image of Atkinson in terms of personality and ambition. In some ways the mirror image was not the way one might have expected it to be. Atkinson was a product of Oxford University, but it was Elton, the Manchester University drama graduate with the *faux* prole-ish stand-up streetwise attitude, whose father was an academic. The contrasts didn't end there. Atkinson had sort of stumbled into a comedy career and felt it could end at any time and it wouldn't be the end of the world if it did. In fact, it was only with *The Black Adder* that he finally changed his occupation on his passport: 'I tried to maintain engineer as a career for as long as possible,' he joked to the *Daily Star*, 'mainly for insurance purposes. You have no idea of the quantum leap in the premium when I made the change.' Elton, on the other hand, had set his heart on an artistic life from an early age. At Manchester he toiled away in the drama department writing plays alone in his caravan and performing them at any opportunity. His college friendship with Rik Mayall and Adrian Edmondson had helped his career and he was now hot property as a writer and a constantly improving stand-up comedian. The two had contrasting talents too. Atkinson's skills and ideas were often physical; Elton was a lover of words – erudite ones and rude ones.

Elton and Richard Curtis worked hard on the second *Blackadder* series despite numerous distractions. At the time they were both single and there were lots of things they would rather do than write. It was a chaotically happy time for Curtis, who would spend much of the day watching television. Eventually, about an hour after the lunch time edition of *Neighbours*, he would start work only stopping to watch the evening repeat. He would do some more work in the evening before stopping for a bite to eat and then would carry on until about three in the morning. It was not a particularly healthy regime, but Curtis was young and able to keep unusual hours.

For Curtis, delaying tactics were as much a part of the creative process as actually writing. To avoid work he would play around with his new computer, opening and closing files and moving icons around and renaming them. Anything to avoid work. But he liked the computer because it made him feel as if he were watching television even when he was not watching television.

Elton and Curtis soon hit a rhythm and found that there was endless comic mileage in similes. When Atkinson's character came out with them they seemed spontaneous, but they were often a struggle to create – certainly the hardest part of the writing process. In *Now That's Funny*, by Joe McGrath and David Bradbury (Methuen, 1998), Richard Curtis shed some light on the process. Ben would send him a line that said, 'You are as stupid – as my knob.' That's what it would always say. We can't use "my knob" so I'd have a go at it.' Eventually, after shuttling between them, the line would sometimes still not be complete when the team got to the rehearsal rooms in west London. Then everybody would have a go until a funny pay-off was agreed upon.

The other key to getting it right was getting the *rhythm* of each episode right. There is an arc to a sitcom episode, and Richard Curtis could tell when he had hit the mark. The plot had to start and information had to be leaked out before he could move to a second plot. Then there was some time to cram in some daftness before concluding by referring back to something in the first half. He could also tell when he had done something good because he wanted to read it to his friends – he never did, but the fact that he wanted to was the sign.

One of Curtis's favourite comic conceits was making the same thing happen over and over again, with increasingly comic results. He did it in sketches in *Not the Nine O'Clock News* and he did it in the film *Four Weddings and a Funeral* – each marriage ratcheted up the comic tension of Hugh Grant's own predicament. And it was a technique used to great effect in *Blackadder II*. In the episode entitled 'Beer', for instance, Blackadder's chums are having a drinking party, and one by one they reveal their false breasts. Finally Melchett manages to trump them all just when they think he has forgotten his costume. With a cry of *'Au contraire'*, he exposes a pair of huge gold breasts.

Though there was a lot of rich dialogue in *Blackadder II*, it was remarkable how Curtis and Elton managed to fillet some of it out, paring things down to the comedy essentials. Instead of building up to a silly name with a string of normal names, as is the comedic tradition, they would just plough straight in with a silly name – one of the drinking chums in 'Beer' is called Piddle; the gaoler in 'Head' is called Ploppy. Similarly Elton would cut to the chase where vulgarity was concerned, never using a double-entendre when a single-entendre would do. With Elton on board the series went from strength to strength.

Blackadder II put the seal on the Blackadder brand. It demonstrated that Atkinson could act, Curtis could write plots and Ben Elton could come up with marvellous one-line put-downs such as 'Your brain is like the four-headed man-eating haddock-fish beast of Aberdeen. It doesn't exist.' Each episode was beautifully self-contained, with a rich diversity of characters, some of whom would flit in and out of the lives of various Blackadders across the centuries.

In episode one, 'Bells', we were introduced to another occasional member of the time-travelling rep company. Gabrielle Glaister, who went on to soap fame as yuppie spouse Patricia Farnham in *Brookside*, played Kate, a young woman from a poor household. Her father tries to persuade her to become a prostitute – it is, after all, a steady job and one you can do from home – but she insists on running away to London and, for no apparent reason apart from the fact that it is the cause of much merriment, in true pantomime style she takes on the identity of a thigh-slapping boy called Bob. Baldrick is promptly sacked and replaced by Bob, who Blackadder finds himself strangely attracted to. (The idea for the cross-dressing and the subsequent romance may have come from Atkinson's awareness of the origins of his middle name. Sebastian in Shakespeare's *Twelfth Night* becomes embroiled in a case of mistaken identity when his sister Viola dresses up as him.) For the first time Curtis was dealing with gender politics, sexuality and machismo. Was Blackadder attracted to Bob because unconsciously he realised Bob was female underneath the codpiece or was something more complex going on? Eventually the truth is revealed and after a rather lame Kiss Me Kate gag, they plan to marry, only for best man Lord Flashheart (a blonde Rik Mayall with a decidedly wobbly moustache) to whisk the bride-to-be away at the altar. If there is a constant theme to Blackadder it is that he is always destined to be thwarted, in life as in love.

In the second episode, 'Head', Blackadder thinks his prospects are looking up when he gets a new job, Minister in Charge of Religious Genocide, in other words, he has to organize executions. But when he carries one out that he should not have, he faces execution himself. Fortunately there's a plan that can save him: 'Tell 'em the plan, duckface,' he says to Lord Percy, in a foreshadowing of the *Four Weddings and a Funeral* character (Curtis recently said that Anna Chancellor's nickname in the film was actually supposed to be 'Fuck-face', but it was toned down for the sake of propriety). Of course, we know Blackadder can't lose his head; there are another four episodes to go.

The series seemed to grow in confidence with each week. In 'Beer' we meet the religious branch of the family, the Whiteadders. They are a bunch of ascetics that could have come out of Aldous Huxley's *The Devils of Loudon*. They are led by his aunt, Lady Whiteadder (Miriam Margolyes), who believes that sitting on a chair that does not have a spike sticking out of its seat is a case of gross self-indulgence. Blackadder is after an inheritance from them and intends to ingratiate himself when they visit. Unfortunately the evening also clashes with a boozy party, so Blackadder has to shuttle between rooms and try to avoid getting drunk. He also has difficulties avoiding letting his motives slip out. As Lady Whiteadder and her husband settle down he remarks, 'I hope you had a pleasant inheritance ... did I say inheritance?' It is a remark that has a very strong ring to it. Blackadder has difficulties resisting the word 'inheritance' in the way Basil Fawlty can't avoid mentioning the war.

Apart from being innovative, *Blackadder II* also showed that the writing team knew their comedy history. In 'Potato', Blackadder decided to compete with Sir Walter Raleigh for the hand of the queen. This meant he had to impress her by sailing around the Cape of Death. To help him in his quest, he seeks out the scrofulous Captain Redbeard Rum (offering him a chance to work with a former Dr Who, Tom Baker), who has no legs and – another *Python* reference? – a dead parrot on his shoulder. When it transpires that Captain Rum can't sail a boat or even find France, Percy is convinced they are going to meet their end: 'We're doomed,' he cries, in a distinctly *Dad's Army*-style homage. Without ever coming close to plagiarism there was often an air of touching on great comedy moments of the past. A whole episode, 'Chains', was devoted to the capture of Blackadder by the Spanish Inquisition, the subject of one of *Monty Python*'s most famous sketches.

Things finally concluded, as they had in the first series, with the main protagonists being killed off – this time by Hugh Laurie as an evil Germanic master of disguise, Prince Ludwig. However, this time there was little chance of the franchise being killed off. Atkinson and Curtis – with the aid of new recruit Ben Elton – had snatched victory from the jaws of defeat the second time around.

It was an odd period for Atkinson. Celebrity had its drawbacks and he tried to pull back, making himself a more private person, retreating to Waterperry wherever possible. It was a difficult balancing act to pull off, being a huge celebrity but retaining a dignified profile, but Atkinson seemed to manage it better than most by growing up. Some of his university contemporaries did notice a significant change in him around this time. Gone was the shaggy-student look, instead here was a well-groomed, well-poised successful man. He looked like a bank manager, he sounded like a bank manager, but he was the funniest man in England.

7

Broadway Malady

Maybe the thought of being mentioned in the same breath as comedy greats at Bob Hope's birthday gala a year earlier had made an impression on Atkinson. In January 1986 he revealed his plans to make his mark in America. Having declined previous offers, he was now planning to take his show to Broadway in October. It was a big step, but he seemed fully aware of the risks, telling the *Daily Express*: 'I know that it is a potential graveyard for English comics. It's something I must plan very carefully and I hope they turn out to see me.'

In preparation for the show he did some small dates in Canada, playing a 500-seat venue in Montreal that was smaller than anything he had done since Edinburgh in 1977. The old routines went down well with the Anglophile crowd and the crowds poured in, but there were other portents that weren't so good. While a passenger in someone's car, a rented Oldsmobile Cutlass, Atkinson was involved in a crash. They were travelling at 70 mph, but according to an article Atkinson wrote for *Car* magazine in November 1992, he passed to the driver 'a cube of chocolate which action instigated the unfortunate chain of events'. It was a somewhat surreal experience. A friend in the back had been asleep during the journey and awoke to find himself inside a vehicle 'rotating around a horizontal axis'. The car had turned over three times, but it was not as serious as it sounded; there was a lot of blood around but on closer inspection it seemed to have been caused by superficial cuts. Thankfully Atkinson had been wearing a seatbelt, which had kept physical damage to a minimum. The group was also put at ease by a number of concerned onlookers who came to their rescue brandishing first-aid kits. Arriving at the hospital the article in *Car* recalled the doctor's initial concern was more about the failure of Atkinson's credit card to leave a satisfactory imprint, which suggested the health scare was not a major one. But was somebody trying to tell him something?

Atkinson and car trouble seemed to go back a long way. Back in 1984 he had broken down on the side of the road in his Aston Martin when a driver pulled up to see if he could offer any assistance. The good Samaritan was racy MP Alan Clark. He later wrote about the incident and his thoughts were published in his scurrilous *Diaries*. He seemed more impressed with Atkinson's DBS V8 than his personality, remarking that he thought him to be 'rather disappointing'.

Atkinson had long harboured ambitions to have a crack at motor-racing on a quasi-professional basis, and at Brand's Hatch he drove round the track in a Renault that had already been in a smash when former Wham! star Andrew Ridgeley was driving it. But motor-racing was an ambition that never went away. A couple of years later he took part in the Renault 5 Turbo Championships. If he had been able to take part in enough races during the season he stood a chance of picking up a new Renault and the £3,000 prize. Cars seemed to run close to comedy as his major passion.

If cars were a major obsession, charity was also becoming a regular activity. Atkinson helped to launch Comic Relief, which, following a live broadcast from a refugee camp in the Sudan in December 1985, staged three all-star comedy shows at London's Shaftesbury Theatre in March 1986. With the success of the second series of *Blackadder* behind him, he was now on an all-time high.

Many of the people, such as Jane Tewson, had already been involved for much of the 80s in comedy-related charity work, such as *Fundamental Frolics* and the weird little festival in Nether Wallop in the autumn of 1984. The organization Charity Projects had worked with Band Aid and had been growing all the time. Richard Curtis had visited Ethiopia in 1985. The poverty reminded him of his childhood years in Manilla where he had seen the sharp contrast between the rich and poor. Here the struggle was starker than ever and it was something he felt he had to try to do something about. What particularly caught his eye was the fact that although the people there suffered poor health and had lost nearly everything, they still clung on to their sense of humour. This link between humour and humanitarian aid would be both enduring and profitable.

With Atkinson as 'ringmaster' for the Comic Relief live shows, they promptly sold out, despite ticket prices as high as £50. It was a chaotic but hugely successful enterprise, with everyone entering into the spirit. One night it was after three o'clock in the morning by the time it got round to Billy Connolly's turn to go onstage. Richard Curtis apologized about the tardy schedule and asked him to do ten minutes. But asking Connolly to keep his act short is like asking the Clyde to freeze over. He did nearly 50 minutes, but nobody was complaining.

Atkinson provided the bridge between the older, established comics, such as Billy Connolly and Smith and Jones, and the newer ones such as Ben Elton – on top form with his tirades against British Rail and the British way of queuing – and Fry and Laurie. He seemed to be the missing link. Agewise he straddled both sides, although interestingly, when BBC1's *Omnibus* screened an edited compilation of the shows, some of the elder statesmen, such as Michael Palin, Graham Chapman and Terry Jones, failed to appear. It was as if television wanted to champion comedy's new wave, and Atkinson along with Billy Connolly were the only acceptable faces of the old guard.

Atkinson chose to showcase some of his new routines. In the sketch entitled A Few Fatal Beatings, Angus Deayton played a concerned parent, Mr Perkins. Atkinson was the stern Scottish schoolmaster explaining to Mr Perkins that his son has been beaten to death for taking a book out of the library without a library card. Even St Bees would not have punished a boy like this, but anyone who had ever had a passing acquaintance with a public school would recognize the essential reality in the incident. The schoolmaster said that afternoon school would have to be cancelled to accommodate the funeral. Then he revealed, to Mr Perkins' initial relief, that he had been joking. Of course he wouldn't be cancelling school for the funeral.

Do Bears?, now a bona fide greatest hit, was revived, though this time in a duet with Kate Bush, who looked decidedly nervous at the start, but soon got the hang of the comedy lark. There was more singing in store for the climax of *Feed the World*. Bob Geldof and Midge Ure took centre stage, but as the entire cast joined in Atkinson also found himself at the front, looking very un-rock-and-roll in his shirt and clean jeans and sharing the microphone with Geldof. It was a strangely casual affair after Live Aid the previous year. At one point during the musical finale a custard pie – or at least a plate of foam – was squashed onto Ben Elton's head and he could be seen sticking two fingers up, like an angry fifth former, at the culprit.

The event was a resounding success, not just because of the money raised, but because it showed that even though Atkinson was decidedly apolitical, comedy itself could be a powerful force for good. Later that year there were further fund-raising shows around the country and to coincide with them some of the main comics involved, led by Lenny Henry, appeared on a special edition of *Wogan*. Henry challenged Wogan to get into the spirit of the charity by attempting to conduct the fastest mass interview of all time. Taking a deep breath, Wogan darted backwards and forwards chatting to as many celebrities as he could. Ben Elton was on one side, Douglas *Hitch-hikers Guide to the Galaxy* Adams was on the other; a youthful Ian Hislop was quizzed next to *Young Ones* co-writer Lise Mayer. Fry and Laurie were on the sofa together. In the middle of the studio floor stood Atkinson, unmissable in a lemon-coloured sweater. As Wogan approached him, an apologetic Lenny Henry intervened, saying: 'I'm sorry Rowan, we just didn't have time for your interview.' Atkinson looked crestfallen, but within seconds the cameras had moved on to someone else. Sometimes, it seemed, Rowan Atkinson could be completely silent when you least expected it.

On 7 March 1986, Atkinson also kicked off the *New Revue*, his first London run – a lengthy three-month residency – since the Globe in 1981. If further proof was needed that he was trying to escape the straight-jacket of his own reputation it could be found in the programme for the Shaftesbury Theatre show: a spoof script talked about Rowan 'pulling a funny face, then another, before doing a funny movement . . . another funny movement only bigger . . . followed by a hilarious funny movement and a surprisingly funny face. There would then be a climax consisting of another funny face, a comical movement and a breathtakingly funny meaningless noise.' Atkinson clearly realized that he had the ability to get laughs out of physical comedy; but the spoof script hinted that he was feeling exasperated by expectations. Now he wanted to take things further.

Ben Elton contributed to the live show, alongside Atkinson and Curtis. By this time Curtis had given up performing to concentrate on his writing, so the new sidekick was Angus Deayton. He unwittingly added to the abiding portrait of the artist as a physical comic with a description of his own role as Atkinson's 'bodyguard': 'If you can call it a body. Perhaps you should call it his strange-bendy-thing-that-holds-his-head-on.'

As if to confirm that Atkinson was still thinking about diversifying into non-English-speaking markets, many of the sketches in his West End show were almost wordless. There was one, written by Curtis and Elton, in which the star played a schoolboy who turns up for exams only to find he has revised the wrong subject. Even though he has more pencils than his nearby neighbours he can't answer the questions. Atkinson showed him trying to cheat, sneaking peeks in any way he could at his neighbour's papers. Although the boy wasn't Mr Bean, the sketch would appear in the very first episode of *Mr Bean* in 1990. These deceptively simple, mostly silent sketches took time to develop. Initial ideas would come but then had to be worked through. Curtis and Atkinson would try to establish ground-rules for this awkward figure. What would he do now? Why would he do this? Then gradually as a sense of character began to emerge, a sketch would evolve.

Other sketches homed in on the problems of communication with varying degrees of decency and taste. There was a skit about three deaf, dumb and blind men who had been killed. Tom was blind and deaf; Dick was deaf and dumb; and Harry was blind and dumb; they had all been involved in a terrible accident with a combine harvester because the one who saw it couldn't warn the others, the one who heard it couldn't see where it was, and the one who could have shouted to the other two could neither hear nor see it. Then there was a song from One-Eyed Jim, the country singer who unwittingly plays guitar back to front. And harking back to *Not the Nine O'Clock News*, there was news for the hard of hearing using increasingly absurd sign language instead of subtitles.

There was a fresh Atkinson seeping in, but the old one had yet to seep out completely. He still seemed to be exorcising the ghosts of St Bees in the sketch in which the headmaster apologizes for beating a boy to death. That malleable body was used to great effect in a new skit in which a passenger on the London Underground, played by Atkinson, is pestered by a bored invisible man, played by no one, who blows annoyingly into the commuter's ear and eventually sticks his fingers up the man's nose, lifting him up and backwards onto his heels.

If some of the sketches seemed dumbed down at times, Atkinson told the press that he was unashamed, even though they might have seemed odd, given his background: 'I'm very aware of being a member of the educated middle class and that sometimes my comedy is aimed at them. But I also like the simpler, less pretentious stuff that appeals much further down the market, like *Blackadder II*.'

The success of his West End show brought some of the old confidence back. He made some rare public appearances with his new girlfriend, BBC make-up artist Sunetra Sastry, who had worked on *Blackadder*. Their first date had been going to see Dire Straits at Wembley Arena. Atkinson was even prepared to make his opinions known on issues outside comedy, speaking out against violence on television and saying that he preferred to watch *Songs of Praise*; he appeared on the religious show as it celebrated its twenty-fifth birthday. *Not the Nine O'Clock News* aficionados may have smiled when they recalled his sketch as the vicar berating his parishioners for only turning up to worship because they knew the *Songs of Praise* cameras were in town.

The new sketches had the mark of Ben Elton upon them, while the older ones and, in particular, the visual and vicar-related sketches, stemmed by Rowan's earlier era. Some critics failed to acknowledge the new work and felt an overwhelming sense of familiarity. In his *Daily Mail* review, the late Jack Tinker confessed to a blinding moment of *déjà vu* during the show. It wasn't that the *New Revue* wasn't full of new material; it was a sense in which 'we have already heard half his funny voices and witnessed one third of his amusing scenes.' There was no element of surprise, just a succession of priest and politicians, according to Tinker. Even aided by Ben Elton, rapidly making a name for himself as a left-wing firebrand, he felt Atkinson's bile wasn't particularly sharp.

Tinker was being somewhat unfair on Atkinson. If his act was familiar that was probably due to the fact that, thanks to *Not the Nine O'Clock News* and *Blackadder*, Atkinson had become ingrained in the nation's psyche over the last seven years. It was not surprising that some of his act gave critics a headache. Atkinson even revisited an old college sketch, chasing a pool of light created by the spot light around the stage. Having caught it he moved it across the stage and burped it out. Michael Coveney in *The Financial Times* suggested this may have been inspired by the clown Popov, though the *Young Ones* was probably just as influential. *The Guardian*'s Michael Billington was fairer, pointing out that while Atkinson had become a national institution he hadn't lost his gift for grotesquerie, which was in itself an achievement. Billington noted the heavier political tone – the Elton influence could be seen in remarks about nuclear missiles at Greenham Common and lesbian protesters. He particularly enjoyed his sketch as the invisible man. Where Benny Hill would have used this power to pinch female bottoms, Atkinson put himself in the position of the victim – the commuter being shunted around by thin air.

Other highlights of the show did away with funny lines and got by on Atkinson's facial and bodily contortions alone. Best of all was his lecture on how to go on a date. Deayton presented the lecture; Atkinson acted it out, appearing behind a door to contrast the behaviour of a Mr Cool, all nonchalance and *savoir faire*, and a Mr Nerd, all butterfingers – a Mr Bean in the making.

Vicars and pedagogues still played a crucial part. There was the rude vicar and his attitude to fellatio and, of course, the Schoolmaster, now so famous it was changed – by Elton – into a knowing postmodern encore. There was now less innuendo, more vulgarity ('Don't let me catch you in the corridor Herpes'); another blast from his *Not the Nine O'Clock News* past was Rawlinson, the Geordie soccer coach – a rare working-class creation – who harangues his team at half-time. It later turns out that they are all members of his family. The song that catalogued increasingly incredible absurdities, *I Believe*, came complete with topical references: 'I believe that a nuclear winter's good for skiing, but I can't believe Norman Tebbit is a human being.'

The intriguing development was the satirical side that Elton was clearly pushing him into. Some moments were more successful than others. A sketch about an ageing, senile Harold MacMillan – hardly topical, though it was used to attack the current government

('Geoffrey Howe wouldn't know a joke if he went home and found one in bed with his wife,' said the fake ex-PM) – recalled Peter Cook's MacMillan impressions at the Establishment Club in Soho around the corner nearly a quarter of a century earlier; but if it was meant as a tribute to Cook it was a fairly obscure one. Milton Shulman in the London *Evening Standard* felt there was a split personality, the visual clown sparring for attention with the verbal wit.

One new sketch broke away from all of these previous formats. Inspired in part by the late-night curries he used to partake of when he was a student, Atkinson played an Indian waiter, forced to deal with a late-night rugby crowd (all unseen, although we gather from Atkinson that one has ordered a Big Mac, while another refers to Alsatian vindaloo). The waiter finally gets the better of them (saying the Shami kebab is the one that looks like shit, 'which is what you are full of'). While there was something uncomfortable about Atkinson's portrayal of an Asian man, this was an intriguing departure from anything he had done before. There wasn't a vicar or a schoolmaster in sight. Unfortunately it was an area of social satire he failed to develop.

The overall conclusion was that Atkinson could still hold an audience's attention for two hours, though Benedict Nightingale in the *New Statesman* felt that the more he spoke the more he spoilt things. John Barber in *The Telegraph* bemoaned his loss of boyish charm and puckishness of the Hampstead Theatre days, but he did conclude that Atkinson could have been a master of the silent screen. He was polished and confident, and even if there was plenty of smut, there was still a layer of maturity to his act that other comics lacked. For every weak gag there were some brilliantly observed, often cruel moments: Christ refusing to be a children's party entertainer despite being able to turn water into wine, for instance. If the routine in which the vicar conducted the funeral of the three disabled men, Tom, Dick and Harry, who had been caught up in a combine harvester, seemed near the knuckle, at least it showed that Atkinson wasn't afraid to dip his toes into the comedy new wave's surf.

Francis Wheen in *Today*, however, did note an obsession with disability – Tom, Dick and Harry, the deaf, One-Eyed Jim who plays the guitar back to front. Wheen noted that Brian Rix from Mencap, who had been seated in front of him, did not seem amused. However, with America in the pipeline, Michael Ratcliffe, writing in *The Observer*, described the *New Revue*, designed complete with steel girders and spiral staircases, courtesy of the old Wireworks team, as a 'very smart Broadway show'.

Atkinson also took the show to the Edinburgh Festival that summer, appearing then for the first time in six years. To say that Atkinson hadn't been in Edinburgh for six years was not strictly true. As well as attending meetings of the Fringe Board, in 1983 he had helped other companies out on the technical side. Edinburgh always seemed to bring out the scientist in Atkinson. One of the first times Festival archivist Michael Dale had met Atkinson, the comic had been trying to fix the photocopier in the Fringe office in the High Street.

But Atkinson hadn't been to Edinburgh for six years as a performer, and comedy was clearly big business now, with the Fringe's comedy crowd glued to the Perrier Awards. Atkinson, of course, was too big for what was, in effect, an award for newcomers to television. Booked to appear as a late-night show at the Edinburgh Playhouse, he was barely part of the Fringe, more a tourist attraction, a must-see alongside the Tattoo and a climb up Arthur's Seat.

Atkinson had gone back to Edinburgh to keep himself occupied and try out some new things before America and to make some money. But there were problems of allowing the ballet onstage. Atkinson's shows needed time to set up and the time just wasn't there for a theatrical show to be organized to his high standards. It did not bode well for the biggest dates in his career since his London début.

In October 1986, Rowan Atkinson made his Broadway début. One omen at least seemed good. He was booked to appear at the Atkinson Theatre. If this was the big test of whether his comedy was international, he certainly failed it – at least as far as the most influential critic in the world was concerned. But then again, his failure might have as much to do with the attitudes and status of the American critics as it has to do with the fundamental Britishness of Rowan Atkinson. The show closed after 14 performances – eight previews and six shows. The closure, which lost backers a reported $500,000, was largely put down to the review of Frank Rich in the *New York Times*. Not for nothing is he called the Butcher of Broadway. In a scathing attack on Atkinson, he concluded that 'the melding of

English and American cultures is not yet complete.'

The star, clearly shaken by the venom of the press – although out of around 33 reviews only a few were negative – called Rich a feudal king with too much power and responded in the *Daily Mail*: 'The only way I'll go back is if I can take out insurance against that man coming anywhere near me.' Calming down a little, he looked on the bright side, calling it a 'disgracefully vicious and irrational attack. The only good thing to come out of the whole venture is that now I will be home for Christmas.' There was a certain amount of relief that it was all over. 'It was like the maths teacher not turning up – thank God I can do something else now. I'm off the hook.' Richard Curtis was equally philosophical, using the kind of reverse logic only an old Harrovian could come up with; he consoled himself with the thought that a fortnight flop was preferable to the long slog of a successful long run.

Rich's review wasn't simply an assault on the star; it was a critique of a lavatorial vein of British humour that has been around since Chaucer: 'It's not inconceivable that this comic's biggest fans at home are products of an upbringing that encourages boys to tame their nasty bowel habits at an early age, with the consequences that their obsession with alimentary byproducts persists right through Oxford and Cambridge.'

A couple of years later, on *Desert Island Discs*, Atkinson was able to look back on Rich's critique with a bit of critical distance of his own. It wasn't the first time he had been described as lavatorial. The first *Black Adder* had been attacked for the same reasons, yet his show had been well received elsewhere. But the Broadway system was unique, and the cost of putting a show on there meant that he had to sell out to survive. In another town he could have run and run even without full houses. And on Broadway the tickets had been selling increasingly well during the previews. Frank Rich just stopped sales dead in their tracks.

Atkinson suddenly found some unlikely supporters in the press. Bob Monkhouse sprang to his defence conceding that 'New York is a tough place. The RSC once did *Julius Caesar* there. When Caesar was stabbed onstage half the audience left because they didn't want to get involved.'

Rich's review found little positive in the show, yet much of the material had stormed it in London. Rich even found fault with the moments he found funny suggesting that even the funny bits were overlong. Were *Rowan Atkinson at the Atkinson* to be edited down to its wittiest jokes however, even its title might have to go.'

Producer Arthur Cantor called Rich's piece 'not a review, a train crash' and pointed to other reviews that had been much more favourable. Clive Barnes in the *New York Post*, for instance, had called it 'very funny, hilarious and sidesplitting', which made you wonder if they had been at the same show. *Newsday* called Atkinson a very droll fellow and even went on to say that he 'brings us a brand of British humour that travels well'.

Maybe the problems were more political than personal. Some saw a certain amount of hubris on Atkinson's part to book a show right on Broadway. Some people said that maybe he should have started off-Broadway and built up a word-of-mouth following. Certainly that was the way Eddie Izzard made a respectable dent in the Big Apple a decade later. Lenny Henry was even more cautious than that, preferring to turn up in clubs and try his luck as an unknown. Then again, very few English comedy stars had made a big impression on the American stage since *Beyond the Fringe* in the 60s. Maybe Atkinson did make the grave mistake of thinking that the Americans would share his reference points of housemasters, vicars and BBC newsreaders, or at least understand them. Frank Rich couldn't see much further than the bottom jokes. Back in England and talking to the *Newcastle Evening Chronicle* about Rich, Atkinson still appeared to be trying to explain the logic of the review to himself: 'Maybe he has some strange complex of his own about being lavatorial and he wasn't going to swallow it.'

Just as the fuss about Broadway was starting to subside, Atkinson appeared on Ned Sherrin's Radio 4 programme *Loose Ends*. The columnist Bernard Levin had recently written about Atkinson's vocalized complaints, which sounded as if he were claiming that 'we wuz robbed' said Sherrin. In his own defence, Atkinson acknowledged on *Loose Ends* that normally in this situation a performer would go away and crawl under a stone, but he had spoken out because he had felt that the whole situation had been 'so bizarre'. He was concerned that the show's closing might have been perceived as an artistic failure, but the problem had not been his but Rich's. Looking for an answer, critics had put it down to failure of the humour to be exported. While Atkinson could understand that this might have been the case with certain Scottish comics who remained nameless and who might have literally had difficulties being understood (possibly he meant Billy Connolly), this did not seem to be the case either. The houses were filling up and were 'enthusiastic as any audience in the world'. Until Rich arrived on the scene. Stephen Fry was also in the radio studio and understood the power of Frank Rich because *Me and My Girl*, which he had been involved in, had transferred from London to Broadway. He too had had a nerve-racking wait as the papers came out. Atkinson accepted that critics were subjective – 'one man's comedy is decidedly another man's tragedy' – but was still trying to find a reason for his experience. Maybe after all, it was down to the differences between America and England; one review could close a show there but not here. In America, offered Sherrin, audiences liked to be in agreement with critics, whereas in England they liked to differ and so would keep going to see something that had had a negative review. Atkinson could only conclude that he had done his best and that there was no pleasing some people: 'At least a third of it was as funny as I had been anywhere and if he didn't like that there was nothing I could do – lavatorial or not – that would have pleased him.'

There was still an abiding sense in which Atkinson felt like an outsider. This man out of time was too small 'c' conservative for the post-punk anarchy of the alternative-comedy scene; and in a world where the word was paramount, he was still an unusually body-conscious physical entertainer. While he shied away from being known only as the Funny Face Man, he did feel that his talents would have been better appreciated in a previous age. In September 1986 he explained his predicament to the *Mail on Sunday*: 'If I had been a contemporary of Charlie Chaplin I feel I might have been able to exploit myself to the full. I am a visual animal.'

By 1987, Atkinson was exorcising the demons of his Broadway nightmare with more live work, setting off on a three-month national tour that included five days at the Oxford Apollo. The provincial previews when he reached the Tyne Theatre were decidedly mixed. David Isaacs in the *Newcastle Journal*, still not convinced that the material was of as high a standard as the performing talent, suggesting that out of a two-hour show was 'at his best for possibly no more than half an hour'. He approved of Deayton's contributions, but agreed in parts with Frank Rich about the juvenile content. Phil Penfold in the *Newcastle Evening Chronicle* compared Atkinson to Marcel Marceau, Nat Jackley (the renowned music-hall star from Sunderland known as the man with the rubber neck) and Jack Benny. But Penfold criticized him for his greatest-hits approach and called him a 'flavour of the night'.

An NSPCC benefit at the Birmingham Hippodrome, however, caught Atkinson at the peak of his powers. The line-up included Bob Monkhouse, Lenny Henry, Dawn French and local-lad-made-good Jasper Carrott (who had replaced Atkinson for the national tour of *The Nerd*). Further down the bill were newcomers Steve Punt and Hugh Dennis. In *Ha Bloody Ha* (Fourth Estate, 1994) by William Cook, Hugh Dennis recalled the impact of Atkinson: 'And then Rowan Atkinson went on. There was a tangible surge of air. We were sitting in a box that was right by the stage, and you could actually feel this air moving forward. It was extraordinary – absolutely extraordinary.'

Early in 1987, Atkinson's first agent, Richard Armitage, had died and Atkinson had contacted Peter Bennett-Jones to be his business partner. Bennett-Jones had studied law at Cambridge and had been involved with the Footlights. He ran the university theatre and in the 1970s became involved in theatre production. He had known Rowan Atkinson for some time, and in 1984 he had worked with Mel Smith and Griff Rhys Jones to set up their independent company, Talkback. He started to work with Atkinson and set up PBJ Management, an artists' representation business with Atkinson as his first client; rather than call himself Atkinson's agent, he preferred to consider himself an *homme d'affaires*. The *Blackadder* franchise could not last for ever, and Atkinson would inevitably want to explore other artistic avenues. Peter Bennett-Jones would be instrumental in developing what would eventually become Mr Bean.

Later in 1987, a live album recorded when the tour reached the Bradford Alhambra on 3 and 4 April was released. The Bradford shows showcased a mixture of new material and old, which he had performed in London the previous year; it reminded audiences that despite the

Broadway experience, Atkinson and Curtis certainly had not lost their appetite to offend. The album release also spawned the single *I Believe*, performed on Channel Four's platform for new comics, *Saturday Live*. Despite being much more well established than most of the acts on the bill that night, Atkinson was happy to contribute to this cult television series. He also chipped in with his old Geordie soccer manager's half-time team talk: 'I don't want to single anyone out, but Duckworth, you were crap.'

Not all of Atkinson's public appearances were quite so well received, however. In June 1987 he took part in The Grand Knockout Tournament, the event more colloquially known as It's A Royal Knockout, and generally regarded as one of the royal family's more misguided public-relations exercises. Luckily for Atkinson, he was only the presenter who introduced the events. The real embarrassment factor was provided by the Duke and Duchess of York, Princess Anne and Prince Edward gallivanting around Alton Towers in medieval garb, looking like extras from *Blackadder*. The best thing you could say about the event was that it was in aid of charity. It would not have been so bad if it had not taken place on a typical June day in the north of England – blustery and grey. Clad all in black right down to his codpiece, Atkinson played Lord Knock of Alton, the master of ceremonies and king of the castle. His wife was played by Carry On star Barbara Windsor – no relation to the royal Windsors. His opening speech was one of the highlights of the day, as he exhorted the participants, who ranged from John Travolta to Cliff Richard to the rest of the *Not The Nine O'Clock News* team, to give it their all: 'for the entertainment of us all, let you fall repeatedly on your bottoms this day.' At least Atkinson did not have to shin across slippery poles for charity like many of the other contributors – he simply had to threaten them with a clip round the ear with a 'wet gauntlet' whenever they were flagging. In fact he was probably one of the few participants to emerge with their dignity reasonably intact. It was only a one-off special, but it set the royalist cause back about a century and made the court of Queen Elizabeth in *Blackadder II* seem like the epitome of aristocratic sophistication. A series might have finished off the monarchy for good.

Meanwhile he continued to take an interest in local activities. In July he spoke at the arts week of the Cheney School in Oxford, and was billed to appear at a benefit barbecue for the Thomley and Bernwood group, which was opposing the extension of the M40 from Waterstock to Wendlebury.

Sometimes live shows had their mishaps. In July he appeared at Montreal's Just for Laughs Festival and was going down a storm at the Theatre Saint Denis until his microphone cut out and he was unable to continue. The tabloids, sniffing around for a scandalous story, claimed that he had walked off in a temper, but in fact, this was not a unique technical problem and he took it in his stride. The Canadian festival was an intriguing and important place to perform, partly because a lot of American television executives would fly in to see the shows and cream off the talent and partly because the festival was split into two languages. The English part was called Just For Laughs, and the French side, Juste Pour Rire. Atkinson donned his red horns again as Toby the Devil, a million miles away from his sinister Mephistopheles at school. This time round the emphasis was purely on the humour of the character rather than the chill factor. It was interesting to see how the professions that Toby condemned to damnation in his British shows were also the people Canadians would like to see consumed by flames. Bank managers in particular seemed to be a universally popular target. While Americans being 'damned in perpetuity' went down understandably well in front of the Canadian contingent – following his Broadway experience it would have been understandable if he meant one American in particular. A topical reference was the addition to the list of anyone who had bought tickets for the Monkees recent reunion tour. Atkinson – and Curtis – were always keen to keep their routines fresh and would regularly reassess them to see if more contemporary references were needed or would improve the lines.

There was also another wordless performance – the news in sign language. Atkinson's own distinctive sign language, developed since *Not the Nine O'Clock News*, utilized every muscle and limb in his body. For halo, he mimed a halo above his head; for Reagan, he impersonated a dribbling, geriatric fool; for Chernobyl, he pretended his skin was flaking off. It was in questionable taste at times, but that had never stopped Atkinson. He was always able to get away with childish mimicry because he added a sense of intelligence to them. Being normal for Atkinson was being someone else. These weren't thoughtless insensitive gestures but a scientifically crafted routine, which somehow made it acceptable.

As the failed American invasion receded into the distance, the effect was less shattering. In a way Frank Rich's review was so vituperative and isolated that Atkinson eventually took it less to heart. Rich had been so dismissive that he couldn't find a constructive thing to say about a show that had been a success elsewhere in the English-speaking world. It was as if he had got out of bed the wrong side that morning and would have harangued the star for the colour of the loo paper in the theatre's toilets if everything else had been to his liking. Life had to go on and in the next decade Atkinson would have the last laugh.

After the doubts about making a second series of *Blackadder*, there was never any debate about whether there would be a third series. The only question was when would it be set. The team provided the answer in 1987, moving the action to the period of 1760–1815 (although strangely, none of the characters ever aged) and the court of the future King George IV, George the foppish Prince Regent. Atkinson was Edmund, no longer a nobleman, but instead the social-climbing butler to the Regent, played with unimpeachable dimness by Hugh Laurie. Blackadder behaved as if he was brighter and more sophisticated than his master – and the frustrating thing was that it was true. He always seemed to get the best lines and was sometimes more perceptive than he realized: he once predicted that in 200 years time he would be played by an actor and that episodes of his life would go out every Thursday at 9.30pm.

Now that the characters and the concept had bedded in, writers Elton and Curtis had more fun than ever playing with historical characters and events of the day. There was a disaster when the only copy of Dr Johnson's dictionary was tossed onto the fire and much hilarity when Edmund Blackadder asked Baldrick to bring him some meat between two slices of bread: 'Like Gerald Lord Sandwich had the other night?' asked his faithful retainer. 'That's right, a round of Geralds.'

Running from 17 September to 12 October 1987, each episode started with someone thumbing through a library as if looking for a bawdy book of the time, maybe something by Henry Fielding, but emerging with an episode title instead. As Atkinson described in the press, it would be less vulgar than *Blackadder*'s past, 'but respectable? never!'

The first episode, for example, was 'Dish and Dishonesty'. An election was looming and there was a fear that the Prince Regent - 'the son of a certified sauerkraut-sucking loon' – would be struck off the civil list if a bill was passed against him. It was decided that a puppet MP needed to be elected. Baldrick was selected with Blackadder acting as his agent ... and the returning officer ... and, it soon transpires, the only man in the constituency of Dunny-on-the-Wold eligible to vote. On the night of the count, real-life political commentator Vincent Hanna interviewed Blackadder, but things, inevitably, don't work out as planned.

The second episode, 'Ink and Incapability', featured Robbie Coltrane as Samuel Johnson, the author of the very first dictionary. Edmund fancies himself as an author too, so they end up vying for the Prince Regent's patronage. Johnson has spent ten years on his tome ('Yes, well I'm a slow reader myself,' retorts Blackadder). Like anyone else, the first thing the Prince does is look up rude words. Unfortunately the dictionary gets thrown on the fire and Blackadder has to attempt to replace it. Meanwhile poets Byron, Coleridge and Shelley – a bit of comedic licence here, they were born in the wrong years, but then again Johnson died in 1784 so he would have been hard-pressed to be around then too – are hanging out in the pie shop of Mrs Miggins (played by another *Blackadder* regular, Helen Atkinson Wood).

'Nob and Nobility' was Curtis and Elton's take on the Scarlet Pimpernel, with Nigel Planer and Tim McInnerney as two prattling fops who may, or may not, be responsible for saving aristos from the guillotine. For Blackadder, the revolution is another potential moneyspinner, and he heads to France only to be captured and nearly upstaged by a heavily accented Chris Barrie, who was just about to find fame as Arnold H. Rimmer in *Red Dwarf*.

In the fourth episode, 'Sense and Senility', Ben Elton had a cameo, sending up his angry radical persona by playing a would-be assassin who attempts to kill the periwigged Prince Regent. The play is the thing here, as Blackadder employs two superstitious old hams – Hugh Paddick and Kenneth Connor – to give the prince acting lessons.

In 'Cape and Capability', Blackadder attempts to marry off the Prince Regent to raise some capital, but it is to no avail even when Baldrick comes up with the first of many cunning plans. The prince's wooing skills leave a lot to be desired, so in the manner of Cyrano de Bergerac, Blackadder has to do the verbal seduction for him. Eventually to solve the money problems at the palace, Blackadder assumes the identity the Shadow, who is halfway to being the new Robin Hood: 'He steals from the rich but he hasn't got round to giving it to the poor yet.'

In the final instalment, 'Duel and Duality', the Prince is still having woman trouble. Having spent the night with two of Wellington's nieces – 'a night of ecstasy with a pair of Wellingtons' – the Iron Duke (a scene-stealing appearance from Stephen Fry) challenges him to a duel. Blackadder is about to swap places with him when he realizes his Scottish cousin McAdder (also played by Atkinson), who happens to be a homicidal maniac – 'madder than Mad Jack McMad, winner of last year's madman contest' – is in town. Blackadder coaxes McAdder to fight in his place. For once things work out rather nicely. Through a farcical twist to events, Blackadder survives – as Prince Regent – and the real prince is shot dead.

By now the plots were becoming richer and stronger and the acting so competitive that it brought out the best in everyone. Even bit-part players such as Helen Atkinson Wood as Mrs Miggins seemed to have got under the skin of their own roles to the point where they were cult figures in their own right. There seemed to be plenty of meat for Atkinson to get his teeth into.

Although the series was very funny when it hit the screens, interviews with the stars suggested that it was less laugh-a-minute off-camera as the supporting cast became more and more concerned about their roles and wanted more creative input. Tim McInnerney had reportedly even pulled out for fear of being typecast – appearing only as Lord Topper in 'Nob and Nobility'. However, he did return for the fourth and final series which seemed to dispel that myth. On-screen over the years Percy had seemed impervious to the constant torrent of abuse, but in reality maybe it was taking its toll. Speaking on *Wogan* in July 1990, McInnerney joked that it was a thankless task being the butt of Rowan Atkinson's jokes. 'It was hell,' he laughed, but maybe he did find it somewhat restricting in artistic terms. The fourth series, however, would change all that, adding a historic layer of tragedy to the sitcom genre.

8

A Tall Story

By August 1987, Atkinson was wondering about the future of *Black-adder*. His anti-hero's prospects did not sound too good, according to an interview with the *Newcastle Evening Chronicle*: 'As I get satisfied with a project and feel that I want to leave it, the public response seems to be always wanting more.' He did not completely write off the possibility of more, saying that the idea of setting a fourth series in early Christian times had been broached. There was also some mutterings about a stage version. An interview in the *Daily Mirror* hinted at backstage difficulties when Atkinson said that it was amazing that the programme ever gets made because 'we're dreadful. It's very democratic because everyone gets involved, but we tear every line apart and discuss each ridiculous little detail of the programme.' Tim McInnerney called it a 'collaborative process', with the script constantly evolving. Even with writers of the calibre of Curtis and Elton, it was a painstaking business getting everyone happy with their lines. Despite the friction, Atkinson still had the full support of Tony Robinson, who even when he wasn't in character as the stupidly loyal Baldrick called Atkinson 'the finest clown of his generation'.

It may have been hard work, but *Blackadder III* was certainly appreciated, picking up a BAFTA in March 1988. In April there was also a more local honour – a real Mrs Miggins Coffee House opened in Beamont Street, Hexham. There were further indications of the influence of *Blackadder*. The style magazine *I-D* appropriated the name Baldrick to describe a sub-cult of Mancunian acid-house pioneers who sported long, lank hair and flared trousers. It seemed ironic that the sitcom's turnip-loving loser was now also the name of a group of youngsters on the cutting edge of fashion.

There was no *Blackadder* series in 1988, but the potential of historical comedy caught on. In March 1988, Channel Four launched *Chelmsford 123*, a good-humoured if haphazard sitcom set during the Roman occupation of Britain and following the squabbles between the Romans and the Celts. The comedy was broader and less sophisticated than *Blackadder*, and the production values were almost non-existent, but it was in such a similarly irreverent vein it is hard to believe that it would ever have been commissioned without Atkinson's success at the BBC. Curiously, it starred and was written by another wave of Oxbridge alumni – Jimmy Mulville, Rory McGrath and Philip Pope. Even more curiously, it lasted for two series, returning in 1990.

In the autumn of 1988, Atkinson went off on a sell-out tour of Australia, where his television programmes – *The Black Adder* had been an Australian co-production – had already made him famous. On his return there was more acclaim when he took part in a show in aid of the Prince's Trust that also included Robin Williams, Elton John, Art Garfunkel and Sarah Brightman. David Frost's introduction was as accurate as it was unctuous when he said of Atkinson that he had expanded the boundaries of comedy in various ways. This time though, unlike his introduction at Bob Hope's birthday bash, he declined to expand the boundaries any further. Looking lean and healthy after his time down under, Atkinson opted for an old *Not the Nine O'Clock News* routine, first performed with Mel Smith, in which they pretended to be origami experts but in fact were doing little more than tearing up large sheets of newspaper. It was an easy act to improvise around, depending on what the newspaper scraps looked like. Angus Deayton joined him onstage to assist and narrate. Between them they came up with some scraps that they claimed resembled a beer mug, skis, a briefcase and even a Honda Prelude. There was one aspect of the act, however, that differed from the way it had been done on *Not the Nine O'Clock News*. Where Smith and Atkinson had played gentle, almost patronizing presenters who had missed their vocation as children's entertainers, here there appeared to be an element of (faked) antagonism between Atkinson and Deayton. Part of the comedy came from the fact that we could sense there was a tension and an inequality between the duo. It was an idea that would soon emerge in the fictional version of Atkinson in the film *The Tall Guy*.

In 1988, Atkinson had another successful venture – his participation in Comic Relief. Comic Relief had started in the mid-80s as a relatively modest affair, but the success of the shows and the attempts to mix fun with fund-raising captured the public imagination. In 1988 the first Red Nose Day was launched. Members of the public were encouraged to purchase a *proboscis plasticus rubus* – a red plastic nose – for charity, or better still do a sponsored walk with jelly in their wellingtons or spend a day in a bath of baked beans. On Friday, 5 February, BBC1's evening schedule was handed over to Comic Relief, and the leading comedians provided the entertainment and manned the phones as donations flooded in. While Lenny Henry and Griff Rhys Jones went off to Africa to film the work of Comic Relief and then present the evening in the studio, others did spontaneous turns in the studio. Rowan Atkinson, Richard Curtis and Ben Elton had always been closely associated with Comic Relief, and in 1988 they did their bit by producing a special one-off 15-minute edition of their award-winning sitcom.

'Blackadder: The Cavalier Years' was set in 1648. Stephen Fry played King Charles I (albeit remarkably like the current Prince Charles, complete with hand-waving gestures) who was fleeing from Oliver Cromwell (Warren Clarke). There were only two men in the country still loyal to the king, Sir Edmund Blackadder and his man-servant Baldrick, and they had to save him from the Roundheads. As ever, they fail miserably with the ever-opportunistic Blackadder bemoaning his fate: 'One measly civil war in the entire history of England and I'm on the wrong bloody side.' He is soon quick to switch sides and denounce Baldrick when he hears that the executioner is to be paid £1,000 for beheading the king.

The Comic Relief insert was a beautifully put-together pocket-sized edition of the award-winning series, and yet it was not without its faults. Not in the performances, but in terms of historical accuracy. Despite being a comedy, the team behind *Blackadder* had always prided itself on having at least a toehold on reality. Yet, perhaps in keeping with their Hitler Diaries rewriting of history, they got the year wrong here. Charles was actually beheaded in 1649. Furthermore, even Blackadder's line about choosing the wrong bloody side for the one civil war in British history was slightly wide of the mark. Charles was actually executed following the second civil war of his reign. There had been one earlier, but problems had not been resolved and Cromwell's republicans once more took on the royalists. Then again, maybe this was conclusive proof that even writers of the calibre of Richard Curtis and Ben Elton would not let a little thing like historical fact stand in the way of a good gag.

Despite being a stickler for discipline in his professional life, Atkinson did overstep the mark while on the road. In July 1988 he pleaded guilty at Newbury Magistrates Court to driving at 114 mph on the M4 in his Aston Martin Zagato; he was disqualified for two weeks and fined £150. That August, on *Desert Island Discs*, he told Sue Lawley that he would like his luxury to be his electric-blue Aston Martin. A nice touch was that he also wanted a tin of wax polish so that he could keep it in pristine condition. He was not even worried about the fact that without petrol he would not be able to drive it. As long as he could build a bamboo garage for it and had plenty of orange dusters with the red edges he would be happy.

The interview with Sue Lawley revealed a deeper side to Atkinson than the public had ever come across. Although he had a remarkably high profile, it was in character rather than as himself. People didn't even really know what his real voice sounded like. He was firm, but polite and well-spoken. If anything a trifle blank, but that in itself was revealing. He was still only 33 years old, but had spent most of the last decade earning his living by playing oddballs and eccentrics. Maybe it was the blank canvas underneath that enabled him to pull these creations out of the bag.

He did reveal to Lawley that he had not always been supremely confident about his talent and there was a time even after the initial flush of fame when he might have returned to a career in electrical engineering or running a haulage firm. Five or six years ago he had had a fear of losing it or thought that maybe he had been a flash in the pan. Now though he sensed he had even more potential: 'I feel I've only attempted about 40 per cent of what I could do.' His only problem was dealing with fame, which could be particularly embarrassing in awkward public situations such as running for a train and missing it and having to stand there when all around you everyone

It started with a *Sneeze*: The Aldwych Theatre, 1988. © Mander & Mitchenson Theatre Collection

A eye-opening performance: *The Sneeze*, 1988. © Mander & Mitchenson Theatre Collection

Age cannot wither him: *The Sneeze*, 1988. © Mander & Mitchenson Theatre Collection

Blackadder, Mark IV, 1989. All present and correct: left to right Tim McInnerney, Tony Robinson, Atkinson, Stephen Fry, Hugh Laurie. © UPPA.

The Final Countdown:
Baldrick (Tony Robinson)
and Blackadder. © UPPA.

Campaigning for Comic
Relief, 1989. © UPPA.

The blind date from hell? Cilla Black and the lucky winner Barbara Churkin cross their fingers as they prepare to meet Mr Bean in a special comedy edition. © Rex Features

Mr Bean in all his gormless glory, 1992. © UPPA.

In 1989 with his BAFTA for
Best Light Entertainment
Performance/Comedy
Performance for *Black
Adder Goes Forth.*

Older and Wiser (and better dressed). *The Not The Nine O'Clock News*
team reconvenes, 1995. Left to right: Griff Rhys Jones, Atkinson, Pamela
Stephenson, Mel Smith. © UPPA.

Racing demon:
Atkinson the driver.
© Rex Features

Première league.
Atkinson and wife
Sunetra attend a
film party dressed
as members of the
Addams Family. ©
Big Pictures

The Comedy Aristocracy. Left to right. Stephen Fry, Ben Elton, Robbie Coltrane, Griff Rhys Jones, Mel Smith, Atkinson. © Rex Features

Coming full circle. The all-over face-shaving routine that he had been doing in revue in the 1970s reaches Hollywood in *Bean: The Ultimate Disaster Movie*, 1997. © Rex Features

Car trouble: Atkinson and
Mel Smith filming *Bean:
The Ultimate Disaster Movie*
outside Harrods in London. ©
Big Pictures

The star and one of his
favourite co-stars: Atkinson
and his Ferrari. © Big Pictures

was thinking 'that's Rowan Atkinson and he's just missed his train.' He wanted the success but he would also like to be the northern middle-class man who likes his friends, fast cars and a modest amount of motor-racing. The problem with being famous was being public property. Then again, without the fame he may not have been in a position to be able to afford a modest amount of motor-racing. He currently had a Lancia and was on to his third Aston Martin. He said that it wasn't actually the speed he enjoyed, but the ownership and the honing of it – being able to take something dirty and turn it into a shining object – which, in a sense was also what he had done with the *Blackadder* cycle.

If his sitcom career was now gleaming, his stage career could still do with some polish. After the mixed reviews for *The Nerd* and Frank Rich's Broadway bashing, he was still keen to prove himself onstage. Television was fine, but there had always been something special about a live appearance. Atkinson's humour was often about the culture of embarrassment and the phenomenon of deflated expectations, and there was an added thrill when the audience was there in person to share in the artist's emotional ups and downs.

Casting around for new challenges, what could be more emotional than Chekhov? Atkinson's next project was to appear in a collection of short stories by the seminal Russian playwright under the umbrella title of *The Sneeze*, a mixture of original one-act plays – light works that catapulted Chekhov into the limelight after a time in the dramatic doldrums – and works adapted from his short stories by a contemporary genius at the drama of manners, writer Michael Frayn (a veteran of the Cambridge Footlights). Atkinson took on a heavy responsibility, appearing in seven of the eight shorts, as well as being involved in the mounting of the production, presented by Michael Codron in association with Atkinson's own company Rowshow Ltd. It seemed on the surface like a huge departure, but the star didn't think it was that much of a digression. *The Bear*, for instance, he described as 'gripping, tragic and terribly funny, with a humour more sadistic than *Blackadder*.' In it Atkinson played a noisy oaf who turns up on a young widow's doorstep to demand payment of a debt and ends up asking her to marry him.

The very title – *The Sneeze* – referred back to one of the enduring motifs of Atkinson's career. On *Not the Nine O'Clock News* he had once played a chef who sneezed on a pizza, thought about it, then served it anyway. Furthermore, the highlight of the sketch featuring the narcoleptic church worshipper had been when he sneezed and had to blow his nose on his jacket pocket lining.

Codron, too, clearly did not have difficulties putting comedians into dramas. He had previously tried to coax John Cleese onto the stage with little success. Cleese was reportedly reluctant to have to say the same words every night. Atkinson, however, was prepared to go down this new avenue and did not see it as a dramatic change in direction. He did, however see it as a challenge and one that he relished.

But if *Blackadder III* was anything to go by – and Atkinson said at the time that the Regency Blackadder incarnation was closest to the real Rowan Atkinson – it was a surprise that he was even entering a theatre, given his opinion of the kind of people who indulged in the dramatic arts: 'a load of stupid actors, strutting around shouting, with their chests thrust out so far you'd think their nipples were attached to a pair of charging elephants'. But at the same time, there was something respectable about the proper theatre. He estimated that about ten per cent of the reason for doing it was so that he had done something his mother could recommend to her friends.

On the eve of the London opening, Atkinson appeared on *Wogan*, though this time his recent *Desert Island Discs* interviewer Sue Lawley was deputizing for the jovial Irish host. Atkinson emphasized that Chekhov was not such an unlikely choice as there was plenty of comedy there, it had just never been brought out. The idea was 'to present him as he has never been presented before'. Besides, he continued, it was hardly a huge departure, it was still a lot of short sketches and some funny voices, including a Geordie accent, the only regional accent he could do with any conviction.

In the plays, which were previewed at the Bradford Alhambra and Newcastle Theatre Royal before opening at London's Aldwych Theatre on 27 September 1988, Atkinson teamed up with two eminent actors for a three-hander that demanded quick changes of both costume and character: Timothy West, who had played so many historical characters in his time, ranging from Edward VII to Churchill, it was a surprise he had never appeared in *Blackadder*; and Cheryl Campbell, best known to television viewers as the errant schoolteacher in Dennis Potter's *Pennies from Heaven*.

Once again, Atkinson was taking a different route to his comic contemporaries. There was nothing unusual about a comedian doing drama – everyone from Stanley Holloway to Alexei Sayle had done their bit of the bard – but the tendency was for funny men to play uncomplicated funny characters such as Bottom or Touchstone. This move only emphasized Atkinson's claims that he wasn't from a stand-up comedy tradition. If anything his roots at St Bees and Durham Chorister School had been in drama and straight theatre. At a tender age he had proved that he could command the stage without recourse to pratfalls. There was nothing wrong with comedy, but Atkinson had always maintained that he simply wasn't a gag merchant. To him *The Sneeze* was his chosen way of 'being serious without being serious'. It seemed a natural way of gaining more theatrical credibility without completely deserting his comedy fanbase, a way for the perennial face-puller to push himself further. As for the possibility of playing some Shakespearean comedy, Atkinson explained in the London *Evening Standard* why he had avoided that path, although he had considered it: 'We even thought of Shakespeare but the parts have been played so often the audience spends the whole evening making comparisons.' Besides, for a performer who specialized in losers, there was plenty of comic mileage to be gleaned from *The Sneeze*, as most of the characters he played in it were, he said, 'miserable downtrodden men'.

Because the Chekhov playlets, directed by Ronald Eyre and designed by Mark Thompson, were short, they were more of a bridge between full-blown dramas and sketches. In its own way, the evening was just like a revue, although Chekhov scholars considered the playwright to have been slumming it when he wrote these brief, lighter works. For Atkinson, on the other hand, this was a broad step upwards in terms of artistic credibility. They may not have been grand dramas, but they did give Atkinson the chance to demonstrate a wide range of mimetic and thespian skills. Chekhov called them farces, but they were not farces in the modern, trousers-down-vicar-at-door sense. As Michael Frayn pointed out, these were farces driven by a sense of outrage over such serious matters as others refusing to recognize a person's right to land, or money or marriage. (Frayn, of course, was very good at the comedy of outrage. A couple of years earlier he had penned *Clockwise*, the movie starring Cleese as a constantly exasperated, punctuality obsessed headmaster).

In the first piece, *Drama*, Atkinson played Pavel Vasilyevich, a writer being rude to a prospective rival. Cheryl Campbell was a would-be playwright, Murashkina, who corners a famous writer (Atkinson) and insists on reading extended extracts from her rather pitiful scribblings. Atkinson's author doesn't need to say much to convey the clear impression that he is bored to tears. As she works through her five acts, he could simply deliver a selection from his broad array of grimaces to display his discomfort. Eventually though he needs to be more decisive to dissuade her, and ends up attacking her with the paper knife.

The short sketch from which the evening took its title was a wordless three-hander in which Atkinson's mimetic skills came into their own. He played a minor government official, Chervyakov, at the ballet who sneezes over the bald head of the uniformed minister Brizzhalov (West), who is seated in front of him. In the original story, the action had then shifted to the office where they both worked the next day. In the play, everything was contained within two rows of theatre seats. Atkinson had to use all of his powers to present a man at the end of his tether, trying to extricate himself from an embarrassing position. At one point he craned forwards trying to confirm the worst consequences of his sneeze through theatre glasses; then he tried to flick the mucus away; then he handed West a note clarifying what he had done, that he had sneezed and not spat, which would have really been a breach of protocol. All of this was done in time with the ballet music from the show that they were both attempting to watch. It was the kind of distinctly un-Chekhovian sketch that Atkinson could have contrived himself in one of his college revues, all knockabout frustration and deceptively co-ordinated twisting limbs, a comedy of manners and a piece that perfectly showed off his unique talents.

The Proposal was all wigs and hypochondria, with Cheryl Campbell as the grandly named Nataya Stepanovna and Atkinson as Lomov attempting to become engaged in a clumsy sort of way. Each time Atkinson asks for her hand in marriage, the conversation between Atkinson and West as his potential father-in-law Chubukov ends in a dispute, either over ownership of nearby land or about whose gun-dog was better, until things reach a hysterical pitch. Maureen Paton in the *Daily Express* was particularly impressed: 'When Rowan Atkinson can even out-act his ginger wig that looks like a dismembered gerbil, you know you are in the presence of a master comedian.'

Atkinson appeared in seven of the eight pieces and worked well against the physically contrasting West. Despite his height and clear onstage presence, Atkinson tended to be given the submissive roles, dominated physically by the substantial size and seniority of West. Typical of this dynamic was *Alien Corn* in which he played another pedagogue, a mute French tutor named Champugne, being bullied by West's brutish Russian landlord. Atkinson becomes a metaphor for France being criticized for everything Gallic, right down to the fact that his country produces such mild mustard. In the *Inspector-General*, Atkinson gets the better of West. Donning a northern accent as the carthorse driver, he realizes that his passenger is an inspector heading for the village and intending to travel incognito. Forewarned, the driver can now get the better of him.

The Evils of Tobacco was a pure pathos-filled Chekhovian monologue at the lectern, mixing comedy and tragedy, with tragedy coming out the winner. Atkinson described this solo piece which opened the second half, as the most serious piece of acting he had ever done, saying 'the laugh freezes on your lips.' He played Nyukhin, a downtrodden husband and teacher, a shambling, scruffy shell of a man. His wife, the head of the boarding school that employs him, has effectively destroyed this hen-pecked man, ruining his life over the years. A lecture in front of a minor provincial audience, which should have been about the perniciousness of smoking, is unconsciously turns into 'The Evils of my Wife', a no-holds barred verbal assault on his spouse, who dismisses him as 'a dummy'. This was a schoolmaster unlike any Atkinson had played before, as he slowly but surely reveals the misery of his marriage, exuding, said Michael Billington in *The Guardian*, 'just the right shrivelled pathos'.

The Bear, however, rammed home the predicament for the eternal clown: Atkinson as Luka was supposed to be playing it straight but according to some reviews he ended up upstaging West and Campbell with a seemingly unintentional funny walk as he left the stage. Chekhov would rather cynically refer to this light money-spinning piece as his 'milch-cow'.

The plays were well received, all things considered; they were hardly Chekhov in top gear, but they did give Atkinson a chance to remind audiences that he was more than just a witty face. Some critics, though, didn't think he was much more than that. In *The Financial Times*, Michael Coveney called *The Sneeze* 'slight but not trite', concluding that at times Atkinson didn't seem to do a great deal more than flare his nostrils, cross his eyes and turn his profile 180 degrees. Comparisons were made with Chaplin, suggesting that Atkinson, once again, could have been a great star of the silent movie era. *Punch*'s Sheridan Morley was lukewarm about the evening as a whole but clearly concluded that Atkinson was a star with great potential as a comedic stage actor: 'The evening survives thanks to the manic intensity of Atkinson.' Even if the production was not a complete success, Atkinson had confirmed that he was a virtuoso character actor.

At this time *Blackadder* was regarded as the best sitcom on television. It was that rare thing, a post-watershed family favourite. Despite the 9.30pm start time, it was probably the most popular programme for playground discussion. Children could even argue that it had some educational value. In the same way that some basic knowledge of history was required to get the jokes in *1066 and All That*, a general grounding in the respective historical periods helped viewers to appreciate *Blackadder*. Though it was not strictly necessary.

For their 45-minute Christmas 1988 special, the team moved away from history and drew their inspiration from literature. In *Blackadder's Christmas Carol*, which went out on 23 December, Curtis and Elton inverted Charles Dickens' seasonal story and turned Ebenezer Blackadder into a decent, honest citizen, kind to his employee Baldrick and generous to little children. But one night he is visited by the Spirit of Christmas in the guise of Robbie Coltrane and sees visions of Christmases past, present and future. In specially shot scenes reuniting the original casts (minus Tim McInnerney or the original Black Adder), we see how nasty the Elizabethan and Regency Blackadders were and we also see a futuristic sci-fi Blackadder – Atkinson in a cling-film outfit, and Baldrick in not much at all. These visions are intended to show the Victorian Blackadder how nice he is. Instead they make him realize what an idiot he is, and that if only he was as nasty as the rest of his family his bank account would benefit enormously. As in the original story he vows to mend his ways. Only here it means turning into the curmudgeon that we expected at the beginning. He has finally realized that 'Bad guys have more fun.' Baldrick's Christmas present, for instance, turns out to be Blackadder's fist – in a sock. But this being the season of goodwill, there is still a moral sting in the tale. Queen Victoria (Miriam Margolyes) and Prince Albert (Jim Broadbent) have decided to make Blackadder a baron and give him £50,000 as a reward for his philanthropy. But when they turn up he thinks they are practical jokers and abuses them and promptly loses his title and booty. Bad guys might have more fun, but it's the good guys who always triumph in the end.

By 1989, Rowan Atkinson had been in showbusiness for little more than ten years but he had done just about everything apart from star in his own Hollywood action blockbuster; although he had found the time to chip in to Nicolas Roeg's children's film *The Witches*, based on a Roald Dahl story; Atkinson played a grumpy hotel manager, Mr Stringer, to Anjelica Huston's vampish lead role. Atkinson's performance in this Warner Brothers project could have easily tipped over into Fawlty-ish exaggeration, but instead he played the role straight, undercutting expectations and allowing the laughs to come from the fact that he did not get exasperated when the windswept seaside Hotel Excelsior (filmed at the Headland Hotel in Newquay, not a million miles from Torquay, where *Fawlty Towers* was set) became overrun by rats. The witches, having their annual convention there, were able to turn children into rodents. Instead, he assumed the role of a boringly efficient jobsworth who likes to see rules obeyed. There was a hint of the future Mr Bean in his role, which seemed to err ever so slightly on the constricting side. It seemed odd that Atkinson had even been cast in this role since it failed to allow him to do what he did best. The only link with his past work was the search to destroy diabolical creatures in *The Black Adder* episode 'Witchsmeller Pursuivant'. But every now and again, there would be hints of his real abilities. His top lip would arch into a bossy snarl. Talking about the restaurant, he had the opportunity to make a meal of saying the word 'cockaleekie'. But for Atkinson-watchers, hoping to see an extension of Blackadder on the big screen, that one word would have been the only moment that gave them any pleasure. It may have broadened his palette, but, unless he wanted to return to being a children's entertainer as he had been on *A Bundle of Bungles*, it did not, on the surface, appear to point him in any particular direction. Film stardom still eluded him.

For Red Nose Day on 10 March 1989, BBC1 once again handed over the evening to a bunch of comedians. This time Billy Connolly trekked movingly through war-torn Mozambique – or Nose and Beak, as his children called it – looking at the work of the organization, while Jonathan Ross joined Lenny Henry and Griff Rhys Jones in the studio. This time round there was no *Blackadder* special but Atkinson did appear in a number of studio-based sketches – the first time he had done this sort of thing since *Not the Nine O'Clock News*. The nice thing about the trail-blazing satire series was that Atkinson had done so many different things that he had avoided being typecast. *Blackadder*, on the other hand, was becoming, if not exactly a millstone, something he was too readily associated with. His stage excursions had stretched him, but because his television performances reached such a large audience, the impact of his stage appearances on his reputation was slight. It had not been great enough to help him break the mould of the scheming historical figures. For Comic Relief II he took the opportunity to play some very different characters. In one recurring sketch he played a surgeon, assisted by Jimmy Nail, who was operating on John Gordon Sinclair, the star of *Gregory's Girl* (one of Atkinson's favourite films). Mid-operation he paused to find a mobile phone to call Comic Relief, much to his patient's discomfort. Later Jane Asher joins the medical team, but turns out to be a vet – unfortunately NHS cuts meant there weren't enough doctors. Atkinson also played a short-haired version of Jeremy Paxman for 'Nosenight', a spoof quiz that cannibalized old political interviews to get politicians to give comic answers to questions. The result was that Robin Cook confessed, for no apparent reason, that 'I was in a major psychiatric hospital only last week.'

Atkinson's career seemed to be pulling in two very different directions. One, given his film aspirations, was Hollywood; the other, given his need to broaden his palette, was into more character-led comedy. If he could reconcile these two areas he would be able to move on. And it looked like he had found a vehicle when he agreed to co-star in *The Appointments of Dennis Jennings*, which was transmitted on BBC2 on 27 March 1989. This was a weird little film for a number of reasons. It was a co-production between the American cable television company Home Box Office and Noel Gay Television, the independent production company that was an arm of the management company that Atkinson's first manager, Richard Armitage, had been involved in. It was also peculiar for Atkinson because his role was somewhere between cameo and co-star. It was clear that the drama, written by Steven Wright and Mike Armstrong, and directed by Dean Parisot, was not really a Hollywood calling card for Atkinson but a vehicle for deadpan American comic Wright – a strange cove with a shock of curly hair over each ear and not much on top. Both comedians had appeared at the Just For Laughs Festival in Montreal in 1987 and the deal had been sealed soon after.

It was certainly a strange kind of double act. Wright's sense of humour was completely at odds with Atkinson. His delivery was a very slow, sleepy drawl; he would, for instance, say his house had been robbed, everything had been stolen and replaced with exact replicas. At times the 30-minute movie seemed little more than a conduit for a endless succession of Wright's gags. Wright played the eponymous Jennings, a waiter who is a regular client of psychiatrist Dr Schooner (Atkinson). It was never explained how a waiter could afford a psychiatrist, but then, as things turned out, this was clearly the kind of comedy where you didn't ask those sort of questions. Atkinson looks severe but smart and avoids the usually tempting German accent lesser talents would have opted for. Similarly Wright sits in a chair where a less imaginative production would have slapped him on a sofa. Clearly this was about as far from the clichéd Woody Allen school of New York shrinkery as one can get.

Little oblique sight-gags that deconstruct common phraseology and idiom add to the pleasure. At one point Jennings is reading a paper, *The London Journal*, and the headline reads 'Time Will No Longer Tell'. Later on, Jennings slumps down in his chair and watches the television, which shows a man in dungarees slumped in his chair. The camera then cuts to a house where a man in dungarees, slumped in his chair, is watching Dennis Jennings on his television.

Following an opening scene in which Jennings is stalking Schooner in a forest, we flash back to three months earlier. As Jennings tells

Schooner about his family problems (he was brought up by his real father and wants to know who his stepfather is), the camera pans around to reveal that Schooner is writing a grocery list in his notepad.

As the meetings continue it soon becomes apparent that the only person less interested in Jennings than Schooner is Jennings's girl-friend (Laurie Metcalfe, better known as Jackie in *Roseanne*). When Jennings is on his way to one appointment, listening to his answer-phone messages on his Walkman, he is told that Schooner cannot make it but that someone else will be there. It turns out to be the doorman. Another time Jennings is confiding in Schooner only for a handyman to emerge from under the desk to tell Jennings to lighten up. These touches give the film the bleak, surreal edge of an early David Lynch movie. Atkinson can do little more than play it straight, but he does play it straight impeccably. In the end a mood of paranoia seems to envelope Jennings, but his neurosis seems justified. When he sees Schooner and some colleagues in a bar chuckling, he thinks they are chuckling about him. And they are – Schooner is showing them a sketch of Jennings he drew when bored during a session. Finally Jennings is watching a news report and in the background we see Schooner kissing his girlfriend outside a Greenwich Village bar. We now understand why he wants to hunt down Schooner, though it still is not made clear why he is hunting him in a forest. Shot with commendable economy and grace, it picked up an Oscar at the 1989 Academy Awards for Best Live Action Short Film. Atkinson's film career seemed to be looking up.

Until this stage, there had not been much overlap between Atkin-son's career and off-duty persona. His job was to appear on the stage and screen to make people laugh. In his casual clothes he was almost like the Cliff Richard of Comedy – your daughters would be safe with him. His press persona seemed to play up to this with quotes such as 'People think because I can make them laugh on the stage, I'll be able to make them laugh in person. That isn't the case at all. I am essen-tially a rather quiet, dull person who just happens to be a performer.' It was a modest, self-deprecating remark for someone who could be good fun in company.

Having conquered the stage and television screen, he now moved into the cinema. *The Tall Guy*, filmed while he was performing in *The Sneeze*, was something of an old pals act. Mel Smith was the director, and Richard Curtis wrote it. In the film, American actor Jeff Goldblum played a struggling performer who gets a job as the side-kick, or fall guy, of comedian Ron Anderson, played by Rowan Atkinson. The character is mean and nasty to Goldblum: on the *Wogan* show, Atkinson described the Anderson character as 'a complete and utter bastard'. There are quite a few scenes in the film that contain echoes of Atkinson himself: its original title was *Camden Town Boy* – recalling the early 8os when both Atkinson and Curtis had lived round the corner from each other in that north London district. Goldblum's role could easily be compared to that of Curtis's and then Angus Deayton's in Atkinson's live show: And just to ram the point home, both the fictional and real entertainers shared the initials R.A. Curtis even revealed in the ITV documentary *The Story of Bean*, in 1997, that when he first sent the script to Rowan, the character of Ron Anderson was actually called Rowan Atkinson. Rowan reputedly contacted Richard and asked him what role he wanted him to play. Not surprisingly, Atkinson made a pre-emptive strike about the similarities between fact and fiction before people assumed that the film character's sadism and cruelty – and the uncharacteristic public bouts of f-word swearing – were all true. He admitted in the press that the film had elements of truth but he hoped 'people will realize my part is grossly exaggerated.'

When *The Tall Guy* opened in April 1989, Atkinson explained where his motivation for playing someone who liked humiliating people came from – even if he wasn't like that himself: 'You only have to go through a fairly mild public-school education to have witnessed cruelty. Comedy may well be my way of taking revenge all these years later.'

There was an intriguing tension in the scenes of Anderson performing onstage with Dexter King (Goldblum). None of the glimpses we see in the movie were actually from Atkinson's routines except for a brief snippet of the changing-into-trunks-in-public sketch when King fails to turn up and gets fired. Instead, we get more fancy dress, though a fondness for religious imagery is retained. Anderson came on in papal robes during one clip and, most famously, they did a double act as dancing nuns ('Life in the Vatican is fun, fun fun/when you're a dancing nun') when a high-kicking King – buoyant from his blossoming romance with Kate Lemon (Emma Thompson) – upstages

Anderson and nearly gets fired. In another scene, King sports a city gent's outfit from the waist up, a dress from the waist down – not something Curtis had ever done onstage. And there was more violence. In a medical sketch Anderson explains the injuries one can cause with different objects by using King as his guinea pig. The assault starts with a slap and culminates in a whack with an iron bar. The main plot was supposed to be the romance between King and Lemon, which, as with so many of the things Atkinson would do, seems to start with a sneeze. King comes down with an allergy, sneezes all over a Madness album as he puts it on the turntable to cheer himself up and goes to the Royal Free Hospital in Belsize Park where Lemon is a nurse.

There were also a number of in-jokes for Atkinson–Curtis obsessives. Curtis himself had probably the smallest cameo in history, one that would make Alfred Hitchcock seem like a screen-hogger; in the corridor in the restaurant when King bumps into Lemon, Curtis fleetingly walks past. At another point, King goes to visit his agent but is clearly not doing very well; two other clients seem to be getting all the offers. Angus Deayton is being courted by Steven Spielberg, while Robin Driscoll (who would later end up working on *Mr Bean*) has Harold Pinter and Arthur Miller. King is offered a Shake 'n' Vac commercial. In the film, Anderson is a slavish fan of the royals. In real life, Atkinson would end up developing an acquaintance with Prince Charles. Anderson drives an Aston Martin, just like Atkinson, though Anderson's has the number plate COM1C. In real life Atkinson would never be so gauche. It is also worth nothing that the special script consultant was Curtis's friend Helen Fielding who later channelled her thoughts on the dating game into *Bridget Jones' Diary*.

The Tall Guy also pointed to the way Atkinson's film career would slowly but surely develop over the forthcoming years. Although the character of this monstrous stage comedian hardly flattered him, it was a shrewd role, more than an extended cameo but not quite the starring part. Curtis was very good at reworking Atkinson's comedy persona for the bigger screen, a trick he would pull off again with Atkinson's trainee vicar, Gerald, in *Four Weddings and a Funeral*. Atkinson's role in *The Tall Guy* was very much a self-contained performance, and although extremely funny, it was part of a sub-plot, playing support to the central narrative, until the end when King takes his revenge on Anderson after seeing him kissing Lemon at an awards ceremony. The role was also memorable because it was the first time Atkinson said 'fuck' on celluloid.

The film was not greeted by rave reviews, but on *Saturday Night at the Movies* on ITV on 1 April 1989, those involved did their utmost to put a positive spin on it. Goldblum had been so keen to do it he had signed the contract eight days after seeing the script. Mel Smith had originally wanted somebody English, and Curtis said he had auditioned over 40 Englishmen in the role but was delighted with Goldblum's performance, comparing his chemistry with Emma Thompson to Spencer Tracy's rapport with Katherine Hepburn. Goldblum spoke particularly fondly of the two days it took to shoot the sex scene with Emma Thompson. They had gone at it 'hammer and tongs' and in the process destroyed most of the set, but the hardest part was getting a slice of toast to stick to Goldblum's bottom as they rolled across the floor.

As for the nagging question of how closely the characters were based on real people, Smith said that Ron Anderson was 'loosely' based on Rowan Atkinson, but – and it wasn't clear how much he was referring specifically to the shambolic-yet-passionate sex scene – Richard Curtis was Jeff Goldblum (although off-camera, Goldblum would sit reading Atkinson's beloved P.G. Wodehouse until Smith cried 'Action!'). Atkinson was relatively forthcoming about his links with Ron Anderson, suggesting that he did not dare let anyone else do it because the audience would only sit there saying, 'You know who that is, and he refused to play the part because he didn't like the sympathies expressed.' He was, he added, delighted to play it: 'There's nothing more fun than playing a very evil part.' At least the film suggested that although, as Atkinson had told Sue Lawley on *Desert Island Discs*, he was not the kind of person who laughed out loud very often, he did have a sense of humour about himself. One of the posters outside the Dukes Theatre where Ron Anderson was performing even featured a poster that read 'Rip-roaring Rubber Ronnie'. It was an adjective that had worn thin years ago, but for the sake of comedy it returned.

At the seventh Just For Laughs Festival in July 1989, Atkinson filmed inserts to go with the Channel Four television transmissions, which went out the following April and were made by Tiger Television. Each programme had its own identity, and Atkinson assumed the character of bland Canadian anchorman Casey Rogers to front them (a succession of tastelessly dull pullovers suggested that Casey Rogers was inspired in part by veteran pop-show presenter Casey Kasem). Rogers/Atkinson welcomed viewers to the show with an intro that sent up the Canadian Tourist Board and the country's perennial image problem. In a Shetland jumper and a smug smirk, Rogers sported a sewn-on badge that read 'Canada Interesting'. Rogers wandered through the woods, camply fondling the trees and singing the praises of the forest and his friend Burt. The action cut to other acts and each time it returned to Casey Rogers he appeared slightly more absurd. Observant viewers may have noted that there seemed to be an increasing number of maple leaves stitched onto his jumper as he would unconvincingly try to goad people into coming to Canada by asking: 'Are you rugged enough to handle it?' By the end of the show he was in the country's National Portrait Gallery but was encountering difficulties picking out pictures of famous compatriots. There was ex-President Trudeau, Joni 'Big Yellow Taxi' Mitchell, but then the trail started to go cold, until desperation showing on his face, he came up with Mahatma Ghandi, who, he claimed, 'came from Canada, or had heard of it'. In fact, the claims Rogers used to drum up trade began to sound increasingly deranged. Canadians had apparently invented everything from insulin to instant mash. And the zipper. The finale featured one of those classic Goodall/Curtis comic numbers except that, according to the credits at least, the script was written by Jon Canter and Lise Mayer (Mayer had co-written *The Young Ones*). Rogers excelled himself with a hymn to his homeland containing such lines as 'I'd rather cut off my dick than leave New Brunswick' and 'I'd rather eat kosher in Nova Scotia.'

Atkinson also used the festival to document some silent material that he was keen to develop. Onstage in Montreal, Atkinson was partnered by Angus Deayton for his now-familiar illustrated lecture, 'Elementary Courting for Men'. Deayton presented the lecture at the lectern while Atkinson played out the instructions. Once again, the advice for the first date was 'Don't look like an idiot' – Atkinson appeared at the onstage door, geeky suited and with the dopiest, drooling expression he could muster. As Atkinson led an imaginary girlfriend to his imaginary car, the spirit of *Monsieur Hulot's Holiday* seemed to hover around him. In the imaginary restaurant there was also an echo of that early *Canned Laughter* as Atkinson's latest nerd attracted the waiter, tasted the wine and bolted the food. The *déjà vu* continued in the imaginary disco where Atkinson proved that in the decade since Robert Box his characters were still unable to dance, instead gyrating as if there was 'something up your bottom or coming out of your bottom.' From there it was just a short step back to the subject's flat for the seduction, with the lights blacking out just as his trousers came down.

Intriguingly, Atkinson was clearly keen to establish the international potential for this character. In order to road-test this wordless character he did a show on a Juste Pour Rire night at the 2000 St Denis Theatre in front of a French-speaking audience. The Montreal Festival was one festival for administration purposes, but there was very little crossover between the French-speaking and English-speaking sides. There had been an attempt at detente with a show entitled *Lost in Translation*, but the title unfortunately came true and the jokes were thin on the ground. If Atkinson could do his act successfully in front of a non-English-speaking audience that was unfamiliar with him, then he would be assured of its success. It was a success, and the tape of the show at Juste Pour Rire was used to show television executives the comic potential of Mr Bean. It was a significant step for Atkinson and a coup for the festival. After more than ten years of slow but sure development, Mr Bean was finally about to blossom.

9

Caught in the Crossfire

Starkey: Where are they bombing today?
Major: Constantinople [Starkey takes a puzzled second glance at the wall map]
Starkey: There is no Constantinople. It's Istanbul now.
Major: I know that.
Starkey: Then why are we going there?
Major: We're not going. They are.
Starkey: Why are they going there?
Major: [tapping his manuscript] Because it says so. See?
Starkey: So that's what we have to call it. Is it dangerous?
Major: Not for those who survive. For those who don't – well, I'd call that dangerous, wouldn't you?

ACT I of We Bombed in New Haven by Joseph Heller

By the late 1980s, British television was involved in a fierce ratings war. While the soaps battled it out to see who could come up with the most compelling unbelievable storylines to grab the viewers, the network chiefs had a different tactic when it came to comedy. Rather than develop new talent and new ideas, they simply waved their cheque book and signed up the most successful acts from the other side. There was nothing intrinsically new about this: Morecambe and Wise had gone from ITV to BBC and back again. But with satellite becoming increasingly popular, video sales to think of and advertising revenue constantly growing, there was more than ever at stake. The ITV companies also had to keep the quality of their programming up so that their franchises would be safe when the government allowed prospective new networks to pitch for them.

In the middle of this competitive market, Britain's top comedy stars would change channels like skilled footballers changed clubs. Channel Four's Vic Reeves and Bob Mortimer and the *Comic Strip* team – many of whom had worked with Rowan Atkinson – would make the same journey. The commercial chiefs needed to hit back, and Rowan Atkinson was the perfect target. He may not have been as hip as the *Comic Strip* but he had huge commercial clout and appealed to viewers of all ages. And of course his first adult television outing, *Rowan Atkinson Presents … Canned Laughter* had been on ITV. In May 1989, it was announced that Rowan Atkinson had signed a reported £250,000-deal with Thames Television. It wasn't clear what the programmes would consist of, but it seemed to mean the imminent demise of *Blackadder*.

It made perfect sense for Thames to ink a deal with Atkinson. Of all the ITV companies, Thames certainly had a good record with international comedy, having had huge success with Benny Hill. But with the advent of political correctness, Hill and his dolly birds were out of favour. His last ITV special had been transmitted on 1 May 1989, and in the same year that Atkinson signed up, Hill was dropped. Atkinson would go on to make Hill's slapstick success seem modest, although his most lucrative work would be done for his own company and distributed through Thames. Atkinson clearly wanted to have more control over his career. He had worked closely with Peter Bennett-Jones for a while now, but in September 1989 the alliance was further formalized when Atkinson became a creative director of Tiger Television, the independent production company that would end up making *Mr Bean*.

Meanwhile back at the BBC, *Blackadder* wasn't going to go down without a bang. The ratings war would seem like a tea party compared to the war that was the setting for the final series. On 28 September 1989, the fourth series, *Blackadder Goes Forth*, was launched. This time round – after considering and rejecting the idea of setting it in the naughty 1890s – the action focused on the fighting on the Western Front in 1917. Atkinson played Captain Edmund Blackadder, the careworn moustachioed descendent of his previous incarnations. Tony Robinson was back as his faithful batman, Private Baldrick, but he had lost a few more brain cells over the generations, as he explained on *Behind the Screen* on BBC2: 'In the first series he was the brightest ... and now he is terminally stupid. It is impossible to see how he actually gets through the day.' In the *Oxford Mail* he joked that Baldrick's stunted development was one of the things holding the series back: 'The biggest problem in the whole series is that we are running out of insults to Baldrick.'

After dim, dashing and devious incarnations, Atkinson's own maturity seemed to have brought out Blackadder's dark side. Edmund Blackadder was simply deadpan, the victim of a humour bypass but prone to the longest one-liners in sitcom history. War had exhausted him and he had no shred of treachery left in him. He just wanted out. The episode titles ran from 'Plan A' to 'Plan E' – each one was an attempt to escape from the horrors of the trenches.

The cycle may have now reached the twentieth century, but in many respects they had gone full circle. The original medieval period had been chosen because the scope for random violence and the unexpected offered great comic potential. In the mud-sodden trenches in France the same primitive conditions seemed to have returned. It was one of the great theories of sitcom lore that the best ones – *Steptoe and Son* in their yard, *Hancock* in East Cheam, *Rising Damp* in Rigsby's grim terrace – were centred on claustrophic scenarios where there was always the desire but never the reality of escape. Where was that more true than in the conflict of the First World War? Each attempt to dig themselves out of their hole seemed to land Blackadder in a deeper one. Despite the bleak subtext, there was still room for plenty of cheap laughs. In one episode, Atkinson's monstrous creation sends up his own comic hero Charlie Chaplin, describing him as being 'about as funny as getting an arrow in your head and then finding a gas bill attached to it'. In Blackadder's opinion Baldrick proves himself to be the only person even less funny than Chaplin by trying to impersonate him using a dead slug as a moustache.

The series that had started six years earlier with Peter Cook being accidentally decapitated at the Battle of Bosworth by the Beeb's anti-hero had a more violent backdrop to it than ever. There was a worry about complaints that it was in bad taste to set a sitcom during a war that some viewers had lived through (although it never seemed to harm *Dad's Army*, or indeed *M*A*S*H* – two of the most enduring comedies ever). The team's equally inevitable reply was that nothing in the series was as absurd as some of the events that really happened, such as messenger pigeons being tried for treason and soldiers being shot by their own side for refusing to wear helmets. As viewers were to find out in the poignant final episode, the series was hardly celebrating war but explicitly condemning the mass slaughter of men whom those in command considered to be little more than cannon fodder.

If *Dad's Army* was a cosier British military antecedent of *Blackadder Goes Forth* (and a big influence on Ben Elton), its closest relation was really *M*A*S*H*, the ratings-record-breaking television spin-off of the Robert Altman movie that certainly seemed to owe something to Joseph Heller's *Catch-22*. *M*A*S*H*, which ran in America from 1972 to 1983, had started off as a fairly lightweight war-zone comedy, but as the show's popularity grew it had the confidence to take more risks. Much-loved characters really died – Colonel Henry Blake was killed in a helicopter crash – while others went through traumatic experiences. And in Hawkeye, played throughout by Alan Alda, the series had a wisecracking lead to compare with Edmund Blackadder. Hawkeye, too, was surrounded by a group of comrades, some loyal, some disloyal, some stupid – Major Frank Burns, Trapper John, Radar O'Reilly. While *M*A*S*H* was set during the Korean War, viewers in America had to be in a disturbingly deep state of denial not to realize that it was a comment on the Vietnam War, which was raging while the series was being transmitted. It was this last factor that gave *M*A*S*H* such a profound strength. *Blackadder* could not quite compete with that, but the team was still committed to producing something that would echo down the years. Like Joseph Heller's play *We Bombed in New Haven*, in which Atkinson as a teenager had played Captain Starkey, *Blackadder Goes Forth* took a mordant view of war, one that exposed war in all its folly and brutality. Unlike *M*A*S*H* or *Catch-22*, the universality of the absurdity of military conflict is made explicit in the initial stage direction of *We Bombed in New Haven*, which states that the play is set whenever and wherever it is being performed.

Blackadder Goes Forth also owed a debt to Joan Littlewood's stirring stage show *Oh What a Lovely War*. This also had a blatant anti-war message, which it communicated through the juxtaposition of an end-of-the-pier show and despatches from the front line. It was a huge triumph on stage (less of a success in the star-studded cinematic version) and proved that an anti-militarism polemic could be made palatable for a contemporary mainstream audience.

The politics of *Blackadder Goes Forth* were clearly defined: the generals were right behind the men – about 35 miles behind the men. If Atkinson had never been particularly political before, with the help of Ben Elton, by now established as Britain's funniest left-winger, he certainly would be in this series. The war was about class conflict as well as national conflict. It was interesting how Edmund's character had worked its way down the social scale – from Prince to just plain officer. He had started off wanting to be king, now he just wanted to survive. Lines about the war being over by Christmas, the only trouble was that no one knew which Christmas, had a convincing ring to them; these men had been fighting for so long they had forgotten what they were fighting about. At times *Blackadder Goes Forth* could have been a documentary, not a sitcom. The original premise of situation tragedy, conjured up in Camden Town in the early 80s, would be truer than ever this time round.

The success of Atkinson's series was clearly down to the attention paid to the smallest details during rehearsals. Voices were raised, but only because everyone was trying to produce the best comedy possible. In the script rooms debates raged over whether 'small sausage' was funnier than 'middle-sized sausage', whether the word 'Congo' was fundamentally more amusing than 'Tanganyika'. Producer John Lloyd, another of Atkinson's long-serving colleagues called the painstaking tweaking process 'plumpelling'. Even the most throwaway remarks would be pored over in minute detail. Richard Curtis would complain that they would never have done this to Shakespeare, to which Lloyd would reply that *he* would have, because some of those plays were far too long. But eventually, when an agreement and a laugh was reached, peace and a round of applause would break out. It was not easy to be possessive about a script. Sometimes it seemed as if whole episodes were flying out of the window because they were not considered funny enough. Passions ran high because it was something everyone cared about so deeply. It was not unheard of for lines to change at the last run-through.

Gallows humour was the main motif. In the episode entitled 'Corporal Punishment', Blackadder is sentenced to death for shooting – and eating – the pigeon carrying orders to attack the enemy. The writers even included a nod to *Dad's Army* by naming two of the firing squad Corporal Jones and Private Frazer. There were plenty of in-jokes for loyal followers since the early days of *Blackadder*. Miranda Richardson cropped up again as Blackadder's love interest Nurse Mary Fletcher-Brown in 'General Hospital'; in 'Major Star' Gabrielle Glaister played Bob, the soldier who is patently female. In the second series, Bob is whisked away by Lord Flashheart, whose swashbuckling descendant Squadron Leader Lord Flashheart also appeared in this series, played once again by the scene-stealing Rik Mayall. The regular supporting cast was more impressive than ever, with a core line-up of performers who were now stars in their own right. Stephen Fry was back as General Sir Anthony Cecil Hogmanay Melchett; Hugh Laurie was in chinless dullard mode once more as Lieutenant The Hon George Colthurst St Barleigh; Tim McInnerney returned after a break as the less-dim Captain Kevin Darling. The simple mention of his surname by Fry was enough to prompt a mass outburst of laughter among the studio audience.

With Fry and Laurie both coming from Cambridge, and McInnerney another Oxford graduate, *Blackadder* might go down as the most middle-class sitcom ever broadcast. Certainly it had the cast with the most degrees. Fry, Laurie and Atkinson had all had similar comfortable middle-class backgrounds. Fry, in fact, would be Atkinson's best man when he married Sunetra Sastry in New York in February 1990.

The wedding was a quiet affair marked by a small gathering in the Russian Tea Rooms. It was, above all, a very English marriage. The paparazzi had hounded Billy Connolly and Pamela Stephenson when they had had a very public relationship. It was clearly preferable for such a private person as Atkinson that his marriage didn't get the same kind of exposure. By marrying someone not directly involved in the forefront of showbusiness, he was able to keep his private affairs out of the limelight. But he was undeniably proud at his nuptials, and when he returned to London he did show off his new bride when he picked up his Showbiz Personality of the Year Award at the Hilton.

Atkinson and Sastry had been together for a while before they married, but one press report of their courtship seemed to typify Atkinson's British reserve off-screen combined with Mr Bean's prat-falls on-screen. Legend has it that he invited her out to dinner and didn't say anything for 15 minutes. He then asked her to pass the ketchup. Then he disappeared into the toilets when his zip broke and he needed to find a safety pin. If this isolated incident provided one picture of Atkinson off-duty as a composite of his comic creations, Stephen Fry offered what is probably the most accurate assessment of Atkinson's complex character to date when he said in *The Observer* that 'Rowan has not an ounce of showbiz in him. It is as if God had an extra jar of comic talent and for a joke gave it to a nerdy, anoraked northern chemist.' Another friend perhaps came almost as close to pinning down Atkinson by revealing that 'he likes nothing better than to be under the lawnmower draining the sump.' His favourite vice was probably kept in the garage in Waterperry and used to secure Aston Martin engine parts when he was working on them.

With his announcement that *Blackadder Goes Forth* would be the final series, Atkinson tacitly acknowledged that there were more problems off-screen than were apparent on-screen. In the *Sun* he said: 'I think we have gone as far as we can go with it. It's a shame because the audience was enjoying it most when we were enjoying making it the least. It's like selling a car – the best time to sell is also the best time to keep it.'

In *Now That's Funny*, Richard Curtis referred to the growing problem of *Blackadder*, which was essentially an embarrassment of comic riches: 'As we got further into the *Blackadders* the number of people who were good at comedy and in the same room and very strong-willed became hard to bear.' Then again, Curtis was quick to acknowledge that the combination of so many creative, talented people had helped to make the programme such a success and because, ultimately the team was on the same wavelength, they were all ultimately pulling in the same direction. But it had clearly been a strain at times because there were so many perfectionists involved. In the *Daily Mirror* Atkinson admitted that conflict over lines had been about more than just whether 'Congo' was funnier than 'Tanganyika'. Whereas perhaps it used to be just me who wanted his script discussed, suddenly everyone wants a major discussion on all their lines.' This was bound to happen with such a gifted cast.

At the heart of these different factions was the relationship between Atkinson and Curtis. It was an intriguing partnership. At times it seemed like the comic equivalent of Wham! with Atkinson the George Michael to Curtis's Andrew Ridgeley, the ungainly one gaining precedence over the more conventionally good-looking one. At the same time, this was creatively a more equal partnership than that of George Michael and Andrew Ridgeley, but how much more equal? Two of Atkinson's less successful ventures, *The Nerd* and *The Sneeze*, for instance, had been pursued without Curtis. Without him, Atkinson always seemed that little bit more vulnerable to criticism. Life seemed to be a joyless struggle for perfection for Atkinson; Curtis seemed to attain success effortlessly.

It was rather like a marriage, albeit a very modern one. Atkinson and Curtis knew they had to make an effort to make things work, and they also knew they had to allow each other a certain amount of space. Atkinson would later work more closely with Ben Elton on *The Thin Blue Line* while Curtis developed a professional relationship with Hugh Grant with *Four Weddings and a Funeral* and Dawn French with *The Vicar of Dibley*. At times it seemed that Curtis's creativity had more breadth to it, more scope, while Atkinson, however talented he might have been, had ploughed a relatively similar furrow ever since he had put his swimming trunks on over his trousers all those years ago.

It was, in a strange sort of way, what anthropologists might have called a polygamous symbiotic relationship. Both seemed to need each other, and with *Blackadder* they had also realized that both of them would thrive if they worked with other like-minded people, hence the incorporation of Fry and Laurie. This all worked out very neatly until the huge success of the series got in the way. Imagine the Beatles containing four John Lennons, albeit four very polite, middle-class, Oxbridge-educated John Lennons. It was as if everyone had inherited Atkinson's perfection disease and all of them were terrified of failure. It made the production process fraught, but it also produced arguably the finest sitcom episode of all time.

Each series of *Blackadder* had ended with members of the cast dead. In previous instalments the deaths had been little more than cartoon killings; however, the final scene of *Blackadder Goes Forth* was much more than black comedy. Melchett, who in the past had simply been grave, was now, said Fry on *Behind the Screen*, 'blustering and quite seriously deranged'. He had ordered his men over the top, and after much prevarication it seemed that they had no choice. In one last attempt to escape, Blackadder calls in a favour from his old chum General Haig – played by sitcom stager Geoffrey Palmer, who is brilliantly revealed in his war-room nonchalantly sweeping whole regiments off his map – but Haig just tells him to stick pencils up his nose and pretend he is mad. Naturally Blackadder has already tried that, but then this is strictly *Catch-22* territory – you would have to be mad to be on the front line; trying to wangle a transfer is con-clusive proof that you are sane. When he realizes the hole he is in, Blackadder's response is typically succinct and as crude as one could get in a BBC1 sitcom: 'I think the phrase rhymes with Clucking Bell.'

The *Blackadder* cycle had never been a show that traded on sen-timentality – think back to Blackadder's Scrooge reversal – but this episode was chilling as no sitcom had ever been, as moving as any war-time drama. No plan, however cunning, could save them now as they stood poised at the edge of their trench. Then everything went quiet: Captain Darling, who, in a particularly dark scene, has been sent out to join them by Melchett, thinks they have been saved: 'Thank God, we've lived through it. The Great War, 1914 to 1917.' Of course, Blackadder is quick to point out that it has gone quiet because not even the British generals would shell their own soldiers. An unusually dignified Captain Edmund Blackadder leads his loyal men over the top – pausing to remind Lieutenant The Hon George Colthurst St Barleigh not to forget his stick – to certain death. As they leapt forward the screen slows down and freezes in a sepia-tinged echo of the final scene in *Butch Cassidy and the Sundance Kid* with Atkinson and Baldrick as a kind of comic Paul Newman and Robert Redford. Howard Goodall's familiar theme strikes a jarring minor chord, the figures disappear and slowly the screen fills with poppies. It just so happened that the episode was lent greater potency by the transmission date – 2 November – little more than a week before Armistice Day. Once audiences had got over the most moving scene in the history of sitcom, they would be left with memories of a truly classic series. The potency of *Blackadder Goes Forth* was emphasized in 1992 when the final episode was screened as part of a BBC series looking at the way conflicts had been covered by television, entitled *War and Peace*.

Blackadder was clearly no mere sitcom but a piece of history in its own right, showing that comedy could dig deeper into the human condition and the follies of mankind. Despite problems with the latter series, Atkinson clearly felt that something more than comedy had been taking place during filming. There had been something creepy about the making of this milestone in sitcom history. In 1992 he reflected on the mood around the very last instalment in *Vox* magazine. Somehow all the elements seemed to fall into place when making that last episode. It suddenly had a realness to it that sitcoms weren't supposed to have: 'There was this awful feeling in the pit of my stomach that "I'm going to die at the end of this programme." This was not like your normal pratfalling comedy death either. There was just this extraordinary feeling of dread that I've never felt before.'

To make things more effective the BBC agreed to increase the budget for the end of the show after Curtis and Elton had convinced them of its importance. Comedy at its best needn't be a poor relation of drama. Woody Allen once said that writing comedy was like sitting at the children's table, but this was comedy at its most mature. The BBC gave the team a bigger studio for an extra day without an audience so that the final scenes could be filmed in a wide shot. Money was also lavished on a recording of the familiar theme in a new mournful tone. And then a long time and a lot of money was spent in the editing process to find exactly the right picture to close with. If nothing else, this was proof that the BBC could function perfectly and put art ahead of accounts. Whether it would do the same today – and whether a producer in an age of budget-conscious producer choice would dare even to ask for more money – is another matter.

It had been a challenging episode, but Atkinson had risen to meet the challenge, too, playing it for laughs for the first two-thirds until things went into a darker area than any sitcom had ever gone before. The feeling of doom for Atkinson felt disturbingly real. And for the viewer too. Over four series and without realizing it until then, the viewer had got to know the characters very well. It was the fact that they were so believable – even though they were acting against type – that made it so effective.

Richard Curtis and Ben Elton's intention had always been to end things on a serious, sombre, provocative note. Elton felt that this was the only way a comedy could be carried off. They had been concerned that the series was going to get a lot of flak and be accused of being in poor taste because of its subject matter, so they knew they had to end it with something serious. Ultimately, though, the wit and skill of the writing and performing overrode any debate about poor taste. The sombre climax had been penned as a pre-emptive apology, but the scenes had such loyal support that an apology was not needed. Atkinson appeared on *Wogan* after the screening and said that he had expected to be lambasted for sending up the horrors of war: 'The ending was to allay that kind of criticism, which in the end never actually came.' There was indeed more praise and plaudits and the show picked up BAFTA awards for Best Comedy and Best Light Performance in 1990. If there had been an award for Best Anti-War Polemic, it would have walked away with that too.

As far as the team were concerned that was the end of the *Blackadder* cycle. Or was it? Richard Curtis actually did work on a script for a fifth series. It was going to be called *The Blackadder Five* and would follow the misadventures of a pop group in the early 60s. Part of the plan was to have the group involved in historical events of the day. This time round Baldrick would actually be the hairless drummer, known as Bald Rick. At one point he would assassinate President Kennedy and with the aid of original footage and editing trickery it would look like he was really there. Atkinson, as Blackadder, would play the band's Machiavellian manager. But it seemed, regrettably, that it wasn't to be. Ben Elton became involved in other projects, as did Curtis and Atkinson. Another high-quality sitcom series would take up eight months of their lives, and by now this in-demand team just didn't have the time.

A story in *Melody Maker* claimed there had been another cunning plan to make Blackadder an evil Tory MP but when ITV launched *The New Statesman* with Rik Mayall, Curtis and co. thought that there was too much overlap. Unfounded rumours flew about in the tabloids that this had caused a rift between Mayall and Atkinson – there was no sign of it when the *Comic Strip* icon had his *Blackadder* cameo as jodhpur-slapping pilot Lord Flashheart.

In 1992, Atkinson himself didn't completely discount the possibility of more television episodes, but considered the prospect to be highly unlikely. Another rumour was that there would be a variant on the Edward and Mrs Simpson story played out by the same team. Atkinson said there were no future plans but did say if there was another series it might be set in the Second World War.

Then there was talk of a *Blackadder* film, but at a time when the British film industry was looking decidedly moribund this also seemed like a long shot. Atkinson himself said it would be unlikely and if it did happen he 'didn't have a clue when it would be set'. It probably was not a good idea. In the 1970s countless sitcoms – from *The Likely Lads* through to *On the Buses* (the most profitable film in the history of Hammer Films; it spawned two sequels and was described generously by Halliwell's *Film Guide* as 'deplorably witless') – had been turned into films but they had only tarnished the images of even the best television shows. Maybe it would be more fitting that the best sitcom since *Fawlty Towers* followed the *Fawlty Towers* principle of less-is-more and didn't outstay its welcome by spreading itself too thinly. Atkinson would prove that a television series could successfully transfer to celluloid but he would do it with *Mr Bean* rather than *Blackadder*.

Besides, there were times when television vehicles had to take second place to motor vehicles in Atkinson's life. He seemed to buy cars like other people bought newspapers. As well as a number of Aston Martins, he also owned a Peugeot 205GTI, which had developed problems when he took it round Silverstone and had never been the same again. In the summer of 1989 he had got rid of the eight-valve Lancia Integrale that had been his way of getting around for two years. Then he tried his luck with the new 16-valve Lancia Integrale. He picked it up from the Belsyre Garage in Oxford and wrote about his experiences in *Car* magazine. After initial fears that he might have shelled out £21,000 for 'a 2,800lb-ovenready-turkey' he was won over, even impressed by the bit of plastic on the floor where his clutch foot tended to make the carpet dirty.

Driving problems sorted, Atkinson had more charity work to attend to. Following the first all-star live-only *Hysteria* show, which raised money for Aids charities in 1987, *Hysteria II* was televised in an edited two-hour version, on Channel Four at 10.30pm on World Aids Day, Friday, 1 December 1989. The line-up – including Atkinson,

John Cleese, Adrian Edmondson, Dawn French, Lenny Henry and Jonathan Ross – might have smacked of the usual suspects, but there was no faulting the cause. Mel Smith and Griff Rhys Jones also appeared, but in a more serious guise than most of their fans were used to, explaining how the proceeds raised from the show would be spent. Atkinson's friend Stephen Fry was integral in organizing the show and directed it too.

Blackadder IV had finished less than a month earlier, so it was something of a surprise that Blackadder was already reappearing at *Hysteria II*. But Atkinson was always prepared to dust off the Blackadder franchise when it was for a good enough cause. He appeared to rapturous applause onstage in his moustachioed Elizabethan incarnation in conversation with an unusually hirsute William Shakespeare (Hugh Laurie). They were having a meeting about some of Will's works. Blackadder, now working as a script editor, had his doubts about them: 'I think we've got a *length* problem,' he explained ominously, harking back to John Lloyd's remarks about Shakespeare being overlong when Richard Curtis had complained about his work being cut. It transpired that some of the greatest works of English literature could do with some judicious editing. The tap dance at the end of *Othello* really had to go. But it was *Hamlet* that provided the biggest problems. The 'To be or not to be ...' soliloquy was apparently on the lumpy side and could do with a bit of trimming. It was all about bums on seats and the audience had to be kept happy: 'Joe Public loves the ghost and the chick who drowns herself,' but the existential gibberish remained a problem. History had turned full circle. During the first series of *The Black Adder*, Shakespeare had been given an acknowledgement in the credits; six years on Blackadder was rewriting the bard.

10

Silent Nights

As a new decade dawned it was time for Rowan Atkinson to unveil his latest creation. On New Years Day 1990, the first 30-minute Mr Bean adventure, directed by John Howard Davies and made for Thames TV by Tiger Television, was screened on ITV at 8pm, attracting an impressive audience of 13 million. The channel may have been new, but the team was not. John Howard Davies had been the BBC's Head of Comedy when *Not the Nine O'Clock News* was commissioned and was now at Thames. He had also been a producer of *Monty Python's Flying Circus* and *Fawlty Towers*. What he did not know about comedy could be written on a pinhead.

Mr Bean was to become the perpetual naughty schoolboy in all of us; the programme's very opening credits seemed to be a coded reference to Atkinson's own schooldays. In the same way that his classmates had called him an alien because of his odd appearance, so Bean dropped down to earth on a beam of light (a device first used in the second episode) – as if he too was from another planet. If so, it was not necessarily a planet with intelligent life; Bean would turn out to be one of television's most gormless icons.

The first episode also made explicit the fact that *Mr Bean* had not just come out of nowhere. The three short films – credited to a writing team of Atkinson/Curtis/Elton – that made up the 24-minute episode (leaving room in the half-hour for adverts) had all grown out of Atkinson's live shows. There was the beach scene in which he attempted to get into his trunks in public; the cheating in the exam scene; and the sneezing scene in church. The character now had a proper outfit – tweedy jacket with leather arm-patches, slightly too short trousers, a shirt and tie. His hair was short and flattened down, like a 50s schoolboy just sent off to school by his mother. He also had a Mini, though in the first episode it was not his distinctive yellow Mini but a tangerine-coloured model. As he got out, the driver's door was locked by means of a padlock; the security-conscious Bean then tossed the key onto the back seat through an open window.

Howard Goodall's music perfectly complemented Bean's other-worldliness (the composer had a bit of experience with aliens by now – he had also written the theme music to BBC2's sci-fi spoof *Red Dwarf*). A Latin choir sang the words that translated as 'Behold the man that is Bean.' As with Blackadder, Goodall had gone for serious music, with the comedy coming through the lyrics – assuming the listener could understand Latin. The music also gave *Mr Bean* a grander introduction, which lent even more bathos to the slapstick comedy. On live shows, the unnamed oddball's incidental music had been played by Goodall on the synthesizer; on television it was a full-scale production job.

Given Atkinson's abiding fondness for vehicles and the presence of this new character's dinky little Mini, maybe a motoring metaphor is the best way of explaining the fundamental difference between *Mr Bean* and *Blackadder*. If *Blackadder* was a Volkswagen Golf, an acquired taste but solid, reliable and always popular, *Mr Bean* was a Ford Escort, lighter, less demanding and very popular indeed. For many viewers this bumbling, mostly silent cross between Jacques Tati, Charlie Chaplin and Frank Spencer was a new sight. People who had followed Rowan Atkinson's career since the late 70s, however, would have experienced more than a hint of *déjà vu*.

There may have also been an element of *déjà vu* for Channel Four viewers with extremely good memories. In 1983 Channel Four launched its very first sitcom, set in Hollywood. *The Optimist* starred Enn Reitel, an actor best known for his many accents (he had a lucrative sideline doing voice-overs for ads). Yet ironically *The Optimist* was silent: each episode followed the visual misadventures of this strange character as he tried to make his way around Los Angeles. It seemed to be an odd piece of casting and maybe that sowed the seeds of its demise. Despite running for two series and 13 episodes – with the second series relocated to London and some words creeping in – *The Optimist* never really captured the public imagination. The funny thing was that *The Optimist* was written by the creator of the Schoolmaster sketch, Richard Sparks. Around the time of *Not the Nine O'Clock News*, Sparks had started to work predominantly abroad, in New Zealand and America, but Channel Four had commissioned his concept. Six years after its finish, *Mr Bean* was born.

Sparks is emphatic that Atkinson did not take his idea. And of course, the seeds of Mr Bean were there long before 1983. But it is intriguing to discover that Sparks had talked to Atkinson about it a few years earlier when he had been trying to write the sitcom: 'I'd found one of the problems of sitcom was being tied down to this verbal thing, which lost a lot of sense of action. I wanted to do an action comedy and around 1979 wrote a script called *The Wind, the Surf and the Moron*. Rowan came to my house in Brixton, sat around and he liked it. It was an idea that we actually took to Rowan because it would have suited him.' The intellectual content of *The Optimist* was decidedly minimal, but it was intended as an adult series, or as Sparks put it: 'for morons'. Sparks went on to say: 'It's not that he pinched my idea or anything. Every sitcom has got a neighbour in it; how many ideas are there? Half of his stage show had no words already, so it was also natural that when someone writes something without words he took it to a guy who does stuff without words. The great rule of television is if it works do it again.'

The début television shorts of *Mr Bean* expanded upon their stage origins. The most notable thing about the first sketch, set in an examination room, is the fact that Bean speaks. He tells his neighbouring student that he has been studying trigonometry, before pulling out two mascots, a pink panther (a reference to his past admiration for Peter Sellers?) and a toy policeman (a prefiguring of his role in *The Thin Blue Line*?). His neighbour, played by Paul Bown, says that he has been studying calculus. When the invigilator, played by stalwart black actor Rudolph Walker – best known for his part in the 70s race-based sitcom *Love Thy Neighbour* – instructs the students to open their envelopes, Bean pulls out a green paper filled with questions about calculus. Bean then attempts to copy his neighbour's paper, in one brilliantly observed moment, sliding across the bench as if on a conveyor belt. His methods get increasingly desperate but fail each time. Then when the exam is finished, it transpires that there is a white paper filled with trigonometry questions still in his envelope.

The swimming trunks sketch made the most of the very English culture of embarrassment, as Bean attempted to put his swimming trunks on at the beach standing next to another man (Roger Sloman, who played Three-Fingered Pete in the very last episode of *The Black Adder*) sitting in a deck chair. Anyone else would have gone elsewhere on the beach, but after countless contortions Bean gets his trunks on before removing his ubiquitous brown trousers. Then when the man sunning himself picks up a white stick, Bean realizes he is blind – he needn't have been embarrassed at all.

The final sketch in the first episode found Atkinson in church, but not as a vicar this time as fans might have expected. Bean is seated next to *Good Life* veteran Richard Briers. Everything that can go wrong in a church does go wrong. He forgets the words to the hymn but that is only the beginning. He then sneezes, discovers he doesn't have a handkerchief and ends up using the lining of his tweedy jacket pocket. During the sermon he falls asleep – nearly into Briers's lap before ending up on the floor. The calamities culminate in him dropping a sweet and retrieving it. In a style that would become typical of Bean behaviour, defeat is snatched from the jaws of victory when he realizes that he has put the sweet into his snot-filled pocket. As the credits rolled, the Mini is totalled, but Bean, an idiot savant who seems to create havoc while getting away with murder, walks away without a scratch on him.

ITV was delighted with the ratings, but the irony was that there was a rumour that he had earlier offered *Bean* to the Beeb and Auntie had turned it down. If true, this was foolish. Bean had been road-tested over the years. Now Atkinson, Curtis and Robin Driscoll, the new writer who replaced Elton after those classic sketches had been used up, would watch Atkinson's old stage-show routines to see what could be successfully adapted for television.

Other ideas, however, were completely new. Despite having carved out his reputation as a pre-eminently verbal writer, Richard Curtis was crucial to getting the silent comedy to work. He would start out by coming up with a small idea at home and then develop it slowly but surely. In his office in west London, Curtis would go through the strange ritual of acting out future *Mr Bean* sketches. It was not the sort of comedy you could write down. For the second episode, 'The Return of Mr Bean', screened on 5 November 1990, Curtis came up, for instance, with the idea of Mr Bean meeting a nameless female member of the royal family at a Royal Film Premiere. For two and a half hours Curtis stood in his room looking at his own body and wondering what Mr Bean would do while he was standing in line. Eventually the team met up in the rehearsal room and the result was Bean getting his finger caught in his flies, with the result that something that looked very rude indeed was protruding when the royal visitor got to him. Luckily this sort of social gaff did not make a habit of happening to Rowan Atkinson in reality. The week before the programme had gone out he was invited to meet Margaret Thatcher at 10 Downing Street. Footballer and fellow northerner Paul Gascoigne was also there. While Gascoigne put his arm around the Prime Minister, a polite handshake was enough for the comedian.

Other ideas were more instinctive. In 'the Trouble with Mr Bean', Bean, late as usual, dresses, shaves and cleans his teeth while driving. At one point he puts his trousers on while sitting in the back seat, steering with his toes and placing a brick on the accelerator. This was based on things Atkinson noticed while travelling on the motorway. He saw other commuters playing with their phones or their radios when they should have been concentrating on the road and took this to its logical conclusion.

Bean was a curious anomaly. Very English, yet very universal. His global popularity confirmed that no single nationality has a monopoly on morons. In meetings, the team would invoke the mantra 'think of the Egyptians'. Rowan Atkinson was remembering those postcard of Phil Collins, George Michael and Duran Duran being snapped up in Venice. The absence of language meant borders were immaterial: or maybe the rest of the world just liked to see the stereotypical dim-witted, awkward Englishman in action – all that was missing was the bowler hat.

Some might have said that the character of Mr Bean was recourse to Atkinson's past and therefore a sign of weakness; he was simply drawing on something that had come naturally to him rather than coming up with something totally new. But maybe it was only as a young man that the comic had the lack of inhibition to attempt a largely visual character. It would certainly be hard to imagine Atkinson in his mid-30s launching a character like Mr Bean unless it had been tried and tested.

The remarkable thing was that the only people who seemed disappointed by *Mr Bean* were the people who had been devoted *Blackadder* fans. If *Blackadder* had not been so epochal and *Mr Bean* such a stylistic contrast, perhaps there would not have been so much criticism. Yet, in some ways, Mr Bean was the more natural of the two creations; it had grown organically ever since that day in the run-up to the Oxford show when Atkinson came up with his act in front of his mirror. Bean also might have been Atkinson's way of coping with his stammer. It had subsided since his youth, but for someone with a speech impediment who chose public performance as a career, it seemed natural to prefer a public performance that was wordless.

Mr Bean was essentially a solo show. Atkinson no longer needed a fall guy because he was now his own fall guy. It worked, but it also put a tremendous amount of pressure on his own performance, which would make or break the programmes. Filming *Blackadder* had been hard, but filming *Bean* could be harder. There were countless retakes in the studios at Teddington, west London, making the days long and arduous.

There was a dilemma: should Bean speak. In some sketches he needed at least to ask a question to kick-start the narrative, but anything more than monosyllables was fiercely resisted – think of the Egyptians. It would be one of the flaws of the *Bean* movie that the character spoke more often. You then ended up thinking that if he could speak why didn't he speak all of the time. It was better to think of him as a wordless creation. The best sketches were clearly the silent ones – a piece set in a library, for instance, where Bean ends up cutting out a page of a precious book that he has damaged, or Bean cleaning his dandruff with his dentist's suction tube.

It was clear from the moment *Mr Bean* was first transmitted that it would be a major mainstream success. Audience research soon showed that the viewers ranged in age from four to a hundred years old. Another indication of the character's success was the fact that people named Bean started writing to the programme saying that their name was now the cause of great embarrassment. Beans in the phone book would now have to go ex-directory. It could have been so different though. In the debate over what to call this nameless character that had been around for years. Atkinson considered Mr White, then he rejected colours and experimented with the sounds of different vegetables before coming up with Bean. It might have been people called Mr Cauliflower or Mr Cabbage that would have to live down an association with this clumsy everyman. As it happened Bean seemed to be a shrewdly appropriate choice of name. According to the *Oxford Dictionary of Surnames*, Bean is a nickname for a man regarded 'as of little importance'.

Mr Bean never came naturally to Atkinson, but there was an instinctive element to him, which arose from the fact that he was so similar to Atkinson the inquisitive boy. The performer admitted in interviews that a lot of Bean was himself as a nine-year-old, which he had also said about *The Nerd*: 'I prefer to look round the back of things rather than take them at face value. Bean, too, is someone who, presented with an advertising hoarding, won't just read it; he'll always want to go round the back, wonder how it's put together, pull out a bolt and "whoops".'

By 1990, however, Rowan Atkinson was not so much a comedian, but more of an industry. And Richard Curtis too was seeking pastures new; although *The Tall Guy*'s takings at the box office hadn't exactly broken the bank, the film had been a useful entrée for Curtis, who was now developing other film projects. In addition to this he was deeply involved in Comic Relief. It could be argued that by relying on the tried and tested team of Ben Elton and Richard Curtis to write the plot of *Mr Bean*, Atkinson closed ranks. However, circumstances now forced him to look elsewhere for collaborators on the *Mr Bean* series. Tiger Aspect put out a tender for writers to submit potential scripts for future episodes of *Mr Bean*.

One of the applicants was Robin Driscoll, an actor with the Cliff Hanger Theatre Company, who specialized in dynamic, physical performances and had close links with the Brighton street-theatre scene. Back in the late 70s and the early 80s Cliff Hanger had also appeared at the Edinburgh Festival at the Wireworks, the performance space set up by Atkinson's Oxford friends Will Bowen, Chris Naylor and Pierre Audi. After the teething troubles with the venues, the company had become established, but still encountered problems. One year Edinburgh's local authority decided that the 800-strong crowd constituted an obstruction. Cliff Hanger simply gathered together its assembled throng, took them down the road and performed in the open air where there was more room. Driscoll clearly had a vivid imagination and a way of choreographing scenes. He submitted some ideas, was taken on and co-wrote four episodes of *Mr Bean* (as well as *Bean – The Ultimate Disaster Movie*). It helped that Driscoll was an experienced trained actor. Rather than attempt the difficult task of trying to put a *Mr Bean* script onto paper, Driscoll would meet up with Atkinson and act his ideas out.

Sometimes Atkinson was able to combine dry runs for *Bean* with his passion for charity appearances. In May 1990, he became a patron of the Oxford Playhouse, alongside Judi Dench. The theatre where he had cut his performing teeth had been forced to close down in 1987 because it did not conform to regulations. He helped to raise money for its permanent reopening by using the theatre to rehearse *Mr Bean*. Bean's silent visual antics suggested that Rowan Atkinson wasn't quite as reluctant to resort to face-pulling as he had been in the late 80s. He seemed confident enough to return to his roots and he had good reason to feel confident.

With *Blackadder* still fresh in people's minds and *Mr Bean* making waves, he spent much of 1990 collecting awards. In March, he picked up a BAFTA for Best Light Entertainment Performer, while *Blackadder Goes Forth* was named Best Comedy Show of the Year. He was also voted BBC Personality of the Year. Capitalizing on his success, the BBC began to rerun all four series, while foreign sales were astonishing, with the series being sold in places as unlikely as Iceland and Hong Kong. *Mr Bean* was also making its mark, picking up three awards at the Montreux Television Festival in the first half of 1990 – the press award, the city award and the coveted Golden Rose.

ITV was keen to have more instalments of *Mr Bean*, but Atkinson wanted to do them as one-offs to keep them special, resisting the opportunity to cash in with a series straight away. It was a strange career decision but another that would be vindicated. It also revealed how much clout he had within the television industry. Benny Hill and Stanley Baxter had been big enough to make occasional specials in the past, but there were few stars who could do it now and fewer executives who would indulge them like this rather than squeeze a series out of them at the earliest opportunity. In all, only 13 *Beans* would be transmitted, with an extra one appearing on a compilation video along with a few unseen sketches. In America that body of work wouldn't even be big enough to constitute a single series.

As ever he seemed to be playing his cards close to his chest. Even Howard Goodall, who had known Rowan since Oxford, said after the Montreux win that 'Nobody knows what goes on inside the inner recesses.' But even the instant success of *Mr Bean*, unlike the faltering first series of *The Black Adder*, couldn't stop Atkinson's angst from resurfacing. Whereas *Blackadder* had taken its time winning awards, there was now instant pressure to continue *Bean*'s winning formula. Atkinson may have been insecure, but producer/director John Howard Davies knew how he ticked: 'He is a very methodical performer. His instincts are great, but he also has an intellectual approach to his stuff that television can accommodate well. I think he's still an electrical engineer at heart – he likes to know how the comic circuitry works.'

With Tiger Television, Atkinson was not just an employee of the broadcasters in the way previous comedy icons such as Tony Hancock had been. He could exercise much more control over his work. But as powerful as he was in the television world, major film success still seemed to elude him. He had once said in the press that he was getting fed up with being offered endless film roles that had been turned down by Dudley Moore and John Cleese: 'villains, butlers and freaks'. The other option was to start to develop his own film projects.

Reports of Atkinson's initial deal with Thames had mentioned that he would be making documentaries for them, but it was only after *Mr Bean* was established that one appeared, on 8 December 1990, and to some fans' surprise it wasn't a comedy at all. *The Driven Man* was a chance for Atkinson to expand upon his passion for fast cars, and he wasted no time in waxing lyrical about his motormania. He was featured at a Renault 5 race, clearly interested but displaying neither emotion nor comic ability as he stood in the crowd craning his neck to catch a glimpse of the action as the cars raced around the track, jockeying for a position. Gradually fantasy took over from reality, and we saw Atkinson, having dispensed with his smartly pressed jeans in favour of a yellow fireproof suit, driving an Elf Turbo. It soon became apparent that this wasn't a fantasy at all. As he said over the commentary: 'This film is about guilt.' On the one hand, he loved everything about cars, from the buying to the polishing; on the other hand, this tireless campaigner for fashionable causes was well aware of the environmental damage they could cause and the danger too. It was this fundamental contradiction in his personality that he set out to explore in *The Driven Man*.

Of course it wasn't the first time his mechanical obsessions had been public knowledge. In the past Atkinson had been happy to engage in conversation about cars and had even appeared on the BBC's *Motor Show* programme. Having first been taken to the Motor Show as a special treat when he was a boy, he was still a frequent visitor. He would eye up the new Renault Clio in the same way someone else might eye up a CD or mobile phone. In the mid-80s he had been regularly buying and selling cars. It wasn't necessarily an investment; he was more interested in the mechanics of different machines than the potential profits. He once bought an unusual Mercedes because he was fascinated by the hydraulic system that moved the seats, but having driven 50 yards in it he realized it wasn't the car for him. He felt rather foolish and sold it after three weeks.

Cars seemed to be his way of escaping from not just comedy but also the outside world. They were a movable but personal space – he could use them as a thick carapace as he negotiated the modern media and all of its complications and intrusions. At times it really seemed as if he preferred cars to people. Even a decade after the event, one of his strongest memories was of passing his HGV test in 1981: 'The thrill of making 2,000 people in a theatre laugh is but a light breeze compared to the tornado of excitement that I felt at that moment.'

The *Driven Man* featured mock psychiatric scenes on the couch, with not one but two real-life shrinks. Under analysis, Atkinson blamed his obsession with cars all on his childhood – during school sports he had preferred to roam around at the back of the field miming gear changes rather than attempt to snatch the ball away from the opposing team. There was something about controlling a car that made him think he was in control of his own destiny. At the same time, he also admitted that his sort of behaviour made him seem like 'a bit of a spas'. And then, of course, there was his mother's Morris Minor, which he had taken on and customized. Driving and per-forming had similar functions for Atkinson. It was all about being in control and proving that he could excel. It also enabled him to be different, and he had always yearned to be different. As a shy man, driving expensive cars was a perverse way to attract attention to himself – but no stranger than coming into the homes of millions every night.

The Driven Man, directed by Mark Chapman, was a step away from comedy, but one that allowed Atkinson to delve deeper into his own psyche. It was one of the few times he felt comfortable being himself on television rather than being a character. As the writer of his own script, there might have been a few embellishments for dramatic effect, but this was certainly the real Rowan on the screen. Even when he confessed to having nightmares about the petrol supply running out, it seemed like a credible anxiety. His solution would be to use chariots. It was easy to get into the psychology of cars: they are womb-like, phallic; they can almost be anything to anyone. But to Atkinson, the epitome of conservatism in his professorial spectacles and green corduroys, they were all about freedom. Endless possibilities. Self-determination. But most of all, it seemed, polishing something until it was flawless.

In what was essentially a serious documentary, Atkinson couldn't resist succumbing to some basic visual comedy. In these halcyon pre-road-rage days, he examined the phenomenon of aggressive drivers by dressing up as a caveman and going on the rampage in a supermarket where a driver who had cut him up was now doing his shopping. Cars were, after all, pretty primitive beasts and maybe the people that drove them were primitive too.

In March 1991, he took part in Comic Relief again. Each year the event had got bigger and bigger, inspired by the achievements of Live Aid to fight famine. This time round though, Atkinson chose to concentrate on the old stage-show favourite, A Few Fatal Beatings, reviving his stern Scottish schoolteacher informing Mr Perkins (Angus Deayton) that his son had died after an infringement of library rules. A showing of the old Constable Savage sketch revealed Atkinson as a bobby whose hair had long surpassed regulation lengths, but whose brutality and prejudice seemed to strike a chord of recognition with the public. In a phone-in poll the sketch was voted as the second-best comedy sketch of all time. The first was, with deadening inevitability, the Dead Parrot sketch. Once again Atkinson seemed to be following in John Cleese's slipstream.

Whereas in the past *Blackadder* might have been wheeled out for charity, now it was the turn of *Mr Bean*. The catchphrase of that year's appeal was 'Let's stonk', and Bean attempted to have a stonking good time by taking part in a sponsored silence. With royalties from video sales beginning to flood in and a lucrative ITV deal bearing fruit for what was only an occasional show, Atkinson could easily afford to contribute to charity events – though time was still a precious commodity.

That summer he was called upon once again by Stephen Fry to appear in the third Hysteria to raise funds for the Aids organization, the Terrence Higgins Trust. The show was staged at the London Palladium on 30 June 1991. Atkinson opted for an unusually restrained cameo, but one that was in keeping with his back catalogue. This time round he called upon all of those straight-laced art-show interviewers he had been doing since *Not the Nine O'Clock News*, but gave this one an unusual quirk – an annoying obsession with names. When his special guest, Elton John, came on (following in the footsteps, said the commentary, of Ian McKellen, Judi Dench and Christopher Biggins) Atkinson kept drawing attention to the fact that Elton's first name sounded like a surname and his surname sounded like a first name. It was a particularly annoying riff and for a while it seemed as if either Elton, in a black Nehru jacket and Greek fisherman's hat, was a very good actor indeed or he was genuinely getting fed up with it. He had that look that was part nervousness, part 'what the hell have I let myself in for?' Eventually Atkinson quoted the line from John's *Your Song* 'You see I've forgotten if they are green or they're blue' and asked him if the same forgetfulness had made him get his own name the wrong way round. Was he jealous of Ben Elton? Warming to the theme, he then said the subject of *Candle in the Wind* was 'Monroe Marilyn' just to irritate John, who seemed on the point of storming offstage when Atkinson got one last question in about why it had taken John so long to get a solo number-one hit – he had just topped the charts with *Sacrifice*. Could he have been held back by having such a 'stupid, bloody pointless name'? At which point Elton John pulls out a gun, leaving Atkinson to sign off with 'what a head dick'.

When Stephen Fry introduced the cast towards the end, there was the faint air of chumminess about it, with Emma Freud singing Atkinson's praises: 'Rowan has a surprisingly pert bottom, his chest hair is dark and matted with a sweet smell of pine unexpectedly emanating from it.' Safe sex advice was offered from a variety of television characters and celebrities. With the assistance of Hugh Laurie and jockey-turned-thriller-writer Dick Francis, Atkinson played a horse about to be mounted – all in the name of health education, of course. As happy as Atkinson was to join in with these events, he never seemed quite as comfortable as the others. Whenever there was an onstage musical get-together, as there was here at the climax (and there had been at the first Comic Relief show), he always stood, stiff as a board. If clapping was involved he tended to do it out of time. It was hard to believe that he had once been a competent drummer. In fact, even as Mr Bean there was a grace and agility to his calamities. As himself, it seemed he could not let it all hang out onstage even if his life depended on it. The public-schoolboy awkwardness could only be shaken off when he donned another personality.

Along with charity work, it was success and breaking new ground rather than money that motivated Atkinson, but that didn't stop him from finally succumbing to the lucrative lure of making adverts. In the early 80s he had a brief stint advertising *The Guardian*, but unlike younger comedians such as Harry Enfield he had resisted doing television commercials for fear that it would dent his credibility. In 1991, however, he did agree to promote Barclaycard for a reported £750,000, which, along with earnings from *Blackadder* videos, would enable him to buy a Kensington townhouse to add to his Waterperry rectory. He seemed fairly unashamed about his earnings, saying in the *Daily Mirror*: 'I uphold the new middle-class tradition of only being funny for financial gain – as opposed to working-class comics who are funny all the time.'

The Barclaycard ads were different to the run-of-the-mill comedians-cashing-in-on-their-fame though. They were directed by Atkinson's old *Not the Nine O'Clock News*/*Blackadder* producer John Lloyd and worked as pocket-sized comedy sketches. Atkinson's character in the credit-card promos was another great bumbler, self-styled super-spy Richard Latham. In each ad he would appear to be teaching his young acolyte Bough, played by Henry Naylor, how to be a secret agent. And in each ad he was hoist by his own petard, falling foul of his own methods while Bough with his Barclaycard came up trumps. Atkinson treated the job as if it was another television series, which in effect it was. 'He loves to get into a role and to know how his character would react in every situation,' said the ad agency copywriter John Matthews in the *TV Times*.

The first ad found the duo in Egypt. While Latham bought an ancient rug for cash in the local market, Bough explained that one of the benefits of Barclaycard was protection if goods were damaged. Latham suggested that little could go wrong on the banks of the Nile, but little did he know that as he spoke the other end of his rug had caught alight on an oil lamp and as he walked away his investment was going up in flames.

According to Matthews, Atkinson agreed to do the ads on condition that they would be a departure from previous television characters: 'Rowan insisted that he would do it only if it was an interesting and original character – not just a rerun of somebody he'd played on television before.' Well, maybe Latham wasn't quite as accident-prone as Mr Bean and he did have lines to say between the mishaps.

It was a frantic schedule. In three weeks the crew filmed in Egypt, Moscow and Westminster, but this was the kind of rollercoaster Atkinson was now on. It was hard to take a break when he was in such demand, and the ads had to be fitted in between shooting schedules for television programmes. It was worth it, however. Over a series of consistently entertaining ads, Latham would prove to be as durable a character as Mr Bean. The money came in handy too. It was all a long way from the old sketch in which he had berated the student in front of him in the queue – for having a Barclaycard.

Things were hardly likely to get easier on the schedule front. In September 1991 it was reported in the *Daily Star* that Atkinson had signed to two movie deals with Fox. Would this finally mark his commercial breakthrough in America? Critically he was now becoming well established there, and in November he picked up another International Emmy for *The Curse of Mr Bean*. In December he was even prepared to have another crack at a live show in America, though this time he steered well clear of the Butcher of Broadway and opted for Boston University's Huntingdon Theatre, falling back on tried and tested material. Two shows over consecutive nights, 21 and 22 December, were filmed by Tiger Television. A longer version was shown on America's cable channel HBO, then a version went out on BBC1 before the inevitable release on video.

Part of the reason behind these shows was the fact that with the success of *Mr Bean*, Atkinson had been contemplating taking a break from stage performances. He wanted to document his past work and used these shows to record the highlights of his 1981 and 1986 shows for posterity. If the material contained few surprises, the set was spectacular. His old friend Will Bowen was still doing the design and had come up with a stark geometric set with more than a nod towards Mondrian.

Boston was a clever choice of location. With Harvard University nearby and a cultured New England anglophile sensibility, it could have almost have been a show in Atkinson's beloved Oxford. It was a tried and tested nursery slope for Brits in America too; Peter Cook and Dudley Moore had also chosen Boston for the warm-up before their 1973 New York show *Good Evening*.

Aided by Angus Deayton, the Boston show could have been a university show, except that it was a million times funnier. It seemed as if Atkinson had something to prove to America, but he wasn't in a hurry to return to New York. Besides, he had been happy with the Broadway show even if the critic Frank Rich was not. Atkinson took few risks as his greatest hits were put down on videotape. Present and correct were the sneezing man in church and the invisible man on the London underground. Half the material was written by Atkinson with Curtis and dated back to their early days together; the rest – apart from Howard Goodall's music – could be credited to the winning *Blackadder* team of Curtis and Elton, the Lennon and McCartney of comedy. And if Curtis was the cuddly McCartney, it was clear where Elton, in his metal-rimmed spectacles and political attitude was coming from. In *Time Out*, Curtis confirmed the long-suspected working practices of the ensemble: 'The tradition has always been that Rowan takes the whole thing very seriously and the rest of us fool around.' The fooling around had to meet with the star's approval, however: 'He is completely unable to do anything he doesn't like onstage because he is so alone there. He is a very rigorous editor.'

One of his well-trodden routines kicked things off at the Boston show. A Warm Welcome, as it had become known, found Toby the Devil as laid-back as ever, trying to be 'informal as well as infernal'.

A Few Fatal Beatings, which followed, may have been flogged to death by now, but it was still worth another outing for posterity's sake. Jesus had a final outing as a magician, turning water into wine and sawing Mary in half: 'thou art, indeed, an all-round family entertainer.'

When sketches were performed in quick succession, it was easy to see themes that had developed over the years. Churches were the most regular location. There was With Friends Like These, in which Atkinson's vicar explained – once again – what he says when young women ask him what the church's position on fellatio is. Of course, It Started with a Sneeze was really where Bean had begun. The Father of the Bride routine sounded as fresh as it had in the 80s, but times had changed. A decade earlier Atkinson might have identified more with the best man, but now, well into his 30s, the stern, curmudgeonly parent seemed to fit him like a glove. As he drunkenly condemned his future son-in-law, the insults rained down thick and fast, a highlight being his frank declaration that 'I spurn you as I would spurn a rabid dog.'

Despite the advent of political correctness, Atkinson was happy to perform old material that had even been criticized at the time. There was another outing for the Tom, Dick and Harry sketch, while Good Loser was his comment on the awards system, playing a friend collecting a gong on somebody else's behalf. The praise comes out grudgingly and when he tries to work out what the winner has that makes him so special, he can only come up with one thing: 'syphilis'.

But whenever it seemed as if Atkinson's speciality was lightweight comedy in dubious taste, he reminded his audience that he was also capable of something with more of a subtext. Guys After The Game reworked his Indian waiter sketch, although the accent was sometimes a little wide of the mark – the Punjab via Cardiff – the comments had a valid point. Atkinson's long-suffering character had to tolerate their tiresome cracks about popadoms and 'paperback raitas' and their vomiting, but he had the last laugh.

Although the material was as strong as ever, there seemed to be a reluctance at times to rework it. But Richard Sparks's Schoolmaster sketch, first reworked in the mid-80s, was now immortalized on video as No one Called Jones. Whereas the original version had reaped the benefits of the English love of innuendo, this time round any potential double entendre was nipped in the bud by the unexpurgated adult version. The class of 1991 included Anus, Arsebandit, Bottom and Clitoris, whose absence prompted the inevitable line, 'Where are you Clitoris?'. The pace may have been slightly faster than back at the Hampstead Theatre, but the delivery was still syllable perfect, though Sparks may not have liked it because he had based the speech on his own father, who would never have said such words. The straight-laced Boston crowd, however, lapped it up, showing that sometimes it is worth fixing something even if it isn't broken. It did not improve on the original, but it did show that there were other potential versions out there. It was Atkinson's way with the words that made them funny. He seemed to relish the childishness of calling for a boy named Myprick and, when he didn't come, calling out 'Has anyone seen Myprick?' Once the ground-rules had been established by the original, they were easy to adapt. The final payoff of course, was that Atkinson's schoolmaster had called the boys together – including Russian exchange student Suckmeoff – to lecture them on smut in the school. The new version was Ben Elton's idea – the real gag was not the rudeness, but the fact that the schoolmaster had no idea that the names were rude.

For Sparks, the rudest thing of all was that it had been rewritten without asking him and it was, after all, based originally on his father: 'I didn't want my father to see someone coming onstage and yelling "clitoris". The dirty version was a little plonkingly obvious.'

The Boston show had to be tweaked a little because the original English version contained frequent references that the team thought the Americans might not understand, but this was a crowd that seemed to appreciate both the sophisticated stuff and the smut. Atkinson was impressed with the director, Tommy Schlamme (a name that Atkinson had great pleasure in enunciating, as if it was on that schoolmaster's register), who was particularly keen on No one Called Jones, and had reassured Atkinson that the Bostonians would go for it. The Indian waiter sketch was probably the only one that lost something in the transatlantic crossing. The late-night post-pub setting didn't really translate because the concept of rowdy hooligans rolling into a tandoori at closing time was alien to Americans. Atkinson pulled it off, but it was a close call.

Back in England, *Mr Bean* was more popular than ever. Fans wanted to know where the inspiration came from, and in the autumn of 1991, he talked frankly about this strange combination of loneliness, childishness and anarchy in the *Daily Mirror*, confirming that this character was basically his alter ego, himself as a child: 'Not only in the sense of his innocence, but also in his viciousness ... when things do not go his way.' Despite the continued success, things didn't come any easier: 'I hate doing the job of Mr Bean. I find being Mr Bean very stressful.' Being a solo act meant that there was little support when things were difficult.

But this was a disingenuous way of looking at things. Atkinson was so obsessive about his comedy that things had been equally problematic in *Blackadder* when there had been a supporting cast. He himself contributed substantially to his stress levels by always trying to get things absolutely perfect. As one Oxford contemporary recalled in *She*, he was just as much of a scientist when he was performing back then, determined to get his equations correct: 'He was infuriating. Everything had to be exactly right – he'd do one little movement over and over, 40 times if necessary, while all the rest of us just had to wait. But the end result was always brilliant.'

Atkinson responded to the accusation: 'I'm not aware that I've ever done anything 40 times – 15 or 20 maybe. I'm aware that I like to get things right and that I have at least a streak of perfectionism.' It wasn't clear whether he was being ironic when he admitted to doing 15 takes – enough to drive any but the most committed supporting cast member to despair. Fortunately Atkinson's successful record meant that he could get that kind of commitment. And no one could say that this scientific approach didn't reap rewards, least of all Atkinson: 'No success has ever surprised me. I didn't assume it would happen, but when it came it just seemed logical in relation to applied effort.'

During the successful run of *Mr Bean*, both Atkinson and Richard Curtis had been looking for ways to diversify. The beauty of *Bean* was that it allowed them to pursue other projects in between episodes during the early 90s. *The Tall Guy* had been a moderate success, and the idea of writing further long scripts certainly appealed to Curtis. Atkinson had dipped his toe back into the big screen's treacherous waters with that cameo in *The Witches*. Then Curtis came up with a new comedy-drama with a dashing attractive young hero, a fragrant supporting role for Atkinson and a romantic happy ending.

Bernard and the Genie was not exactly a Hollywood production. It was made for the BBC by Talkback/Attaboy productions and transmitted on 23 December 1991. Directed by Paul Weiland, who also worked on a number of editions of *Mr Bean*, it was a strange drama that had a child-like simplicity; however, it went out in an evening slot normally associated with programmes for adults – rather like *Mr Bean*, in fact.

As would be the case with a later, much more lucrative Richard Curtis script, Rowan Atkinson was not the star of *Bernard and the Genie*. It was Lenny Henry who played the Genie complete with bright-yellow designer threads and braids in his hair, summoned up by a latter-day Aladdin, Bernard Bottle, played by the young Scottish actor Alan Cumming. Bottle worked for a firm of high-class but dodgy antique dealers, Krisbys; Atkinson played his devilish boss, Charles Pinkworth. He looked every inch the evil city shark in his tailored pin-stripe suit and beard, which seemed inspired by De Niro's beard when he played a devilish figure in the movie *Angel Heart*, with Mickey Rourke. It appeared clear from his first appearance that Atkinson wanted to do something different with this role. The eccentric manner of speaking that Curtis had devised for him – 'Elucidate ye', 'Sit ye' – sounded initially as if it had been written for someone with a more colourful character, such as Stephen Fry. But Atkinson soon made the part his own as he dismissed Bottle from the company for failing to rip off enough old ladies with a curt 'I sack ye.' Pinkworth lacks humanity big style. He even sacks a staff member who says maybe Bottle should have been given a second chance. It was a fiendish part that made Ron Anderson in *The Tall Guy* seem positively philanthropic and most of the Blackadders seem like bumbling fools.

The drama seemed very much like a fairy-tale in reverse. In the manner of Irvine Welsh's *Granton Star Cause*, everything that can go wrong promptly goes wrong for our protagonist. No sooner has he lost his job than he loses his girlfriend to his rival. It is only when he finally gets round to rubbing a dusty old lamp that things begin to look up. With his new friend they soon go on a spree. There are some nice jokes as Bottle wishes for the Mona Lisa, then wishes he could look like Bob Geldof only to turn into the real Bob Geldof. He keeps

the Mona Lisa, but decides that he prefers looking like Bernard Bottle. On his return to his flat, however, Pinkworth and the police are waiting for him. Having slipped into Bottle's flat to steal a list of antiques, Pinkworth spots the recently stolen Mona Lisa. But the genie is able to turn the clock back, pinch back the list and change the picture for one of Kylie Minogue.

After a spot of romance and some more fantasy, the finale finds Pinkworth getting his just desserts. He is doorstepped by real-life political pundit Vincent Hanna – who had previously interviewed Blackadder during 'Dish and Dishonesty' – and it is announced that he has spontaneously donated £100 million to charity. Howard Goodall's Motown pastiche theme-tune strikes up, the credits roll and Atkinson has notched up another mean and moody role on his c.v.

By the end of 1991 there was no doubting that having had the courage to end *Blackadder* on a high note, Atkinson's rise had continued. In two glorious years everything he touched turned to gold – everything, that is, except Thames Television, the company that had helped to tempt him away from the BBC. In the fierce ratings war, things got dirty in 1991. Thames Television lost its London television franchise; one of the conspiracy theories was that this was the Tory Party's revenge on the station that broadcast *Death on the Rock*, a damning documentary about the killing of suspected IRA terrorists in Gibraltar. *Mr Bean*, however, was indestructible. When Carlton Television took over ITV's London franchise on 1 January 1992, *Mr Bean* would continue to be made and would go from strength to strength.

11

The Unbearable Lightness of Bean?

Comic Relief had always staged Red Nose Day in alternate years, but this did not mean the fund-raising had to stop in the intervening period. Other methods were used to collect money, and the most successful of these was the charity single. Most famously French and Saunders had teamed up with Bananarama to put out their cover version of the Beatles' *Help*. In the spring of 1992, Rowan Atkinson in the guise of Mr Bean also revived a pop classic. This one suddenly had a topical edge. A general election was looming, and Mr Bean decided to stand as a spoof candidate in a spoof election, choosing *Elected* by Alice Cooper as his campaign song. As a teenager Atkinson had been partial to minor doses of heavy metal, but it was still odd to see his creation being backed by Bruce Dickenson, the erstwhile leather-clad vocalist from Iron Maiden. The video that accompanied the single shuttled between Dickenson and Bean, but while Dickenson performed as if in concert, Bean was seen on the campaign trail canvassing door to door and snatching photo opportunities with passing babies. In keeping with Bean's craven, self-interested personality, any bribes, ranging from cash to televisions, were gratefully received.

The mock campaign even had a manifesto. If Bean was voted in, having a beard would become a criminal offence; there would be no tax cuts, only haircuts. Pollution in the English Channel would be solved by stopping anyone who lived in Dover from going to the toilet. Angus Deayton, finding fame in his own right as the question-master on BBC2's *Have I Got News for You*, cropped up as the Returning Officer when the results of the poll were announced. But unbeknown to the other candidates – who included a life-sized dolphin, Postman Pat and Bean-co-writer Robin Driscoll – Bean had switched the ballot boxes and, just as Edmund Blackadder had done, had rigged the result. Victory went to the Bean poll, and Deayton spoke for the nation when he responded with 'Have mercy on us all.' But despite plenty of television coverage and the increasing popularity of *Mr Bean*, there was a poll that *Elected* failed to win – in the charts it peaked at Number 7.

Given Rowan Atkinson's scientific outlook on life, it is surprising that it wasn't until the 90s that he actually applied this analytical sensibility to comedy as a whole rather than just the making of his own comedy. In 1992 the balance was redressed when his production company made, in association with Showtime in America and TV3 in New Zealand, the six-part series *Funny Business*, which the BBC started transmitting on 22 November. This was a serious documentary series about the world of humour that looked at all sorts of different comedic genres. It was also a chance for Atkinson to theorize about his own heroes in between sending up this self-same academic approach by appearing as both a professor and his bright-green lycra-leotarded demonstrator Kevin Bartholemew. Atkinson, assisted by Robin Driscoll and Felicity Montagu, appeared only in the first episode. The programme, directed by David Hinton who co-wrote it with Atkinson and Robin Driscoll, had some difficulty straddling genres. Docu-comedy would be the best way to describe it.

On the one hand, it appeared to be a spoof lecture – presented by a greying, made-up Rowan Atkinson M.Sc. (Oxon), in a green corduroy jacket and waistcoat ensemble, from the Benjamin P. Hill (Benny Hill?) Memorial Library in the city of dreaming spires; but on the other hand, it also seemed to be a genuine attempt to get to the very root of the nature of visual comedy. Atkinson in academic mode, for instance, wondered why Charlie Chaplin was no longer popular while W.C. Fields continued to thrive. Chaplin – a primitive pratfalling precursor of Bean – peddled a kind of innocence that was no longer fashionable, while Fields – in some ways a role model for the various incarnations of Blackadder – tapped into a vein of self-centred cynicism that had become part of the British psyche in the Thatcherite late 80s.

Atkinson was typically modest about the enterprise, suggesting that it was not a comedy thesis to end all comedy theses, merely six films with comedy as their subject. They were not attempting to be the last word in comedy documentaries. Each one had a different style and his opening lecture was basically a serious documentary in an ironic style. In fact it owed some of its style to the corporate Video Arts films he had written and starred in a decade earlier – this was also an educational training film, but the business it was tackling was the funny business.

Although in name the executive producer of the entire series, Atkinson concentrated his efforts on getting his own film right. There were obvious contrasts between visual comedy and verbal comedy, and less obvious ones too. Atkinson believed that visual comedy came from deep within; compared with spoken comedy it was more essential, more honest. He sang the praises of one of his idols when promoting the programme and played down his own mimetic skills at the same time: 'Peter Sellers was one of the greatest comedy performers ever, yet I think he only ever had one visual character, in *The Pink Panther*. Mr Bean is mine. I think I'll never find another one.' In fact Sellers, one of the first case studies of the documentary, was used to illustrate the way that visual gags are often as much a part of humour today as they were in the silent era. We saw him fall into water, fly through the air, come a cropper and generally show a facility for physical humour that few had been able to match in the intervening years. Except, perhaps, Atkinson.

The autobiographical elements of the documentary were unavoidable. It drew considerable source material from Atkinson's own career. Once again we saw the face-shaving sketch, the silent-piano-recital sketch and the making-coffee-in-the-mouth sketch. Although these were performed by 'Kevin Bartholemew', Bartholemew was another version of Atkinson, closer to Atkinson than Ron Anderson had been in *The Tall Guy*. The commentary also talked about Bartholemew in a way that devoted Atkinson watchers whose memories stretched back to the one-man mime troupe Alternative Car Park in *Not the Nine O'Clock News* would have instantly recognized. For Bartholemew, 'his body is his tool.'

While references to Peter Sellers and Jacques Tati were explicit nods to Atkinson's major influences (every now and again, Atkinson lit a pipe – another nod to Tati's perennial prop?), the choice of other clips also suggested Atkinson's much-admired antecedents. The programme would not have been complete without John Cleese as Basil Fawlty, slamming Manuel's head into the wall. In another clip Bartholemew was seen mocking a policeman by goosestepping behind him, but the high kicks did not recall Nazi totalitarianism so much as *Python*'s Ministry of Silly Walks and Cleese as Fawlty in full flight in the famous 'Germans' episode when he can contain his mixture of paranoia and xenophobia no longer and starts marching through the hotel, much to the displeasure and dismay of his Teutonic guests. And through Cleese, of course, we end up with Jacques Tati, whose legs seemed to have a mind of their own. The French clown had once said that, 'Film comedy is all a matter of legs.'

In some respects it was almost as if Atkinson's Visual Comedy lecture was giving away some of the trade secrets behind Mr Bean (and, at the same time lending some intellectual credibility to a character whom the chattering classes had yet to embrace in the way they had embraced Blackadder). This was particularly ironic, as *Bean* was transmitted on ITV and this was part of a BBC series. Atkinson revealed, for instance, his painstaking attention to detail when he pointed out that even the slightest of differences in outfits could make a difference to a character – as in the world of high fashion, you could sink or swim depending on the length of a trouser leg. Body language could also speak volumes. In demonstrating how to get the most out of the classic blocked hosepipe gag, Atkinson seemed to be putting into place the essential building blocks of Bean's character. There was the 'comedy of stupidity' – looking down a hosepipe and getting sprayed with water; 'aggressive attitude' – passing the blocked hose to a cute little girl so that she was soaked; and the 'crude attitude' – standing side-on to the camera so that it appears that you are urinating in public when in fact you are holding the hose at your side and watering some flowers. Bean, at varying times, possesses all these traits. Atkinson also observed that while some comedians used out-of-the ordinary props to create their visual comedy, it could also be done with banal household objects (demonstrated at the sink with a bar of badly behaved slippery soap). He could even have been asserting some kind of Bean manifesto when he suggested that 'the physical comedian is an alien. He comes from the other side of the looking glass.' It was a thesis that had certainly served Atkinson well over the last 15 years. Perhaps when his schoolfriends had described him as an alien they had actually done him a favour, bestowing an identity upon him that would prove to be an enduring one.

Atkinson may not have been a scholar of the silent-movie era, but he was certainly up to speed when it came to his favourites. As well as the inevitable Chaplin and director Mack Sennett and the lesser-known Hollywood genius Harry Langdon, he also showed clips of very early films by the French master George Méliès, whose visual tricks had been the basis for much movie magic over the years. A more recent example of screen magic combined Atkinson's beloved Ferraris and his two old chums Mel Smith and Griff Rhys Jones. In a sketch from their BBC series they played executives comparing security devices: Smith secured his car with a sophisticated electronic alarm; Rhys Jones made sure no one would steal his when he was away by pressing a button and turning it into a Robin Reliant. Video trickery made it change in a flash.

But historical expert or not, the references to Chaplin's perfectionism could have been references to Atkinson himself as he remarked how Chaplin would painstakingly reshoot scenes that seemed to be satisfactory to everyone else until he was happy with them. The same rigid, analytical approach was applied to the filming of *Mr Bean*. Ideas would be hatched before shooting began and then discussed on location. By the time the film crew turned up, the plot would already be rigidly mapped out on a storyboard, on which the antics of Mr Bean resembled cartoon capers out of a children's comic. It was up to Atkinson to make these pictures flesh and he went about the process with great care.

By now Atkinson was becoming something of an elder statesman in the comedy world, middle class and advancing towards middle age. Even those young Turks that had come up after him, such as French and Saunders or Mayall and Edmondson who had cropped up in *Blackadder*, were fast becoming part of the establishment. But continued success didn't seem to have made him any more outgoing and neither did it make him feel any closer to perfection. In May 1992 he made his discomfort and ambivalence about his profession clear in the *Sunday Express*: 'I don't mind the meetings and preparation before a programme but I can't stand the performing. Showbusiness is a sandwich with a vicious filling. Even though I hate the filling I like the sandwich.' Most tellingly, he called the quest for the perfect joke 'the disease of comedians'.

He was still looking at ways of knocking his film career into shape, but it seemed to have caused more problems than it was worth: it was so full of worries, thought Atkinson, the only reason to do it was to stretch yourself.' In desperation for the right cinematic vehicle maybe he would consider bringing back *Blackadder* for a feature-length escapade. He nearly donned leggings not for Blackadder, but for Mel Brooks, when there was talk that he might play the lead in the Hollywood director's Sherwood Forest spoof, *Robin Hood – Men in Tights*. It did not happen but it would have been an intriguing pairing; the seasoned American gag merchant had previously made one of Hollywood's few post-talkies films without dialogue – or at least almost without dialogue: in *Silent Movie*, Marcel Marceau, the voiceless mime artist, had the only line.

Trips to America a couple of times a year resulted in a lot of talk but fewer deals, but these trips were necessary to remind Hollywood that Atkinson existed. Having spent time in America, he was aware of a Los Angeles saying: 'To make money do TV, to make a reputation do film.' A brief appearance alongside Charlie Sheen in *Hot Shots! Part Deux*, made in California by Twentieth Century Fox, wasn't quite enough to establish his reputation, but at least it kept his face on the screen so that Hollywood knew he existed. Although this was a major movie, by his own admission it was hardly a major role. In his regular column in *Car* magazine Atkinson discussed the American love affair with automobiles and his role in *Hot Shots!*: 'And when I say tiny I mean tiny – if you ever see the film, don't blink.'

It was a bizarre role for Atkinson, to say the least, with very little to connect it to any of his previous work. *Hot Shots! Part Deux* was the latest film from Jim Abrahams, best known for his work on the *Naked Gun* cycle with the Zucker brothers, which played equally fast and loose with the American police force. (Coincidentally, Atkinson's long-time collaborator John Lloyd directed the highly successful series of Red Rock beer commercials loosely inspired by the films and starring the same actor Leslie Neilsen.) Like the *Naked Gun* films, *Hot Shots* was peppered with sight gags, but unlike the kind seen in *Mr Bean*. These were quickfire post-modern jokes, often spewed out at blink-and-you'll-miss-it speed, but at other times they did share a sense of childishness with *Mr Bean*. Often the film would play around with scale and the cinematic conventions of special effects and set-pieces. For instance, a military helicopter landed and then turned out to be a tiny toy helicopter. Two protagonists had a sword fight in the manner of Errol Flynn and Basil Rathbone; as their shadows continued to duel, the characters could be seen in the foreground taking a breather. And one point their swords became *Star Wars*-style light-sabres. The film was very silly, but also remarkably cine-literate – even the Gallic title was a nod to the French *cinéaste* tradition, though Jacques Tati did not warrant a mention.

Atkinson played Dexter Hayman, a British soldier who had been taken hostage in the Middle East. The leader of the country, complete with thick moustache and army outfit, was a dead ringer for Saddam Hussein, but the film-makers weren't about to make a fragile political relationship even more fragile by naming him Hussein. However, this was a decidedly dodgy tinpot dictator. The film kicked off with a botched assassination attempt when a crack regiment attempted to kill him in bed and only succeeded in chasing him around in his nightshirt. With Hayman being held hostage and an American election looming, President Tug Benson (Loyd Bridges) needed to boost his popularity. His advisers suggested that a daring rescue mission would do just the trick (Jimmy Carter had attempted the same thing for real in the 70s). The star of the original *Hot Shots*, heroic Rambo-clone Topper Harley, played by Sheen with rippling muscles and matching hair, was called in to do the job. Eventually, after countless corny sight gags and surreal *trompe l'oiles*, Hayman is rescued by Harley. In Atkinson's only really significant speech in the film he comes over all heroic and, his voice cracking with pain, says that he can't leave: 'I can't walk …' It sounds as if he has been brutally tortured. '… They've tied my shoelaces together.' The joke, now up and running, as it were, continues to the end of the film.

Not possessing the intelligence to cut the shoelaces, Harley carries Hayman back to the chopper and freedom. But along the way it soon transpires that Hayman is a pretty difficult cove. He complains about the quality of the local drinking water and gets fussy about Harley's sweatiness and the way he is carrying him. Hayman is a vain, difficult and cynical monster who is maybe not that far removed from Black-adder after all. Instead of thinking about getting back to his wife, all he can think about is becoming a celebrity and being invited onto daytime chat shows. Eventually Harley and Hayman reach the rest of their group where his wife, Ramada Rodham Hayman (Valeria Golino), awaits him. Unfortunately she falls for Harley and Hayman, shuffling backwards to take a picture of them in order to illustrate his escapades when he appears on Oprah Winfrey's show, topples off the edge of the cliff.

It certainly was not the kind of film that would make Atkinson a name in America, given that the style of humour was so far removed from his own; but at the same time, the very fact that he could be cast in what was a lightweight but big-time film showed that he was making tentative inroads. Minor inroads admittedly, but inroads nonetheless.

Amid the speculation about a *Blackadder* revival, there was no stopping the strange, mute clot known as Mr Bean, who slept with a teddy bear by his side. *The Diary of Mr Bean* (Boxtree, 1992) written by Atkinson and Robin Driscoll, was at the top of the bestsellers list, when another Atkinson nearly stole Rowan's thunder. His older brother Rodney Atkinson made the papers when according to press reports he accused Foreign Secretary Douglas Hurd of undermining the British constitution in his dealings with the Maastricht Treaty. In a declaration that sounded like a tirade rejected during a *Blackadder* script conference, Rodney claimed Hurd had flouted the 1795 Treason Act. Political commentators wryly wondered whether he would call for the death penalty to be invoked. To date, however, Douglas Hurd has yet to be thrown into the tower or beheaded.

At this point it seemed as if *Mr Bean* was set to conquer the world, unless, of course, something happened to stop Atkinson from making more episodes. There was a small scare in October 1992, during filming the seventh and eighth instalments of *Mr Bean*. After the sixth take during which he had to put a suitcase onto a reception desk Atkinson felt a pain in his neck. He was filming again within 48 hours, but he was careful to take things easy for the next few weeks. The part was so physically taxing that it wasn't even clear what had precipitated the injury. There was something about Bean's peculiar posture that could put a strain on the actor's well-being. Every movement was based around the neck, which had to remain perfectly still. If Atkinson was not in good physical shape it would be difficult to continue. The very nature of Bean being off-beam meant that becoming him was at odds with Atkinson's normal posture. Fortunately the sporadic nature of the shows meant that over the course of time the recording was a fairly low impact and there were months off during which he could relax. Then again, he was approaching 40 and he could not be Bean for ever.

It clearly wasn't a serious injury though. In the middle of October he appeared on ITV's *The Des O'Connor Show* in character to promote *The Diary of Mr Bean* and the latest videos and then on the children's Saturday morning show *Live and Kicking* where he created havoc. These Bean appearances were a great advantage for Atkinson. He was becoming increasingly reluctant to do interviews and talk about himself but by sending this half-witted alter ego on his behalf he was able to get exposure without actually exposing himself. A couple of years later he appeared on the daytime ITV magazine *This Morning with Richard and Judy* in character again – not only did he not have to talk about himself, but once again he was like a walking bumbling advert for whichever *Mr Bean* spin-off he was promoting at the time.

On *The Des O'Connor Show* most guests have to give some of themselves away in order to promote their product. But Atkinson was able to come on as Mr Bean (the other main guest that week was Pavarotti), carrying a plastic bag and a polaroid camera and leave without breaking the illusion. Bean did speak however, explaining to O'Connor that he was nervous because when he saw how many people there were in the audience he realized he did not have enough biscuits to go round. We did get a little insight into Mr Bean's private life. He confessed that his hobbies were 'newts and country dancing'. It contrasted dramatically with the previous time Atkinson had encountered Des O'Connor on television. It had been a decade earlier and they had both been guests on Michael Parkinson's show. Back then they both reminisced happily about their early days in show-business. He had been guarded in the late 80s, but the muted critical response to Mr Bean – very much at odds with its commercial success – had made him more wary of the press than ever.

In the early 90s, Atkinson settled into family life. His wife gave birth to a boy and a girl, Ben and Lily. Parenthood may have been part of the inspiration behind *Mind the Baby, Mr Bean*, in which our intrepid hero's Mini hooks a pram and he finds himself lumbered with a baby at the seaside (Southsea, to be precise). The nappy gags virtually wrote themselves and the cute setpieces flew thick and fast. Bean looked at this new addition and – selfish at the best of times – decided he wasn't going to let it spoil his day, choosing to go on the rides regardless. Eventually he buys some balloons, straps them to the buggy and the baby flies away. Using his initiative he shoots the balloons and the baby falls – landing just where a relieved mother finds it. Sometimes Bean's mischief could result in good, but then he had got the baby into the mess in the first place.

It was an episode where comedy and tragedy became uncomfortable bedfellows. *Mind the Baby, Mr Bean* was scheduled to be transmitted on 17 February 1993, but this was the week that three-year-old Jamie Bulger was abducted and murdered in Liverpool. Sensing that the disappearance of an infant in a fictional programme might still be sensitive, the edition was postponed for over a year, until 25 April 1994. Fortunately an innocuous edition, *Mr Bean in Room 426* had been completed for later transmission and was rushed out in the allotted slot. In this episode, Bean has an altercation with the guest in an adjoining room, runs down a corridor naked and ends up doing some cross-dressing. There was also a cameo from veteran drag artiste Danny la Rue.

At times it could be formulaic but that didn't stop *Mr Bean* from being funny. It was clearly crafted with care and a huge amount of attention. Even when it wasn't totally original – a gag, for instance, in which Bean has to go out of the room with the television aerial to get a good picture was remarkably similar to a joke done on Hancock 30 years earlier – Atkinson's contorted comical features made it funny. *Bean* was the comedy of embarrassment at its best, whether it was getting his finger stuck in his zip or getting his head stuck inside a turkey in *Merry Christmas Mr Bean*.

It was a character that could extract humour from almost any situation. This was put to good use during the 1993 Comic Relief evening when Mr Bean took part in a special one-off edition of *Blind Date with Cilla Black*. As he larked about and made a fool of himself on his stool the audience laughter made the woman, 'Tracey', on the other side of the screen think he was the most attractive choice and inevitably selected him. But when the screen pulled back so that they could finally see each other, the viewer might have expected her to shy away. Instead it was Bean who refused to kiss Tracey. The path of true love was clearly not going to run smoothly. In an echo of *Rowan Atkinson Presents ... Canned Laughter* we see the date that followed, a success for him, if not for her.

But by 1993 there seemed to be no stopping this quirky, annoying everyman. The inclusion of videos in airline in-flight entertainment packages had helped to make *Bean* a global success. The ubiquitous *Mr Bean* episodes had become the lingua franca of international travel. The success of the character could in part be put down to the growth in long-haul travel and the desperate need for family-orientated in-flight entertainment. Where other shows had to be either subtitled or edited, *Mr Bean* fit the bill so perfectly it seemed as if it had been made with mass airline consumption in mind. In fact, such was Atkinson's all-round popularity that even the *Blackadders* began to make regular on-board appearances. This did, however, cause unexpected problems. According to Richard Curtis, speaking to *Cult TV* magazine, Atkinson has never watched *Blackadder*. When they were travelling it inevitably turned up on the in-flight channel and Curtis tried to make him watch it, but Atkinson gave up after just 15 minutes because he was so self-conscious.

Even when his programmes weren't on television, Atkinson's profile was still constantly high because of his accident-prone Richard Latham in the Barclaycard ads. In May 1994, having previously set a rug alight, smashed a wedding gift and set off the emergency alarms on a diplomat's visit, he now ejected his MI7 boss from his Aston Martin.

The Aston Martin element was a nod to James Bond, but it was also a nod to Atkinson's own penchant for the brand. Over the years he had had four Aston Martins, picking up his first one, a red V8 with a honey-beige hide, when he was 26. He had had a less happy time with the next one, a Vantage. Then there was the Zagato, and finally the Virage – Atkinson became the proud owner of the tenth one to be produced in February 1990. Aston Martin owners were indeed a rare breed. Atkinson had once been at an owner's gathering where, as well as realizing he was one of the poorest people in the room, he also realized he was one of the most normal. One man he met said he only used his V8 Vantage to travel from Leeds to London to have his nails manicured at Harrods. Another explained how he used his to travel to the south of France, but never went alone – he always took a giant teddy bear in a Union Jack T-shirt. Maybe he was a Mr Bean fan. By comparison, someone who played a silent imbecile for a living seemed rather conventional.

Latham meant Atkinson needed more room on the awards shelf: when BAFTA created a new award for ads, he was the first person to scoop it, alongside Maureen Lipman, who got her gong for her enduring British Telecom ads. The Barclaycard ads also revealed just how much Atkinson loved his cars. Director John Lloyd once recalled that when filming an ad in New York he wanted Atkinson to look all wistful and romantic. He suggested that he think about his wife Sunetra, who was standing nearby. Sunetra, on the other hand, told him to think of his Aston Martin. Atkinson did as he was told and according to Lloyd produced just the kind of lovestricken look the scene required.

Atkinson's familiar profile was less prominent when he voiced the bird Zazu in Disney's *The Lion King*, spending the summer of 1993 working on it in London. With a large beak and deep set eyes, Zazu seemed to have been created with Atkinson in mind. It was a classic comic sidekick that Disney films seemed to specialize in. Zazu was the faithful retainer of the old king and the young prince Simba, but when the evil brother snatched the throne in a manner not a million miles from Hamlet, Zazu had to adapt quickly. Appearing in a cartoon found Atkinson in good company acting alongside Jeremy Irons and Whoopi Goldberg and singing, with Jason Weaver and Laura Williams, the jaunty 'I Just Can't Wait to Be King'. He was beginning to choose his film work carefully now, becoming more cautious about his celluloid outings: 'I don't want to take so many risks. It is better to make no films than bad films.'

With *The Lion King* this superstar managed to maintain his anonymity. The children watching it in their droves may have also had *Mr Bean* videos on their shelves, but since Atkinson hardly spoke in Bean they would have been unlikely to recognize Atkinson's voice.

At the London premier on 6 October 1994, the stars were out in force. If the cast of *The Lion King* was diverse, the audience was even more eclectic. Boy George sang its praises; golfer Nick Faldo chipped in; Richard Branson raved about the movie; and Sylvester Stallone seemed overwhelmed by the production. Atkinson was present with Sunetra, but it was left to his erstwhile straight man Angus Deayton to pay tribute when interviewed by Carlton Television: 'It's worth seeing just to see, or hear, Rowan Atkinson singing alone.'

The trajectory may have been an odd one, but Atkinson had parlayed his unusual talents into a film career. It was an area where, unlike live performance, he could not exercise as much control as he would have liked. With his live work and television he had worked predominantly with close friends. Films had been a tougher prospect. *The Tall Guy* had been the only time that he had really been among people he knew well on a film set, and even *The Tall Guy* had originally started out as a film for London Weekend Television. Hollywood was a monster that it was hard to beat, but he and Curtis were about to come up with a David that could take on Goliath.

The reviews may have been variable, but there was no denying that *Four Weddings and a Funeral*, released in 1994, was a hit. Written by Richard Curtis it went on to become the most successful British film to date. If the film made Hugh Grant a bankable star in America, Atkinson's part as the tongue-tied trainee vicar Gerald was more in keeping with his cinematic cameos of the past, but it still upped his profile in America to a degree hitherto only hoped for. *Four Weddings* was a very grown-up, mature affair. Where in the past Curtis had given parts to chums and had just stuck a moustache on them, here there was a rigorous selection process; but we can safely assume that Rowan was the best person for his part, given that it had been written with him in mind. As for the screenplay, Curtis had toiled over it for years, drawing inspiration from the countless nuptials he had found himself attending in his early thirties.

Some people suggested that *Four Weddings and a Funeral* was little more than a succession of sketches – there was even a rumour that an early cut was deemed *too* funny. One scene was reputedly cut just for this reason. One scene that did appear in the final movie was actually written by Richard Curtis for *Mr Bean*. This was the scene in which Hugh Grant has to hide behind a curtain in the hotel room while the newly weds make love on the bed. One could imagine Mr Bean getting into this scrape, but maybe not at 8pm on ITV. But it was no surprise that the final edit was a big hit. It seemed to tap into the American love of British misfits that had made *A Fish Called*

Wanda such a success (like *Wanda*, and *The Tall Guy*, it had Anglo-American leads) and it had a dashing romantic hero at the heart of it. In retrospect how could it fail?

Atkinson had always resisted this sort of freakish part in the past – the kind that might have been offered to John Cleese or Dudley Moore – but given that his friend had written it he could hardly turn it down. Presiding over the marriage ceremony of Bernard and Lydia, Gerald found that nerves soon got the better of him: their names were mispronounced; they were blessed in the name of the father, the son and the holy goat; and the holy spiggot was on hand to greet Bernard's awful wedded wife. The ceremony may have been a disaster, but the film could hardly have done Atkinson's Hollywood prospects any harm.

It was an unusual project and, at first glance it seemed like an unusual director. Mike Newell was not known for his comedy work. Among other films, he had been responsible for bringing Miranda Richardson into the public eye in *Dance with a Stranger*. But back in 1968 he had made a television version of the Jack Rosenthal story, *Ready When You Are Mr McGill*, which was something of a comic masterpiece, so there was a lot of confidence in Newell. The success of *Four Weddings* came after a hitch in the financing, which caused a delay, but in the end these gave Curtis a chance to make sure the script was just so – and the casting too, since in the end everyone had to be auditioned twice.

Four Weddings was a success because it had an honesty and integrity to it. In the same way that *The Tall Guy* echoed Richard and Rowan's Camden Town years, *Four Weddings* reflected the fact that they were moving up in the world and that most of their friends were in their early 30s and getting married – at least they were in their early 30s when the project was first thought up – they were pushing 40 now. This didn't stop them from being surprised at its success, particularly in America. When the producers, Working Title, had projected global figures they reputedly had zero dollars by the American column.

While it worked as a film, it had all the winning hallmarks of Curtis's triumphant television work. In the same way that Baldrick would constantly come up with cunning plans, so Curtis employed the device of having four weddings just so that he could make the same marriage gags over and over again with slight variants. Likewise Hugh Grant's character constantly said 'fuck' and Rowan's Father Gerald kept botching his lines. It was that comic trick of repeating things but making them bigger each time. Now the next challenge was to make Rowan Atkinson's career even bigger.

It was a challenge, however, that Atkinson would have to meet, in part, without Curtis. While they continued to collaborate and develop a movie vehicle for Mr Bean, Curtis was becoming busy elsewhere. In November 1994, his new series, *The Vicar of Dibley*, starring Dawn French, started on BBC1. It seemed to have all the traits of the classic British sitcom, much in the way *The Thin Blue Line* would a year later. French was the new vicar in a quaint country parish populated by a collection of eccentrics and idiots who made Baldrick look like a rocket scientist. If it was not for the fact that the situation in this situation comedy was based around the reluctance of a traditional parish to accept a female vicar, it would have been easy to imagine Atkinson in the role. After all, with the assistance of Richard Curtis he had been portraying comedy clergymen for nearly 20 years. In March 1999, Curtis explained to the magazine *Broadcast* his reasons for writing the role, reasons that could just as easily have applied to the vicars that Atkinson had played, from the vicar who did not know what fellatio was, right through to Father Gerald: 'I'm interested in the comedy of the awkwardness of goodness. For most of us the funny things happen when we try to be nice to people, to accommodate our little fibs and smooth things over in embarrassing situations.' There was also the additional fact that comedy often came out of confinement, and what could be more confining than a dog collar. Apart from, maybe, an Englishman such as Atkinson in a dog collar?

Over the years Atkinson had very shrewdly been able to combine his love of cars with his career. He had written for *Car* magazine, talked about vehicles on *The Driven Man* for ITV, and had been in an Aston Martin for Barclaycard. He was also able to combine his passion when he played great British eccentric Sir Henry 'Tim' Birkin in *Full Throttle*, part of the BBC series *Heroes and Villains*, made by Tiger Aspect and directed by Mark Chapman, who had also worked on *The Driven Man*. The drama was transmitted on 2 February 1995 and it found Atkinson sampling the delights of some classic old racing cars, Bentleys in particular. It was a fairly straight role, but it was clearly the cars as much as the chance to stretch himself artistically that was the main attraction. Speaking to *The Guardian* in 1997, Chapman elaborated: 'Rowan's very placid and easy, a real gentleman, but he is a very fast driver ... One of the big attractions was that he got to train up on an old Bentley – nothing very dangerous but he drove it round a circuit at high speeds.'

As Atkinson explained at the programme's press launch, he had come across the story because Sir Henry Birkin was an ancestor of one of the directors of *Mr Bean*, John Birkin. Having heard about this strange chap who was part of society but who refused to conform, it rang bells with Atkinson: 'I love all things intrinsically English and there is something terribly British about eccentricity. Sadly there is not enough of it around these days.' Birkin had spent his fortune on a racing career after the First World War but had died in a particularly eccentric and tragic way. After the 1933 Tripoli Grand Prix he fancied a cigarette and, leaning out of the car to light it, he burnt his arm on the hot exhaust pipe. According to the film he thought nothing of it at the time. But blood poisoning set in and three weeks later he died.

Dramatized by Kit Hesketh-Harvey, *Full Throttle* had its light moments, but essentially this was Atkinson's first straight dramatic role on television and his first dramatic role anywhere since his stage forays in the mid-80s. But Sir Henry Birkin was relatively easy to play because Atkinson could approach Birkin's genuine eccentricities as if they were comic tics. The story takes the form as flashbacks. Birkin decides to have his autobiography ghost-written; he needs the money (he doesn't seem that broke, but he does have expensive tastes) and invites a young writer up to his Norfolk estate to take notes. The journey there is a hair-raising trip from Mayfair – Birkin has a rule that if he can get to the Norfolk border in an hour he is allowed to treat himself to eggs and bacon in a cafe. Together they mull over possible titles for his story: 'Driving Force', 'Spinning Wheels' and 'Racing Demon'. As his story unfolds, it soon becomes apparent that he is certainly driven by demons to take risks and go further than anybody else. In the First World War he flew Sopwiths with his two brothers. Afterwards he could not face office life, or working for his father's lace business, he preferred 'living in the shadow of death' – an unspoken contrast with Atkinson, who chose the less life-threatening adrenaline rush of performance over a technical life, or working for his father's farming business.

Birkin was certainly Atkinson's most seriously romantic character to date. There was even a bona fide bedroom scene with his wife Audrey, though Atkinson did have pink and white striped pyjamas on at the time. But Birkin's marriage did not last. He put shooting and cars before Audrey and she finally walked out on him. Having semi-retired he then returned to the racing circuit and made up for lost time, winning at Brooklands and later at Le Mans. Meanwhile, his father (Geoffrey Palmer in a very fetching tweed suit) still wanted him to join the family business – 'Can you not see the excitement in lace?' he pleaded. But the chances of Birkin following his father were about as high as the chances of Atkinson giving up comedy for farming.

Sometimes Birkin's heroics just seemed to have come straight out of a *Boy's Own* adventure comic. In one race at Le Mans his Bentley got a puncture from a horseshoe nail. Three miles from the pits the wheelrim collapsed. Birkin had refused to carry a jack because he wanted his car to be as light as possible, so he now had to run all the way to the pits to get help – hitching a lift would have got him disqualified and he had to complete the course to qualify for the following year. Eventually the car was repaired and he finished, beating lap records in the process.

But like Atkinson and his work, Birkin could be obsessive about his racing. He developed his own turbocharged car – the Blower Bentley – to compete with Mercedes. In the final showdown, Birkin's Bentley is used as a sacrificial pacemaker. After much jostling for position with the Germans it develops a fault and Birkin has to pull out; but further down the road the Mercedes breaks down too. Birkin claims it as a moral and technical victory over both the Germans and the British racing establishment and declines a desk job with Bentley, preferring to become a driver for hire. This, however is his downfall. He got a letter of congratulations from Mussolini after winning a race in an Alfa Romeo, but Tripoli soon followed. There he drove a Maserati and he leaned out thinking there was a rail there as there was in the Bentley. Instead he touched the red-hot exhaust. The frame froze, as it had done at the end of *Blackadder IV*.

Apart from cars, the parallels between Birkin and Atkinson were pretty thin on the ground. Both like the fine things of life, but where Birkin took risks that put his life in danger, Atkinson's risks barely even put his career in danger. *Mr Bean* might have gone against the grain of British contemporary comedy but you would be hard-pressed to call Atkinson a maverick. Each step had been shrewdly thought through, from opting for the ensemble comedy of *Not the Nine O'Clock News* to trying out Mr Bean at the Just For Laughs Festival. What they did both share was a tremendous focus, though even there they differed. Birkin thought about cars 24 hours a day. Atkinson was obsessive at work, but at home he was able to unwind. You might not even realize Rowan Atkinson earnt his living as a comedian if you saw him pottering about at home. Birkin never pottered.

There was another contrast between them. Where Birkin had been determined to outwit the Mercedes, Atkinson had, after some faltering preludes, actually been bowled over by them. In the summer of 1992 he had bought a Mercedes 500E. It was his third foray into the company. He had first bought that odd overlong 600, which he had promptly sold within the month, having, as he explained in *Car* magazine in November 1992, 'discovered what it's like to become Pope and then be told that you have to drive yourself around (it's embarrassing)'. He had then bought a 450 SEL 6.9 and this was the natural follow-on motor, fulfilling his requirements of a car that was very fast, very rare and very discreet. With one difference though. This was a left-hand-drive model – and he picked it up for £17,000 less than list price because it had done 900 miles. Perhaps left-hand drive appealed to him. It did mean that when parking in places where he might be noticed by the public, he could get out on the pavement side and disappear into a building rather than have to walk round the car to reach his destination.

Cars were Atkinson's true love and whenever he took time off from filming it was a fair bet that he would be under one or in one. He was able to indulge his passion on the race-track in real life as well as in *Full Throttle*. He had taken the Mercedes for a spin around the Bruntingthorpe circuit, where its performance could be tested under various conditions and against the clock.

By 1995 though, he was looking for a different car to add to his collection. After 14 years of almost continual ownership of an Aston

Martin – as well as various other cars – he opted for a new Ferrari 456GT. After deliberating over the colour scheme and finally opting for red leather, green carpet and green body, he ordered his car and waited. When he went to pick it up, he was surprised to discover that the dealer would only deliver the car against cleared funds, while Atkinson had expected to pay – a sum not unadjacent to £156,445 minus the deposit – by cheque. In the past his relationship with dealers when he had been buying Astons and Lancias had meant that his cheque was good enough. With Ferrari, however, company policy meant that things were not that simple. But he did finally pick the car up in October 1995. It was everything he had hoped for – except that he would have preferred an old-style steering wheel without an airbag and had been given the standard fitting, but he eventually grew to like it. It seemed like the perfect car for a spin in the country, though some country residents did not see it that way. On one trip he hit a pheasant that had been crossing the road, presumably under the misapprehension that it was a chicken. Writing about the incident in *Car*, Atkinson reassured himself that it was a quick, painless death: 'The speed was such that it could not have suffered. At least not physically. It might, on reflection, have regretted some of its pension contributions, but otherwise it went without pain.'

By 1995, *Mr Bean* had outstripped the commercial popularity of *Blackadder*. It had become the bestselling video ever, selling 600,000 copies in two months in Germany alone, and the programme had been sold to 82 countries to date. In England, though, the fan bases of the two series seemed almost mutually exclusive, divided by class and age. In *The Sunday Times* Atkinson tried to explain why *Bean* was ignored by the chattering classes: 'It's because it has no intellectual conceit or irony or subtext whatsoever. It's the sheer manifestness of it, I think, which is sort of irritating to those who tend to look for more depth in comedy.'

Even Atkinson would have to admit that depth was the one thing lacking in this comedy dumb show. Part of the success of *Mr Bean* was lucky timing; part of the success was comic genius. Atkinson had realized years ago that the secret of international success was coming up with an act that would work as well in Cairo as in Croydon. It was very much a case of 'No verbal jokes please, we don't speak English.' *Bean* was following this rubric with unprecedented success, appealing to all nations regardless of language and all ages too. It was a truly worldwide hit, arguably the biggest British sitcom ever.

Atkinson was not really surprised at the success of *Mr Bean*. He had always had faith in the character and faith in the notion of purely visual comedy, even though it was very much at odds with the kind of comedy that usually appeared on television. There had been the occasional stabs at silent comedy in the past (*The Plank*, with Eric Sykes, and *Futtocks End*, with Ronnie Barker), but television was very much regarded as a verbal medium. Which was odd really, since radio ought to be the verbal medium and television ought to be the visual medium.

What really bemused Atkinson about *Mr Bean*, though, was the way it had drawn in precisely the demographic that had missed out on *Blackadder*, in terms of both age and class. It seemed to be the very young and the very old who went for *Bean*, an audience that had never really taken to Atkinson in a big way until now. *Blackadder*, on the other hand, had followed *The Young Ones* as the top student cult sitcom – but it had also been a major ratings success with the rest of the population between the ages of 15 and 50. *Blackadder* was hip, post-watershed and BBC1; *Bean* was as square as you would expect from a sitcom that went out on ITV at 8pm. *Blackadder* fans seemed to miss the verbal wit and would never forgive Atkinson for killing off their hero. As far as Atkinson was concerned, Britain was now a divided nation. There was even a class division too, with *Bean* appealing broadly to a working-and upper-class audience, whereas *Blackadder* was very much a kind of middle-class centred programme because of its metaphors and allegories.

What really annoyed Atkinson was when critics wrote off *Bean* as a poor facsimile of comics from Hollywood's silent age. When *Mr Bean* had first come out there had been a review that described it as 'rehashed Harold Lloyd'. Yet at the time Atkinson barely knew who Harold Lloyd was; about all he knew was the famous still of a man in glasses hanging from a clock, so he certainly could not have been in a position to be plagiarist. On the other hand, his major influence, Jacques Tati, was inspired by the silent pioneers, so there clearly was a lineage, but Mr Bean was no mere Anglicized, updated Monsieur Hulot. He was a much more contemporary product. His nastiness seemed to have the whiff of Thatcherism about it. Hulot was benign;

Bean was vindictive. At the end of the day of course, there are just only so many silent gags one can do and maybe Atkinson was drawing on this limited source and putting Bean's own spin and twist on them. It was interesting to notice that despite the endless scrapes he got into he was never physically injured. He doesn't even get a custard pie in the face, but the people around him suffer the effects of his actions. Look back at most silent comics and they were invariably the butt of physical disasters.

In some ways Atkinson was now so close to Bean it was hard to spot the join enough to talk about influences. Atkinson had lived with variants of Mr Bean, for over 12 years now. Making new programmes he learnt more about Bean and refined him. It was like throwing mud at a wall. The team would see what would stick and hopefully each time they made a programme more would stick.

After taking a creative back seat during the writing process of *Blackadder*, Atkinson had more input with *Bean*. It seemed to be the kind of comedy that came most naturally to him. The original live material had been written in tandem with Richard Curtis, and now Robin Driscoll contributed to the television version. The beauty of *Mr Bean* was the fact that it was an occasional series and, therefore, never outstayed its welcome. Its fans didn't tire of it and its star found the time to diversify. The very last episode of 14 (one was a video-only release), 'Goodnight Mr Bean', was transmitted on 30 October 1995. There was talk of doing a film, but there was a question mark over whether Atkinson would do any more helpings of Bean for television. Richard Curtis wouldn't discount anything. The answer depended upon one man, he explained, and funnily his answer echoed the title of Atkinson's very first film appearance: 'It's up to Rowan, but you can never say never again.'

As a brilliant physical comic he could always make it funny – even if it took ages in rehearsals for him to be happy with his performance – but after five years it seemed to have stopped developing. It came as no surprise then to hear that Mr Bean was to be put on ice for a while so that Atkinson could work on an all-new comedy with Ben Elton.

12

Copper-Bottomed Success

For someone who is an intensely private man, Rowan Atkinson had made a habit of not staying out of the limelight for too long. The very first *Mr Bean* was transmitted within two months of the last *Blackadder* but the launch of his third television persona came even more quickly. Within two weeks of the transmission of the thirteenth *Mr Bean*, Atkinson made his television début as Inspector Raymond Fowler in *The Thin Blue Line*. After a cynic and an idiot, Atkinson was now a back-to-basics idealist, albeit a rather bumbling one. But two questions remained: could he ever be as critically acclaimed as he was for *Blackadder*, and what would he be like without Richard Curtis contributing to the scripts?

To call *The Thin Blue Line* an all-new comedy when it first appeared at 8.30pm on 13 November 1995 seemed somewhat inaccurate. Broadly speaking it was *Dad's Army* in a police station with a non-pension-age cast. But look deeper and there were distinctive signs of both Elton and Atkinson's preoccupations. Atkinson had made a habit of shuttling between strict authority figures and sad pathetic creatures. If Mr Bean was one of the latter, Fowler was one of the former, although at times his authority was not as authoritative as he would like it to be.

Atkinson played Inspector Fowler with Mainwaringish pomposity and was surrounded by a supporting team of off-the-peg stereotypes, many played by actors who had worked in Atkinson-related projects before – the long-suffering girlfriend (Sgt Patricia Dawkins, played by Serena Evans), the oddball constable (PC Kevin Goody, James Dreyfus), the keen Asian (WPC Maggie Habib, Mina Anwar), the nostalgic veteran (PC Gladstone, Rudolph Walker, the *Love Thy Neighbour* veteran who had been in the very first *Mr Bean*). And in the same way that the *Dad's Army* platoon was in constant conflict with the air-raid patrol and the church where it used to meet, so Fowler's uniformed police were up against their own enemy within: their plain-clothed colleagues who thought they were in *The Sweeney* – DI Grim (David Haig, the moustachioed comic actor who had played one of the grooms in *Four Weddings and a Funeral*) and DC Kray (Kevin Allen, who left after the first series and had also had a small part in *Bernard and the Genie*) and Detective Boyle (Mark Addy) who joined for the second series before making it big in *The Full Monty*. It was no surprise that Ben Elton admitted that he was unashamedly trying to write a populist ensemble sitcom in the tradition of *Dad's Army*. Even Howard Goodall's jaunty whistled theme tuned seemed to be echoing police series of bygone days, *Dixon of Dock Green* in particular.

The Thin Blue Line marked the emergence of – some of the time at least – a new, stately Atkinson. He didn't even need to do any face-pulling. James Dreyfus, who played PC Goody, seemed to have taken on that mantle, contorting his features and limbs and constantly upstaging the rest of the cast, milking each laugh for its last drop. As Atkinson had learnt from his own hero John Cleese, there was little one can do in front of an audience that can get a big laugh as easily as a silly walk.

Inspector Raymond Fowler was another role that had elements of Atkinson running through it like letters through a stick of rock. Certainly his love of procedure and rules must have appealed to Atkinson's ordered mind. In the *Sun*, Atkinson admitted that he identified with his latest character and explained why: 'I liked the part immediately because Fowler is a man with some amusing contradictions. He has to live in the modern world but he wishes it was different. Fowler rings bells with me. I can identify with Fowler's point of view.'

He was less keen, however, on the innuendo, which seemed to be Elton's preoccupation. It always bubbled to the surface when he worked with Atkinson. It was Elton who introduced the single entendres into *Blackadder* and now he added a few double entendres here: 'I would like to meet the man who can get inside my trousers,' says

Fowler during a speech on how to avoid pickpockets. Nearly an entire episode seemed to be devoted to PC Goody's 'coming out' – the gag being that everyone in the police station thought it meant he was about to reveal that he was gay when in fact everyone watching at home knew that he meant he was going to come out for an after-hours drink with his colleagues.

The humour was strangely innocent, almost a throwback to the Ealing comedies or Will Hay, with not a sniff of post-modern irony to it. There was a tendency to look for meaning that probably was not there. Was the station in a place called Gasforth because Atkinson was born in Gosforth? Fowler's girlfriend, Sgt Dawkins, had once found him in bed with a model – the glue had stuck bits of balsa wood to the sheets (the chances of sex taking place seemed minimal. It was as if Fowler had been slipped some bromide during National Service and had developed a taste for it). *The Thin Blue Line* could be seen as a metaphor for Britain in the early 90s – multicultural and messed up – with Atkinson as the John Major figure, the kind of overgrown teenager who makes model aeroplanes and wears a vest under his pyjama jacket.

As had become the norm, scenes would be rehearsed endlessly until Atkinson felt he had got things right. He admitted he was a perfectionist and conceded that it wasn't always such a good thing: 'Perfectionism is more of a disease than a quality. It reduces you to a person who worries too much and that isn't healthy for anyone.' It was something of an achievement that this time round he was only 'healthily nervous' at the prospect of a new project that he considered, with typically English restraint, to be 'reasonably accomplished. That is not to say it will be popular. You just have to fling it up the flagpole and see if anyone salutes.'

Atkinson had sensibly stuck with someone whose writing he had confidence in, though critics might argue that this is indicative of a fundamental conservatism in his choice of projects – throughout his career he has invariably played safe, never gone out on a limb. At the launch of *The Thin Blue Line* he elaborated on the difficulties of constantly coming up with new ideas. 'It is always difficult to know what to do next. It's so much a matter of chance. There are hundreds of extremely talented actors but very few good writers, so we twiddle our thumbs until someone comes up with something suitable.' The only problem with Elton was the penchant for vulgarity. Atkinson would wince when he heard some of Elton's ideas, worrying about whether they were suitable for family viewing. Inspector Raymond Fowler would have probably had the same concerns. Atkinson was now a father of two in his 40s and his views on good and bad taste suggested he was rushing headlong into a mid-life crisis. He disagreed, but then in many respects he had always seemed middle-aged: 'I don't think I'm in any mid-life crisis, but your perspective shifts as you get into your 40s. Suddenly I have a different view than when I was doing *Not the Nine O'Clock News*.'

Inspector Fowler was the culmination of a succession of parts that had all reflected elements of either Atkinson's own personality or of the world he had grown up in. It was something he acknowledged himself in interviews to promote *The Thin Blue Line*: 'The common link between my parts is that they are establishment – soldiers, vicars, policemen ... which must relate significantly to my upbringing.' He had become a great portrayer of the establishment, but that didn't mean he took it too seriously. Even though he had been known to do readings in his local village church that didn't stop him from mocking the clergy. He had the good sense to know that there is something inherently funny as well as painful about being English and middle class: 'You can believe in the Establishment but, by gum, there's a lot to laugh at about it.'

The first series of *The Thin Blue Line* had a strange charm, but there was never quite the Ben Elton twist that one expected. Gasforth was like *Twin Peaks* without the perversity. The crimes that seemed to be committed could have almost been drawn from the pages of *Beano*, such was their innocence. And the police were about as far removed from the savage Constable Savage as you could imagine. In real life Goody, a man with a penchant for keeping Curly Wurly chocolate bars in his truncheon pocket, would surely have never made it through the rigours of Hendon Police College. Credibility was stretched even further by Fowler, who seems far too naive to be in command. When his student son Bill (named after Fowler's favourite television series) brings his girlfriend back, he thinks they are revising for exams together. Suddenly the cuddly satire of *Not the Nine O'Clock News* seemed like the cutting edge of comedy. In fact, just before *The Thin Blue Line* was launched, BBC had been screening reruns of Atkinson's first comedy series. Admittedly John Lloyd had edited the shows down and distilled them, but the best moments actually stood the test of time pretty well. There was a cynicism to them that the rest of the world had now caught up with. By contrast, *The Thin Blue Line* seemed to hark back to a non-existent golden age of character comedy, when everyone simply had their stock foibles and quirks and delivered them on cue.

Ben Elton, who less than ten years earlier had been the voice of youth, had now portrayed an extraordinarily romanticized view of young people. In 'Kids Today' the station set out to tackle juvenile crime – the answer was a short camping trip. Fowler as ever is amazed by the drink and drugs that are consumed nowadays. In his day, he adds, ecstasy was building a model of the Forth Bridge. This expedition did at least provide a brilliant cameo for Stephen Fry as veteran yomper Brigadier Blaster Sump, a man with a beard like dense foliage who, after giving the group a lecture, shoos them away by lifting up his kilt. The expedition does not work out though because the party absconds.

This was a world where master villains had names such as Terry the Tank. It would not have been a surprise if he turned up in a striped jersey and a mask, carrying a sack with the word Swag on it. In 'The Honeytrap' Fowler, a copper who always does things by the book, reluctantly agrees to the modern methods of the plain-clothed branch and lets Habib entrap Terry the Tank so that the case can be solved in time for her to join the rest of the pub quiz team. Unfortunately, through a typical set of crossed wires, Sgt Dawkins ends up thinking Fowler has made special arrangements because he is having an affair. The truth comes out though and it appears that Raymond and Patricia have been reconciled. The episode closes with him in bed saying, 'I love you, I love you, I love you.' Then the camera pulls back to reveal that he is saying it adoringly to the pub quiz trophy.

Crossed purposes seemed an easy way to get a laugh. In 'The Queen's Birthday Present' Fowler happened to be celebrating his tenth anniversary with Sgt Dawkins at the same time that the Queen was celebrating her birthday. Throw in PC Goody pursuing Habib and all the ingredients were there for a write-it-yourself comedy of errors. If there was any cynicism in this series it was a cynicism for modern life.

The first series of *The Thin Blue Line* received respectable reviews and respectable viewing figures but it was not a spectacular success. Like the first series of *Blackadder*, things did not seem to be in their right place. Surely PC Goody was gay – he was certainly camp. But if so, how was it that he was romantically pursuing PC Habib? And would partners really be allowed to work in the same police station? Possibly, but probably not when they were of different rank and probably not on the same shifts, which could have created problems for the plots if they were never seen together. And how did Fowler ever get promoted to the rank of Inspector anyway? The BBC was certainly confident about the series, having commissioned a Christmas special straight after the first run, but would the confidence be vindicated?

By the time the series had gone out there was clearly a sense that some tweaking was needed. The second series followed a year and a day after the first one and, sure enough, there had been some changes. The major change was moving the transmission time to 9.30pm. Once this had been done, everything else seemed to make more sense. Before the watershed it had just seemed too innocent: now Ben Elton had a bit more freedom. His scripts could tackle more serious subjects and use more realistic language. After a nervous beginning when there had been some doubts about the choice of Atkinson's career move, he seemed to have struck gold yet again. This was a new, confident Atkinson who had his own comic identity. There had never been any fears as there had been with *Blackadder* that doing something contemporary would make people compare it with *Fawlty Towers*; this time round it was following unashamedly in the footsteps of a situation comedy classic, but Atkinson felt he could compete with it.

It was an indication how the secret of sitcom is not the sit, but the com. There was certainly nothing new about the situation. There had been countless police station sitcoms in the past. In fact Robin Driscoll had been involved in one of the more recent attempt to crack this conundrum. He and other members of his theatre company Cliff Hanger had been responsible for *Mornin' Sarge*, which had one series on BBC2 in 1989 and followed the antics of a group of PCs and plain-clothed officers in Middleford Police Station. It too had the same ring of displaced innocence about it, but the chemistry was not quite there.

In Elton's second series the characters were still clichéd but seemed better at being clichéd. *The Thin Blue Line* seemed to have acquired ironic quote marks. In the middle of this, Atkinson, strangely, was playing it like a straight man. This seemed to get even more laughs than when he tried to be funny. In the manner of the police series *Dixon of Dock Green*, he started each edition of the second series at his desk with a little saying, which the episode would then proceed to act out.

In 'Ism Ism Ism', for instance, Fowler's introduction started with a little story and concluded with 'Appearances, as we shall see, are often like bus timetables, highly misleading'. It turns out to be a busy day in Gasforth. In a hi-tech nod to the movie *Rear Window*, it transpires that Sgt Dawkins thinks she has seen someone being attacked on the close-circuit television. At the same time there is a report that an illegal asylum seeker is in the town, a European Inspector is due to visit, as is a gay spokesman, and DI Grim is applying to join the local version of the Masons, the Todgers. As it turns out, the alleged beating is actually a meeting of the Todgers, the asylum seeker is in fact the diplomat, and the flamboyant visitor to the station (played by Melvyn Hayes of *It Ain't Half Hot Mum*) is not gay, but the chief Todger. Appearances have indeed proved to be deceiving.

In the process of lecturing his team on the evils of racism, however, Fowler does come up with one of the best scenes of the series, which also refers back to Atkinson's past work. When he mentions real police chief Paul Condon, Goody starts giggling because his name sounds like 'condom'; in a long-winded but very well-articulated allegory, Atkinson pretends to be an alien to show how racism occurs; and the rhyming expletive 'trucking tanker', a close cousin of Blackadder's 'clucking bell', is incorporated.

As with the first series, the theme of kids today being different to kids 30 years ago continued. In 'Alternative Culture,' Habib's sister Nazia comes to visit and turns out to be a user of cannabis. When the team raid a local rave and she is carrying it, PC Habib takes it off her sister only for one of DI Grim's sniffer dogs to catch Habib with the cannabis. It seems like nothing can save her. Fowler knows she is the best copper in the station but he does things by the book and she must be charged. Until, that is, Fowler is able to catch the plain-clothed mob drinking after hours. A deal is done so that both charges are dropped. In the end, the evidence is mistaken for a bovril cube and drunk by the notoriously tight-fisted visiting auditor, who promptly pays for the station's much-needed new toilets.

Elton did have a good way of weaving storylines together into a tight 30-minute script. In 'Come on You Blues', the constabulary has to police the local team's second round FA Cup match against Chelsea, and Fowler thinks that if things work out, this might put him in line for an MBE. Unfortunately the team fails to turn up – they have been arrested on the day of the match. In the Christmas special another mix-up involving presents means that PC Habib ends up with a puncture kit from PC Goody, and Sgt Dawkins – much to her evident delight – thinks she is going to get some sexy lingerie from Fowler. The subject may have been the police force, but maybe police farce was a better description.

When the second series had started, Ben Elton conceded in the *Radio Times* that it was hardly a ground-breaking departure, which, he claimed, was what would make it a success. While Atkinson thought the idea of a police station was pretty unoriginal, that was what attracted the writer to it: 'In comedy the obvious is often very good. You've got a vast wealth of background knowledge of television police stations that have gone before. You don't have to establish anything. It's just a sitcom full of completely flawed and fumbling but basically decent people.' He was eternally grateful that his old collaborator had agreed to choose his project out of the countless he was regularly offered. Others might have called Atkinson insecure or reluctant to take risks; working with Elton was another example of sticking with the people he knows – it could be said that the more successful he has become the less inclined he is to take a leap into the complete unknown – but fortunately for Atkinson his old colleagues also happen to be some of the most talented and creative people in the entertainment industry.

Some of Atkinson's older characters managed to make a slight return in less controversial style. In January 1997, the British Army's Combat Service Unit in Aldershot adopted a Blackadder motif for their flag, which flew proudly above their barracks. This minor triumph, however, paled into insignificance when news from America started to leak out. Behind the scenes bigger international deals than ever were being negotiated. The latest Tinseltown tittle-tattle was that Atkinson was being paid $4.5 million by a Hollywood studio to make a Mr Bean movie. Atkinson was certainly making waves in America. Following on from *Blackadder*'s cable success, *Mr Bean* was now building up a following on smaller channels over there. And in March 1996, Atkinson had appeared on the *Tonight Show with Jay Leno* and brought his career full circle by shocking a whole new audience with his ancient routine in which he put on his swimming costume without removing his trousers. He then whipped his trousers off in front of Leno and fellow guest David Duchovny of the *X-Files* to reveal a pair of tartan trunks. Luckily Frank Rich was not now working as a television critic or Atkinson's latest invasion might have been stopped in its tracks.

It was an old trick but one which went down a storm; a defining moment that cemented Atkinson's relationship with America. After the disappointments on Broadway he had become a player again. There was talk of his appearing as fellow northerner Stan Laurel in a biopic, gossip about his shows, acclaim as a cross between Benny Hill and Jim Carrey. The future was in Atkinson's hands.

13

Malice in Lalaland

While the ubiquitous rumour mills ground into action, the reality of a *Mr Bean* movie finally began to take shape in the summer of 1996. But it had been a long process. The idea had been floated for years. By 1993 it had actually got as far as the meetings stage. During this time Richard Curtis had come up with various scenarios in which Mr Bean could create havoc, and the one that seemed to stick was sending him to stay with an American family. By May 1995, Curtis set himself the task of writing a version. Working Title, the team behind both *The Tall Guy* and *Four Weddings and a Funeral*, were involved in the project, which was a good sign. Curtis's partner Emma Freud was due to give birth to their second baby in June so he knew he had a fairly fixed deadline. By the end of July the screenplay was in enough of a workable state to discuss it with Rowan Atkinson at Curtis's house in Oxfordshire. Unfortunately Atkinson had a number of criticisms, including concern over Mr Bean having a lot of dialogue. Suggestions were taken onboard and the script was passed on to collaborator Robin Driscoll. Driscoll promptly chopped out lots of dialogue and added more plot. The script had to be constantly fine-tuned for the big screen. Each element had to fit together as neatly and run as smoothly as the cogs in the gears of one of Atkinson's beloved Ferraris. Whereas the *Mr Bean* television series could be constructed in the rehearsal room, for the big screen the jokes came first and then the rehearsal period was used to work out how to link them all together.

By November this core trio was able to have a rehearsal, working through the results to date and numerous packets of biscuits. The outcome of this workshopping was more refinement to the script. Atkinson, who really had the final say, had been unhappy about elements in the past, but eventually a draft appeared that met with his approval. Insofar as a film can be said to be definitely happening, it was eventually all systems go.

It certainly made sense for Atkinson to opt for his own project. In the past he had joked that he had been a choice behind John Cleese and Dudley Moore, but in the Hollywood scheme of things in the 90s he was now also competing with established American stars such as stand-up comic turned hyperactive malleable family entertainer Robin Williams. If a script came to him he could usually work out who had rejected it. There had reportedly, for instance, been the possibility of a part in *The First Wives Club,* starring Diane Keaton, Goldie Hawn and Bette Midler, but Atkinson did not appear in it.

With Atkinson's old friend Mel Smith directing, filming started on *Mr Bean – The Ultimate Disaster Movie* on 1 September 1996. While Curtis stayed in London overseeing various other projects, Driscoll was on-set in America and very proud to have his own chair with his name on the back. Though Driscoll joked that he chose to sit in other chairs so that he did not obscure his name.

It was an ambitious project that took Mr Bean out of his basic bedsit environment and into another world entirely. He was now an attendant at the Royal National Gallery who, through a combination of good fortune, mistaken identity and the efforts of his superiors to get him out of the way, finds himself on a three-month sabbatical in Los Angeles, where he is believed to be Dr Bean, a Professor of Art. While there, he is supposed to present the inaugural speech marking the return of the great American portrait of Whistler's Mother to its native land from Paris.

In essence the story was a basic fish-out-of-water plot, the kind of thing that had inspired *Crocodile Dundee* in the 80s, but there was a lot more going on here. In *OK* magazine, Atkinson pointed out that the contrasting location was almost incidental: 'Mr Bean can find almost anything alien. Just a tap can be a problem, an enemy, a challenge.' He did acknowledge changes to the television incarnation: 'For the first time ever, Mr Bean takes responsibility for his own actions.' When his actions end in disaster he wants to make amends, 'which is a side of him we've never seen before.' Bean would be a fish out of water anywhere, but America provided some new opportunities for him to mess things up. In terms of the plot, this meant that there couldn't just be self-contained sketches strung together; each action would have a consequence for the storyline and unlike a cartoon, where damage would be magically rectified in the next sequence, here it was all for real. Insofar, that is, as a movie could be real.

For the movie incarnation, Bean would be a more three-dimensional character. He spoke a little, he had a date of birth, 15 September 1956, and there was even the possibility of giving him a first name: Julian was floated for a while, but dropped. In the television version, it was four episodes before we even saw that Bean had a home. The movie was the first time he had a job. At the same time, the film started by harking back directly to *Rowan Atkinson Presents ... Canned Laughter*. There, once more, was that shaving routine, right at the outset. Shortly afterwards Bean is in a panic that would make the White Rabbit in *Alice in Wonderland* seem the epitome of calm. In the process of preparing to go to work in the morning Bean breaks a cup. There is only one way to drink his coffee – he puts the powder, sugar and milk in his mouth, pours in the water from the kettle and jumps up and down. It was a familiar routine but still something of a surprise to see it in a film that expected a sizeable pre-teen audience. Wasn't there a chance that children everywhere might end up copying him and subsequently blocking up the emergency wards with a mass outbreak of scalded mouths?

By his own admission Richard Curtis had depended on Bean ideas that had already been done, but this time round they cropped up in a grander, more operatic style better suited to the big screen. When Bean travels to America he unwittingly pops a paper bag that another passenger has been sick into. The vomit is explosive and explicitly illustrated. In 'Mr Bean Rides Again', transmitted on ITV on 17 February 1992 at the time many people would be eating, Atkinson does the same trick with a bag into which boy next to him has thrown up. But in the television version, as Atkinson's hands approach the bag the screen blacks out. The basic art-gallery plot also had its roots in the early 80s, though in a piece that never saw the light of day. Curtis had written a short sketch, 'The Restorer', about a character called Mr Smith who in an expert restorer of classic paintings. Unfortunately he is just about to set to work on the Mona Lisa when a accident causes two paint bottles to be switched and he promptly paints La Giaconda's eyes black. He then goes to great lengths trying to solve the problem without anyone finding out. In the process the picture ends up on the gallery window ledge where pigeons leave more mess on it. In the best traditions of farce, Smith does solve the problem, only for it to occur again in the final scene.

With the *Bean* film, the team had returned to Atkinson's old adage. Richard Curtis told *The Sunday Telegraph*: 'If we wanted a sign that said haberdashery, Ro would say "will they get it in Egypt?" and we'd have a pair of underpants instead.'

Despite the long gestation and the proven track-record of the writers, there still seemed to be holes in the plot. Why exactly was the head of the Royal National Gallery so supportive of Mr Bean while the others wanted 'the worst employee in the gallery's history' sacked? Was the head as senile as Bean was dysfunctional?

When *Mr Bean* transfers to America, however, the plot moves further away from his stage origins, into echoes of Peter Sellers' memorable film *Being There*. Bean is collected from the airport by the Grierson Gallery's art lover David Langley (Peter MacNichol), who has decided to put Bean up for two months in his own colourful modernist home. Being with other people and causing havoc was redolent of *Monsieur Hulot's Holiday* and *The Nerd*. (Writer Harry Shue had been killed in a plane crash in September 1985 so was hardly in a position to complain – besides Atkinson had had considerable input into the character of the nerd). At first David is bemused by Bean, but then, as in *Being There* – and *The Emperor's New Clothes* – he thinks that Bean's ostensibly dumb pronouncements are actually profound. When David asks him what he does, he simply replies, 'I sit in the corner and look at the paintings.' This takes on a strange zen-like significance. Mr Bean, of course, had never really spoken before, and in the film his dialogue was kept to a minimum. The more he said, the less profound it sounded.

As well as some of the more obvious moments, the film also contained some nice coded back-references. When they visit the Pacific Palisades Park 'ride of doom' on Santa Monica pier, Bean pulls a screwdriver from his pocket to tinker with the electronics and make it more death-defying. And at another point David's young son Kevin says in passing to Bean, 'Catch you around, Moonman.' It was as if

Atkinson the schoolboy scientist-cum-alien had never gone away.

When Mr Bean and David have to quickly cook Thanksgiving lunch, Bean looks knowingly at a huge turkey carcass, recalling but not succumbing to the scene in *Merry Christmas Mr Bean* (not to be confused with the David Bowie movie *Merry Christmas Mr Lawrence*) when he ends up stuffing himself into an enormous turkey. This reference, however, was not supposed to be so coded. In the script the scene had replayed the scenario where Bean gets his head stuck when he fishes inside the bird looking for his lost wristwatch, but the scene did not make the final film version.

It had taken numerous years to get the script into a workable shape so that the essence of Bean the television icon would survive. The pivotal moment, however, was one that Atkinson had been doing for years in his live show. It was that sneeze again. While examining the painting, he sneezes on it. Wiping it off, he uses a hankie that has ink on it from an earlier mishap. Wiping the ink off he uses fluid that removes the original paint. The masterpiece is ruined and he has to somehow make amends. Eventually he covers his tracks by replacing it with a poster version from the merchandising department.

The scene in which the sneeze takes place is strangely multi-layered. Bean goes to sneeze, then on the verge, he stops. It's classic slapstick scenario, but deconstructing it a little makes it much more interesting. While children may not have known it, every adult viewer would know that he was still about to sneeze. So maybe, they would be thinking, the writers surely aren't going to be that obvious and make him sneeze in the end after all. But in fact, what Curtis and Driscoll seemed to do was to confound our expectations of subversion by doing the most obvious thing – making Bean sneeze. The laugh was achieved by actually doing the most expected thing. It was the same, in fact, as *The Thin Blue Line*. We expected it to be subversive and it was funny precisely because it was not subversive. It was a reversal of the famous *Not the Nine O'Clock News* sketch where Atkinson walked down a street and avoided hitting the lamppost. In the end he falls down an open trapdoor. If the same double-bluff tactic had been employed then, he would have still ended up hitting another lamppost.

A new motif in the film was the presence of M&M chocolate sweets. Scenes were worked out with precision. But when it came to tossing M&Ms into his mouth, Atkinson could not quite master it, so there was always a cut-away after he tossed one into the air and another one dropped into his mouth. In rehearsal they would often hit his teeth and bounce off. The sweets may have smacked of blatant product placement – what real home ever kept an inverted pyramid-shaped bowl full of chocolates on its coffee table? – but they were pivotal to one of the subplots. Towards the end, Atkinson's Los Angeles Police Department nemesis, Detective Brutus (Richard Gant), has been shot and is in hospital. Bean is mistaken for a doctor and has been dressed in surgical gown and mask and left with Brutus. Pottering around he tosses an M&M up, but it bounces off his mask and into Brutus's exposed chest. This is not the sort of thing you see very often in comedies, but in the American sitcom *Seinfeld*, in an episode called 'The Junior Mint', comedian Jerry Seinfeld had misplaced some confectionary while observing an operation and his sweet had also ended up inside the patient. In the *Bean* version, however, the star fishes around for the sweet and pulls the bullet out by mistake. Not wanting people to know he has interfered he puts it back, fishes some more until he finds his M&M, washes it and – waste not want not – eats it. Later on in the hospital scene, Atkinson, Curtis and Driscoll probably drew some inspiration from *Mr Bean Rides Again*. In that episode a pedestrian who has a heart attack is revived with an electric shock provided by Bean brandishing a car's jump leads. In the movie he is about to give David's comatose daughter Jennifer a shock, but instead gives one to himself – he then flies through the air, lands on Jennifer and revives her.

As with *Four Weddings and a Funeral*, the makers of the *Bean* film were keen to get the pace and narrative flow right even if that meant cutting out successful scenes. Things were extremely disciplined and after initial screenings in America there were more changes. The running time was kept tight, bearing in mind a large segment of the audience would be children. Big set-pieces did not make it to the final cut. Not only did the turkey fail to stick to Bean's head, there was very little of London in the finished movie. In fact a whole scene in which Bean and his Mini cause havoc around Harrods did not get in. While Bean transferred to America, his beloved Mini stayed at home.

Even the pivotal scene, in which Bean rushes around trying to clean up the painting was dramatically shortened. He was supposed to have appeared on a ledge unbeknown to the museum staff standing below, but by the time the film was released that was, metaphorically speaking, out of the window. Even the ending had a couple of variants. In one, the scene was supposed to cut to three years later, when an earthquake knocks the fake replacement off the wall and in the process it falls out of the frame and the guard realizes it is just a poster (Bean has the real, damaged one on his bedsit wall back in London). In another version, Bean returns to London expecting to get his job back at the gallery. He arrives to find the place deserted and the pictures all gone. A cleaner tells him that the gallery has moved, so Bean drives off. As he departs the entire staff emerges from hiding and breathes a collective sigh of relief. Except that having driven off he realizes he still has his security pass and he drives back to return it. It would seem that there is no escape from Bean.

Filming took place in and around Los Angeles, and Atkinson flew his wife and children to America during the shoot. It wasn't just his family that was temporarily transplanted. The homesick British crew had to be supplied with PG Tips and marmite. Some of the American customs didn't go down too well. Mel Smith had to cut down on his beloved cigars because of draconian anti-smoking regulations. But maybe, just for once, smoking really could be a health hazard. During the autumn of 1996 there were serious forest fires in the part of California where the movie was being shot. The elements seemed to be doing their best to get in the way. There were also strong Santa Ana winds, floods, and subsequently landslides.

The rain didn't just make the set wet, it caused a stink. Green rabbit pellets had been laid down to simulate fresh grass, but when they became moist they were particularly pungent. For Smith, who had directed Rowan in London's West End, it was not always a bundle of laughs. In 1997 he told *The Times*: 'It wasn't a riot. If you want to have a laugh, you do serious dramas. "King Lear" is the one to do if you want to have a good time.'

Soon Bean was causing heads to turn while wobbling on a skateboard on Venice Beach. It was an indication of the groundswell of support for Mr Bean that while *Baywatch* was being filmed further down the coast, the crowds were gathered around this unlikely Englishman with the caterpillar eyebrows. Rowan Atkinson had come a long way from his father's farm in the north-east of England.

Any fears that the film was not going to be a hit were soon allayed when it opened around the world. By the time it reached Canada it coincided with the release of the sci-fi blockbuster *Starship Troopers* yet it got into the North American top ten on its Canadian takings alone. *Daily Variety* called it a 'classic'. At screenings everywhere adults choked with laughter alongside children.

The promotion of the film was equally successful in Los Angeles. Mr Bean's face grinned out from the most sought-after billboard on Sunset Strip. The film was an unqualified success, making $200 million before even television and video deals come into it. A conservative estimate put the final figure closer to $400 million. Not bad for a children's entertainer.

The film opened successfully in Australia, where it did better than George Clooney's *Batman and Robin* at the box office. But the promotional process in London was a more delicate one, since the critics had never embraced Bean in the way the public had. If the television series had prompted occasionally outbursts, the movie release prompted a fusillade of fury. When the film opened Matthew Sweet in *The Independent on Sunday* accused Atkinson of dumbing down by even dropping the 'Mr' from his name because it was not a word used in some languages. If that was the case though, would a non-English-speaking demographic have grasped the meaning, never mind the irony of the phrase 'The Ultimate Disaster Movie'? (Actually, in America it did become known simply as *Bean*.) Sweet went on to point out why he believed *Bean* was such a success as in-flight entertainment: 'Half-asleep between bouts of air-sickness is undoubtedly the best way to watch it.' Once more Atkinson was upbraided for aiming gags at nine-year-old boys. Sweet suggested that *Bean* would insult the intelligence of blue-green algae.

The Independent's Ryan Gilbey started by singing the praises of Atkinson's famous face only to conceal a sucker punch. With a face like that, the only other thing necessary for a hit would be a decent script: 'And that's exactly what *Bean* needs.' Gilbert described the character as 'like Mr Magoo with added malice and mucus.'

According to the London *Evening Standard* on 29 July, Atkinson had taken the penthouse suite at the St James Club to perform the task of personally publicizing his new film. The article suggested that the relationship with the press had not been improved when someone compared his son Benjamin to Mr Bean Junior. The monster that Atkinson and Curtis had created was out of control. The *Standard* suggested that friends call him 'a motor mechanic dreaming he is an actor'. Although in his smart suit and silk tie, Atkinson looked more like a member of royalty than a grease monkey.

In *The Daily Telegraph* on 6 August, Atkinson reflected on the cynicism of the British press and explained why the film had already opened in Australia: 'If there's a chance of opening a British film anywhere but here it's not a bad idea.' He did admit that he wasn't averse to a spot of cynicism himself though, confessing to being a fan of the waspish quiz show fronted by his old fall guy Angus Deayton: 'I enjoy *Have I Got News for You*, which is concentrated negativity. But it's different if you're a victim of it.' In *Woman's Own* he confessed that his own children had never seen *Mr Bean*: 'I won't expose them to him as they're still too young.' He went on to expand on how his creation was the personification of maladjusted social disgrace: 'Mr Bean is not a nice man, not the kind of person one would choose to have dinner with. He's a nightmare. Normally the custard pie ends up on somebody else's face and he walks away from it all.'

Atkinson was constantly asked where he ended and Bean began, and he was finally able to come up with a connection that explained how the role came so naturally: 'There must be something deep within me that Mr Bean captures.' In *The Daily Telegraph*, Atkinson let Sue Summers in on a secret: 'In some ways it's the easiest acting job I've ever had, because I feel I'm inside Mr Bean looking out. Quite a bit of me is Mr Bean already.' As if to emphasize the point, the picture of Bean used to promote the film revealed the fictional character toying with a screwdriver, just as the real Atkinson had been doing on a regular basis as a student 20 years earlier.

At the British premiere at the Chelsea Cinema on 5 August 1997, there was a Bean-like minor mishap. The film started late and the microphone used for the opening address played up. According to the *Evening Standard*, Atkinson made a jokey speech that, given his intensity about comedy, was maybe closer to the bone than the assembled realized: 'If you enjoy watching the film half as much as I have enjoyed making it, I'm afraid you will have a pretty rotten evening. So I hope you enjoy it.'

The party that followed the premiere was certainly an enjoyable event. Chelsea's Old Town Hall was packed with over a thousand partygoers sporting masks and scoffing M&Ms in the kids room. The walls were adorned with framed old masters – artfully grafitti'd on. The party boasted a mixture of film names, pop stars and the Oxbridge mafia: Boyzone and Rod Stewart mingled with Angus Deayton, Harry Enfield, Clive Anderson, Griff Rhys Jones, Trevor Nunn, Richard Curtis and Emma Freud. And Atkinson gave the publicity campaign a boost with a public appearance.

By then success was already on the cards anyway. For a movie that had cost £8 million to make it was not faring so badly, having taken over £10 million in Australia in three weeks and £2 million in 11 days in Holland. At the premiere in Australia a smart double-breasted suit had not stopped Atkinson from being gently mobbed by Bean-ites.

The critics had about as little success in spoiling the film's success as the television critics had had with the ITV version. In its first three days in Britain, it took £2.5 million at the box office, a new record. Even *Four Weddings and a Funeral*, the most successful British film to date, had taken only £1.4 million in the same period. Even the single was a hit in England. Boyzone's 'Picture of You' rocketed up the charts with Atkinson joining the band – all decked out in Bean tweeds – for the video shoot in Forest Hill. By 25 September the movie had also been a hit in Brazil, Germany and Serbia. At home Bean was a prophet without honour, but at least he would show a profit.

Reviews of the film in Britain continued to be decidedly mixed, which probably justified the decision to open the film in Australia. In the *Daily Mail*, Christopher Tookey took it to task for inaccuracy. Why would the National Gallery – renamed the Royal National Gallery, probably to pander to American's love of British heritage – employ this Olympic blunderer as a security guard? Why, in a world of marketing and focus groups, was the Gallery run by a committee straight out of an Ealing comedy? How does this imbecile succeed in reprogramming a computer to turn a mildly chilling amusement ride into a horrific rollercoaster? After continuing to unpick a film that should never have been taken seriously in the first place, Tookey concluded that the film would not help Atkinson break into the American market. The *Mirror*, in a more generous moment, suggested that the film was 'a series of disconnected droll episodes'. But by and large the tabloids lapped *Bean* up while the broadsheets remained as devoutly sniffy as ever.

The release of *Bean* signalled some changes for Atkinson. In October he parted company with Barclaycard after seven years. In the final *Bond* spoof, his woman boss – as with the real 007, so the ads had to move with the times – gives him the choice of capturing an enemy spy or facing a charge of treason. Following a powerboat chase around Sicily, Latham has to hide and dons a blonde wig and smart playboy outfit. The enemy is just about to intercept him when he pays by Barclaycard; they promptly lose the scent, thinking that no one as stupid as Latham, would use Barclaycard – until now he had always mocked this magic piece of plastic. After 17 missions, the ads had finally left their mark on their dim-witted star character. There was later talk of reviving Latham as an Austin Powers-type spoof superhero, but Atkinson would be too busy with other projects to pursue this on this side of the millenium.

Besides, he neither seemed to need the money nor had any immediate inclination to work. There was a rumour that he was going to take a year off to polish his cars. According to the *Mirror*, he celebrated the success of the movie by buying a Mclaren F1 racing car for £650,000 – a second-hand one that could still do 0 to 60 in 3.2 seconds. And Sunetra took delivery of a VW Polo.

He certainly was not in any hurry to return to work. There was also a rumour that a *Bean* cartoon was in the pipeline. That would certainly be one way of helping Atkinson stay out of the limelight. Ironically Atkinson had the attention that he did not want, and his creation had nothing. At heart *Bean* was a deeply lonely character. This had come across gradually in the television episodes. We saw how he lived on his own, except for his teddy bear. We saw how he had the saddest New Year's party – in 'Do It Yourself Mr Bean' he coats twigs in marmite instead of buying Twiglets and in the end his guests desert him. At Christmas he sends himself Christmas cards. It is a wonder that he ever got a girlfriend (Matilda Ziegler), and even more of a wonder that he succeeds in holding on to her. In the *Bean* film there was one pivotal scene that would have spelt out his predicament and made Bean a more sympathetic character. Bean shows his photo album to David, but it soon becomes apparent that he has taken all the photos himself at arm's length, and no one else is in them. The only photo of a family is not Bean's family – it is rather poignantly stuck next to a picture of Bean. However, this scene was cut. Maybe this was just too downbeat for a movie that had to have a feelgood factor.

What we do see at the end of the film, is that David's family becomes Bean's family. Kevin even ends up dressing the same as Bean, and when Bean returns to London we get a fleeting glimpse of pictures of his new American family on his bedsit wall. It's a touching moment, incidental but also central to Bean's personality. Richard Curtis has joked that the way he understands Bean is to think of him as someone who was abandoned at six for being too annoying and had to bring himself up. Every now and again that sense of abandonment comes across, and these moments have much more emotional impact than all the chaos that Bean causes put together.

In October in *The Express*, psychotherapist Arlene Gorodensky explained the appeal of Bean: 'His fascination with bodily secretions gets the most laughs, fuelled by our sense of disgust and disbelief. This is mainly because it permits us to regress into a state of infantile self-absorption when the pursuit of sheer pleasure was acceptable.' So now you know.

But the success of the film did not stop critics from attacking it. The bigger the profits, the heavier the brickbats. This antipathy reached its apotheosis with a 'snub' at the BAFTA Awards in the spring of 1998. The film received no nominations despite grossing £216 millions, level with *The Full Monty*, just behind *Four Weddings and a Funeral* and still rising. This lack of appreciation contrasted sharply with the public response abroad. At a press conference in Japan where *Bean* was about to open Atkinson had been mobbed by fans. Of course, box office success is not the same as critical acclaim. But rather than taking things too personally, Atkinson should note that compared to other countries, Britain is not a big fan of physical comedy. In France, for instance, Jerry Lewis is a national hero, while here he is bracketed alongside Norman Wisdom – who himself is an unlikely icon in Albania.

Atkinson's agent Peter Bennett-Jones complained that at the Evening Standard Film Awards, Bean had been dismissed as 'a four-letter word' and condemned as 'the unfunniest film of the year'. In

The Daily Telegraph on 23 February, Bennett-Jones, having already got wind of the snub, had said: 'The way the film has been treated in Britain you would think that we had made something with leprosy.' The Best Film shortlist featured *The Full Monty* alongside *LA Confidential*, *Wilde*, *Donnie Brasco* and *The Wings of a Dove*. The results would be announced on 19 April, but for *Bean* the interest was over.

In a letter to *The Daily Telegraph* on 17 March 1998, Atkinson was the first to admit that *Bean* was not the first film phenomenon to enjoy popular appeal and a critical mauling at the same time, but, he went on, 'I have to say that it is difficult to think of examples where the gulf between popular perception and the media's perception is as wide as it is with Mr Bean.'

Having taken a year off, Atkinson now appeared to be using some of his free time to write letters to the press. He wrote to complain to *The Sunday Telegraph* following Alan Stanbrook's review of the *Bean* video release on 22 March 1998. Stanbrook had written that *Bean* could have convinced no one that the poster of Whistler's mother was the painting, and Atkinson felt he had to defend his project. He said that the audience at the opening only saw it briefly before a glass security box descended to block it. It was a minor point in Stanbrook's review, but Atkinson was clearly sensitive to criticism, which he considered unfair.

Meanwhile the world continued to succumb to the movie's charms. Japan soon gave in too. The movie took $3 million in its first three weeks, while there was a story that Rover in Japan was marketing 200 Mini Mayfairs with black bonnets *à la* Bean – despite the fact that the Mini did not even appear in the finished film. In fact, *Bean* had a deeper impact in the Orient than even Atkinson might have expected. In June 1998, *The Guardian* reported that graduates of Tokyo's National Personnel Authority had voted Bean as the boss they would most like to work for. A survey of 788 high-flyers put Bean ahead of three major baseball-team managers. Japan's own slap-stick icon Tora San had died in 1997, and Bean was seen as a natural successor by many. San used to try to help people and make a fool of himself in the process. Some critics suggested that fans had now transferred their allegiance to Bean – although other commentators suggested that the selection of Bean as a possible mover and shaker said something even deeper about the economic malaise currently hitting the Far East.

Sometimes the fame of Mr Bean was overwhelming, though not always positive. Among younger comedians, for instance, even those who had grown up and loved Blackadder, Atkinson was now seen as a member of the cosy establishment and a legitimate target. Stand-up performer Stewart Lee's Edinburgh Festival show in 1998 took the form of a lecture on comedy, and part of the lecture criticized Mr Bean. In the same summer I was parking outside a comedy club in Battersea. I had a Mini at the time and as I parked a passer-by felt that it was perfectly acceptable to shout, 'Oi, Mr Bean' at me, just because of the car I was in. The passer-by turned out to be Jeff Green, whose show I was on my way to review.

Actor Nick Hancock also had an interesting Bean-related experience, but one that indicates the extent of the character's travels. In 1998, Hancock was filming a documentary about Iran's involvement in the World Cup and at one of the matches everyone started staring at him. It turned out they recognized him from his fleeting appearance in *Mr Bean Goes to Town* in 1991.

Yet in the past there had been even stranger Bean-related incidents. When Terry Venables gave up the post of England football manager in 1996 various names were floated as successor during a BBC Radio 5 phone-in. Kevin Keegan was a front runner. There was a strong body of support for ex-captain Bryan Robson. Some people even thought Glenn Hoddle was a serious candidate. Then one caller rang up and suggested Rowan Atkinson. The DJ asked the caller if he really thought the man who plays Mr Bean should be put in charge of the England soccer team. The caller replied he meant the veteran manager who had had more clubs than Jack Nicklaus and then it dawned on everyone. 'Oh, Ron Atkinson.'

One more, even stranger Bean sighting shows just how international he is. According to a report from the Far East, a group of Burmese rebels were crawling up to an outpost of government troops, but when they looked in on them everything was quiet, except that every now and again there was an explosion of laughter. The soldiers turned out to be absorbed by a *Mr Bean* video.

14

The Second Coming

Things seemed to have a habit of going full circle for Rowan Atkinson. In the build-up to the release of the *Bean* movie, a general election had been called in Britain. In 1979, Atkinson's burgeoning television career had been put on hold when the election that would consign the Labour Party to the opposition benches was called and *Not the Nine O'Clock News* was pulled from the schedules. In the run-up to the 1997 election, which returned Labour to power, once again any programmes with political content had to be kept off the screens. But at 9pm on 1 May the polling booths closed and normal transmission could be resumed. The BBC wanted to appear on the ball and the first thing they screened was the first episode from *Blackadder III*, 'Dish and Dishonesty', in which Baldrick becomes an MP in the decidedly rotten borough of Dunny-on-the-Wold. It was as if the arc was complete. And with *Bean – The Ultimate Disaster Movie*, Atkinson had reached the other side of the rainbow.

The end of 1997 marked the end of a chapter for Atkinson. With *Bean – The Ultimate Disaster Movie* doing big business, he also released the complete set of small-screen *Bean* episodes for the first time on two videos. As well as the 13 that had aired, there was one that had never been transmitted, 'Hair by Mr Bean of London'. Bean is standing around in a barber shop when a busy mum brings her son in and, thinking Bean is the barber, asks him to give her son a quick haircut. Before you can say Fringe Festival he has shaved the boy's hair off.

There were two other sketches that had never gone out. One was on each video so completists would have no choice but to buy both of them. In one he misses his bus but is reluctant to queue for another and particularly does not want to be stuck behind a blind man (Robin Driscoll), whom he nearly kills by faking the sound of a bus so that the man walks into the road. In the second sketch, 'The Library', there are shades of the *Bean* movie plot in his destruction of a priceless rare book. Tracing a picture, Bean makes a mistake and uses liquid paper and then closes the book, spreading the liquid paper across the page. Typically he tries to blame the man sitting opposite, by switching books, but he is soon found out.

Atkinson had admirers everywhere. He was easily the most popular comic in Germany, thanks more to the universally understandable Mr Bean than the final series of *Blackadder*. Germans found solace in the profoundly stupid Mr Bean. Perhaps he was a conduit for their humour, which seemed to be excluded from other areas of their life. As well as record-breaking video sales, the spin-offs were rather attractive. Atkinson was even reportedly approached by a German bank to do ads in the role of Mr Bean but he declined. However, he had not always turned down ads for Mr Bean; he did one for a Norwegian grocery store REMA 1000 in which he could be seen counting sweets in packets to see which contained the most and squirting mayonnaise across the floor the see which tube was better value.

And of course, Mr Bean headed a high-profile campaign for M&Ms (previous recent incumbents had been footballer Ruud Gullit and designer Jean Paul Gaultier). If Mr Bean had ever had any credibility, these ads certainly put a big dent in it as he was seen rather stupidly at a bowling alley with the animated chocolate sweets. The M&M presence in the Bean movie was also rather overwhelming.

Tapping into the lingua franca of visual comedy had its hairier moments, though. In Holland, Atkinson was in a video store signing copies of *Mr Bean*. The shop was inundated with the kind of crowd one might expect if a pop star had been paying a visit. The pushing and shoving eventually became too much, and Atkinson had to be escorted off the premises via the back door. This was the kind of perk that went with success which hadn't been sought.

Other perks were more attractive. In 1997, Atkinson's company Hindmeck reportedly gave him a 17 per cent pay rise, putting him in the top bracket of British-based earners with an annual take-home pay of £1,341,750. This might not have been a huge figure for a pop star, but there were certainly few indigenous comedians who could come close to this figure. John Cleese possibly, Billy Connolly maybe, but few others – certainly few who were UK residents.

Despite Atkinson's wealth he did not forget his origins, ploughing some of his profits into his own past. Oxford University's Experimental Theatre Group, for instance, was able to start again, due in part to a donation from Atkinson, and in 1997 it returned to the scene of his triumphs, the Oxford Playhouse. The *Bean* phenomenon was certainly profitable thanks to numerous merchandizing deals. The team behind *Bean -The Ultimate Disaster Movie* was clearly aware of this during filming. There is a scene in which the marketing team discuss the spin-offs of the return of *Whistler's Mother*. They have come up with what appears to be every franchised cash-in you can imagine from edible Whistler's cookies, to a sexy pin-up poster – *Whistler's Sister*. This scene, however, is followed promptly by the sight of Mr Bean tossing M&Ms into the air on the plane over the Atlantic. The irony, unintentional or not, did not go unnoticed.

Back in the days of *Blackadder*, merchandising was minimal. You could buy the video and that was about it. With *Not the Nine O'Clock News* there were initially only books and vinyl albums. Now there were all manner of *Bean* books and spin-offs. But the issue of money appeared to be a difficult one for Atkinson. A report in *The Sunday Times* in January 1998 by Andrew Alderson suggested that the success of the Mr Bean movie had made Rowan Atkinson the country's highest-paid actor, earning £11.25 million in the previous year, taking into account fees, percentage of film takings and records at Companies House. It was estimated that Atkinson had earnt 7.5 per cent of the total takings from the movie, which had reportedly grossed £136 million that year. The fact that he had stopped doing Barclaycard adverts was a drop in the ocean by comparison. The following week Atkinson responded by letter, denying that he had received 7.5 per cent of the box office gross. He also put it on record that Mr Bean was not based on his brother Rodney, as had been suggested by another newspaper. At least, however, he had a sense of humour about the matter: 'If you think that anyone with financial acumen would base a character on a close relative, and thereby risk having to share the proceeds ... in the manner that one is forced to share gobstoppers, then you're very much mistaken.' *The Sunday Times* responded by saying that its calculation was based on 2.5 per cent share of the box office gross for his acting and a 5 per cent share for his producing role.

After *Bean – The Ultimate Disaster Movie*, Atkinson decided to take that year off. He had certainly earnt it and he could also afford it. Meanwhile Richard Curtis set to work on his follow-up to *Four Weddings and a Funeral* – an equal, not a sequel, much in the manner that *Fierce Creatures* had reunited the team behind *A Fish Called Wanda*. Atkinson did not take part this time round.

Despite Atkinson's huge success in the 90s, the critics could never quite forget *Blackadder*. When Atkinson did grant interviews – an increasingly rare occurrence except in character as Bean – it was a question that frequently came up. In the *Daily Mail* on 30 July 1997, Atkinson discussed his character: 'Blackadder could have an interesting perspective on the millennium and the last 2,000 years of British history.' The report hinted that he and Curtis were thinking of a *Blackadder* movie. In the *Mirror*, Richard Curtis seemed equally cautiously optimistic that the blackguard would be back: 'There have been rumblings we would do something at the turn of the century.'

And when he was not giving interviews there were always rumours to be going on with. On 29 January 1998, the *Mirror* reported that there were plans afoot for a biblical *Blackadder*. This would have seemed odd for a number of reasons. Apart from the perfect sense of finality of *Blackadder IV*, the series – specials excluded – had always proceeded forwards in time. Even for a series that played fast and loose with history, there would be something anachronistic about travelling back 2,000 years in time. According to journalist Chris Hughes, Atkinson would play a scheming thirteenth apostle, and Ben Elton, Stephen Fry and Hugh Laurie would also appear. There was no suggestion of who would play Jesus, but a rather clumsy mocked-up picture showed Atkinson and Tony Robinson in distinctly unconvincing beards, long hair and robes. A quote from a BBC insider – it might have been the cleaner for all we knew – suggested that talks were already under way, although it might be a controversial project. There would always be Christian groups ready to lobby television when they got even the merest sniff of anything remotely blasphemous. And if the series were transmitted around the time of the two-thousandth anniversary of the birth of Jesus, there would immediately be something for them to get into a righteous lather about just as they had done over *The Life of Brian*. Inevitably Atkinson did not comment on the piece. Nor was there any word from Richard Curtis, Ben Elton, Stephen Fry or Hugh Laurie. Tony Robinson didn't admit that the rumour was true, but, according to the *Mirror*, didn't deny it either.

Maybe the creative tensions during *Blackadder IV* had ebbed away. Plenty of 80s pop groups were getting back together despite much more acrimonious splits, so why shouldn't this group? They were, after all, still friends. The only tensions had been on the set. Robinson certainly seemed open to the idea, saying: 'I know many of us have gone on to do other work. But when it comes to *Blackadder* it's very much a mates thing for us. It's a bit like asking your friends to come back for a fun reunion – which will really mean something in 2000.' On 21 February, however, the *TV Times* spoilt the fun, quoting Richard Curtis as saying that the thirteenth-apostle idea won't now be happening. There had been rumblings but they had come to nothing.

The magazine *Cult TV* also speculated on the future of *Blackadder* in early 1998, and there Curtis seemed a little more optimistic about something being afoot. The BBC had just embarked on repeats of the entire cycle, suggesting that although the year would mark a sense of closure to *Blackadder*, it might also be a way of testing the waters to see if there was the requisite interest for another outing. There were young adults out there who only knew Atkinson as the teddy-cuddling, Mini-driving silent Mr Bean. What would they make of his garrulous anti-hero?

Cult TV suggested that there was talk of a *Blackadder* for the new millennium. In an interview with the magazine, Curtis categorically dismissed the possibility of a *Blackadder* movie, but certainly did not discount a tantalizing return to television in some form. His statement was a decidedly cautious, guarded, qualified yes: 'There are millennium plans for *Blackadder*, possibly, but they always end up conflicting with a million other plans. To give a little hint would be sheer and untrue madness, but there may be something.'

By the autumn of 1998, the plot thickened. When the complete *Blackadder* scripts were published, entitled *Blackadder: The Whole Damn Dynasty*, with all royalties going to Comic Relief, the story behind the book seemed to rekindle the original *Hitler Diaries* idea and the possibility of a link to the millennium. In a mock press release, the publishers, Michael Joseph, claimed that the documents on which the book was based had just been found during excavations at the Millennium Dome building site. Among the papers, new stories were revealed about other branches of the family – the first Blackadder, Emun, had apparently been a Druid overseeing the building of Stonehenge. One of the workmen was known as Bad Reek because of the smell that he gave off. During the Hundred Years War the entire family had hidden under some stairs in Northumberland. And Cardinal Blackadder had been a great chum of Henry VII. They liked nothing better than spending time together at Hampton Court, 'stuffing each other's orifices with lightly-oiled lampreys'. However, if a future *Blackadder* series were being planned, Ben Elton was either being extremely tight-lipped or had not been informed. At a BBC spring launch that March he dismissed the tabloid reports.

Other tabloid stories did seem to have come basis. In December 1998 it was reported in the London *Evening Standard* that Atkinson had been sighted in a car with Norman Tebbit. Tebbit was quoted as saying: 'Yes, I know Rowan, and we did go for a spin.' The one-time Tory frontbencher added that they had discussed their shared interest in cars rather than politics, and the newspaper item signed off by remarking that it could not imagine Norman Tebbit joining in with some of the old *Not the Nine O'Clock News* classics such as 'Gob on You'. Fortunately for Lord Tebbit's feelings, it overlooked the fact that in the 'I Believe' episode Atkinson had sung: 'I believe a nuclear winter's good for skiing, but I can't believe Norman Tebbit is a human being.'

The 'Millennium' rumours were the latest evidence that Atkinson had become an integral fibre in the British cultural fabric. Atkinson was so popular that sometimes he could not stop himself from being appropriated. In South Wales, tattooist Steve Joyce paid £300 to have a huge image of Mr Bean tattooed on his upper thigh. According to the *Mirror* he commented: 'This is as good a way as any to keep me smiling through the day.'

The image of Mr Bean was already being used by New Labour. Designer Michael Johnson was approached by the British Council to design 12 posters to stress both continuity and change under Tony Blair. Among other places, the pictures would go up in classrooms around the world where English was taught. Johnson decided to split each picture down the vertical middle. The left half represented old Britain – though not necessarily a bad Britain – while the right represented the new Britain. Cleverly Johnson joined up the images in the centre, so that the back end of a horse by George Stubbs linked up with the front end of a sheep by Damien Hirst; Geoff Hurst and Michael Owen kicked a ball together. Mr Bean was rather strangely united with Ernie the fastest Milkman in the West, created by Benny Hill, the comedian who had gone out of favour in the politically correct 80s. Did this mean that Bean was the new Benny Hill? It was probably the least successful of the images. Whereas there was no denying the lasting cultural worth of, say, Hurst or Stubbs, Benny Hill's legacy was more questionable – naff even – making the connection with Bean less than clear. Besides, although there was an undeniable Englishness to Bean, his reluctance to speak had made him a universal everyman. And, Atkinson had said that one of his influences was Jacques Tati, the French clown. Bean may have been an instantly recognizable icon, but did his fans in other countries actually realize he was English?

In early 1999 the *Blackadder* story suddenly seemed to resurface. In January, Maggie Brown's Media Diary in *The Daily Telegraph* suggested that *Blackadder would* actually be involved in the Millennium experience. She continued that Tiger Aspect was unhappy that the story had leaked out. She add that there was a feeling that there was also the risk that it would look as if Atkinson was being cajoled into rescuing the much-maligned Dome.

There would be a pleasing symmetry to making another, even grander *Blackadder*. Richard Curtis had claimed in *Now That's Funny* that the secret of his comedy writing was about 'the same thing happening again, but bigger.' That could almost be taken as a metaphor for Rowan Atkinson's entire career. In two decades he has gone from sketch to sitcom to film. Some of the same movements he had done in the Oxford Revue show had ended up, 20 years later, on the cinema screen in Hollywood. Each character he had created had conquered more and more of the world. *Blackadder* had grown and grown in stature over the years, even, some might argue, transcending *Fawlty Towers*. Why not cap everything with the biggest *Blackadder* yet?

One of the few things holding it back could be Richard Curtis's workload. Comic Relief took up a third of his time, he had two small children and he was heavily involved in the *Notting Hill* film. But by the end of March 1999, Red Nose Day was over for another two years, *Notting Hill* had wrapped and, well, what was more important – bringing up two children or bringing back *Blackadder*?

If the spirit of *Blackadder* was haunting Rowan Atkinson, it wasn't exactly ignoring Ben Elton either. In the absence of public pronouncements from the star, Elton was constantly probed about plans. If *Blackadder* was not coming back, what about *The Thin Blue Line*? Elton seemed keen for Rowan to return to work, but the star seemed adamant that he wanted time off after the *Bean* movie. The difficulty was getting Rowan out from under the bonnet of his cars. While in the 80s he had worked furiously, now there seemed to be a new calm to his career. At times it seemed as if Atkinson was perfectly content to play with his children, read the latest John le Carré or tootle about in one of his vehicles.

All of this talk about Atkinson's classic historical creation seemed to put his contemporary copper sitcom in the shade. It was criticized for being traditional and soft – portraying a character with 50s policing attitudes in a 90s world rife with corruption scandals and low morale. In contrast, *Blackadder* had been mould-breakingly edgy. Elton, who was also about to attempt to revive variety with his solo BBC show – solo, that was, apart from a comeback from Ronnie Corbett – saw nothing wrong in being old-fashioned. If anything it was even more of a challenge for this bastion of the comedy new wave: 'It takes a lot of work to be this traditional; it is a lot easier to be edgy. I don't care whether *The Thin Blue Line* is abrasive or traditional. I just hope it is funny.'

Elton was rapidly becoming a public spokesperson for Atkinson *in absentia*. In late 1998, he appeared on a number of shows to promote *Blackadder: The Whole Damn Dynasty*. On Channel Four's lowbrow *TFI Friday*, he told Chris Evans that even when Rowan had passed on, his gravestone would carry the words: 'I know you are dead, but when's the next *Blackadder*?' On the high-brow BBC2 chat show *Face-To-Face*, it didn't take interrogator Jeremy Isaacs long before the question of Atkinson's comic virtues and attention to detail surfaced again. Elton harked back to the failings of the first series and the problems in the way it was filmed: 'Rowan falling off a horse at 200 metres is no funnier than than anyone else ... but Rowan falling off a horse at two feet is just about the funniest thing you could ever see.'

But apparently we would never see this again. Unlike all of those 80s rock bands that got together when the right incentive came along, there wouldn't be a *Blackadder* reunion tour with accompanying commemorative mugs and T-shirts. We would not be treated to the sight of middle-aged men larking about in silly costumes – that would be left to Culture Club.

And yet, it turned out, we might not have heard the last of the dynasty after all. Maybe all it took was an invitation from someone with significantly more influence than the BBC's Director-General to get Rowan Atkinson into some breeches. Like the proverbial bad penny he did turn up again. In the autumn of 1998, the tabloid newspapers reported that the Princes William and Harry were helping to plan a special surprise fiftieth birthday party for their father. This would include Rowan Atkinson in a specially written *Blackadder* to be performed at Highgrove. The rumours indeed turned out to be true. On 28 October, Rowan Atkinson and Stephen Fry joined the cream of contemporary comedy at the Lyceum Theatre to celebrate the half-century of Prince Charles. Atkinson was booked to open the show. Howard Goodall's instantly recognizable theme, this time on a harpsichord, chimed out as the curtains opened to reveal Blackadder apparently hard at work at his desk. This was a semi-reprise of the bewigged Blackadder in the black-and-white ensemble he had sported in Comic Relief's 'The Cavalier Years'. This time he was Privy Councillor but his allegiance to the crown seemed decided wobbly. 'There, that should do it,' he announced. He had just written a letter turning down an invitation to join in with the celebrations to mark another year that King Charles had survived with his 'head and shoulders intact'. As if he had never been away in the ensuing nine years, the crown prince of put-downs then reeled off a litany of comical things he would rather do than go to the king's party, which took in going to Cornwall and marrying a pig and hacking off his big toe, 'slicing it, mixing it with beetroot and serving it to Clapham as a light summer salad'. Blackadder's reason for not attending was that the king's parties were famously dull events.

At this point Stephen Fry as King Charles turned up and made matters better by inviting Blackadder to organize the party. Of course, now things were looking up and he was 'as excited as a masochist who has just been arrested by the Spanish Inquisition' – a reference that, ever since *Monty Python* had sent up the Spanish Inquisition and threatened victims with the dreaded comfy chair, has been guaranteed to get a laugh. For once a *Blackadder* moment ended on a happy note, but since there were obvious contemporary parallels, Blackadder could hardly remain a curmudgeon. Instead he bowed out with an uncharacteristic 'Let the revelries begin.'

Atkinson must have been doing something right. As well as appearing at the public show, which was eventually transmitted on ITV on 14 November, he was also invited to Prince Charles's private party where he performed for the royal family in the Orchard Room along with Stephen Fry and Emma Thompson. Apart from the presence of Camilla Parker Bowles, the only other story to compete with the *Blackadder* return was the news that Charles's niece Zara Phillips had had her tongue pierced with a metal stud.

Slowly but surely every road started to look as if it was leading to a *Blackadder* revival. In the spring of 1999, Britain appeared to have gone costume-drama crazy. *Blackadder* seemed a forerunner of a new trend. You could not turn on the television without seeing a screen awash with crinolene. If it was not *The Scarlet Pimpernel*, it was *Vanity Fair*. In the cinema there was Cate Blanchett as *Elizabeth* (filmed in part at Alnwick Castle, where the *The Black Adder* had been shot), as odd in her own way as Miranda Richardson's Queenie. And there was *Shakespeare in Love*, with Joseph Fiennes as the bard in a biography that messed around with the historical period just as much as *Blackadder* had. At one point Shakespeare is seen working on a love story entitled *Romeo and Ethel*. Richard Curtis might have been happy to use that gag, but he might have drawn the line at a London ferryman remarking 'I had that Christopher Marlowe in the boat once.' Like *Blackadder*, the movie *Shakespeare in Love* realized there was considerable scope for comedy just by virtue of having men wearing tights and codpieces. With clothing being as integral to the narrative of this film as it was to the BBC series, at times it seemed as if *Blackadder II* was a rough draft for *Shakespeare in Love* – or maybe that should be ruff draft? One thing was for sure. In 1999 the spirit of *Blackadder*-past cast a heavy shadow over the present. The film *Plunkett and Macleane*, starring Robert Carlyle and Johnny Lee Miller, following the misadventures of two highwaymen in 1748, also seemed to follow in the anarchic tradition of *Blackadder*. Trailers for the film featured the anti-Robin Hood catchline 'They rob from the rich ... and that's it.' In *Blackadder III* Atkinson's own anti-hero had also toyed with a life of crime in 'Cape and Capability'. His plan was to emulate the notorious thief known as the Shadow, who was halfway towards being Robin Hood. Halfway because 'he steals from the rich but he hasn't got round to giving it to the poor yet.'

A more concrete confirmation that Blackadder would make a return came about in January 1999. Following various rumours, on January 17 *The Sunday Times* revealed that there was a comeback in the pipeline. There were plans to make a *Blackadder* film to be shown in the Millennium Dome. In early January a two-page written proposal had been submitted to Jenny Page, the chief executive of New Millennium Experience Company. The suggestion was that the film would take the form of a comic tour, from Roman occupation to the present day, and it was endorsed by Michael Grade, the chairman of the Dome's creative advisory panel. The initial plan was for the film to be screened in the Dome's Sky-sponsored 'Baby Auditorium' at hourly intervals. Atkinson as Blackadder would open and close it and play other historical comic characters throughout in what sounded like a New Labour version of *1066 and All That*.

It was ironic that Grade was now a supporter: he had been the executive who nearly cancelled the character after the first series. There had been delicate negotiations since November 1998, with Alan Yentob, the BBC's Controller, and PR guru Matthew Freud, all looking at the scheme's potential (so Elton hadn't known anything after all back in March). The report hinted at reasons why the series had stopped: 'Tensions between the Blackadder team ... led to its demise in 1989 at the height of its popularity.' There was also talk that an *Only Fools and Horses* film might be made if *Blackadder* failed to materialize. While that sitcom had garnered the highest-ever ratings for its final Christmas special, *Blackadder* somehow seemed more apt. What would best symbolize Britain? A scheming loser whose family had been close to the seat of power for a thousand years or a south-London wide boy? A spokesman for the New Millennium Experience Company seemed to be talking about Atkinson himself when he said: 'The 30-minute film shown in Sky's zone will be based on one of Britain's greatest cultural exports – our sense of humour.' If Blackadder's cunning plan could not save the Dome, what could?

Sure enough, on 24 April 1999, the *Guardian's* arts news section printed a fuller, firmer confirmation of Blackadder's return, based on remarks made by Tony Robinson at the Montreux Television Festival. *Blackadder Back and Forth* would, it reported, cost £3 million and would reunite Lord Blackadder with his humble serf Baldrick. The duo would then travel through time, stopping off at various historical landmarks.

According to the *Guardian's* story, Baldrick builds a time machine out of Weetabix boxes on the even of the new millennium. The two comic characters would then set off on a voyage of discovery, answering the such burning historical questions as 'Elizabeth I: virgin or big ginger tease?' joked Robinson. Everyone from Glenda Jackson to Cate Blanchett and the original Queenie Miranda Richardson, seemed to be in the running for the role of the first Elizabeth, while regulars such as Rik Mayall, Ade Edmondson, Miriam Margolyes and Nigel Planer were also said to be included alongside Dawn French and Jennifer Saunders, contemporaries who had not starred in the original run. Executive producer Geoffrey Perkins described the latest plot. 'The aim of the Dome is to inspire, inform and educate. If people come out having learned just a little bit about British history than they knew when they went in then we will have done our job.'

The film would not just make history, but remake it. Writers Richard Curtis and Ben Elton were said to be planning to alter the result of the England v. Argentina World Cup 1998 match. There was a rumour that the makers wanted David Beckham to appear so that Blackadder could prevent him from being sent off. As rumoured the film would be screened on two 20-metre-wide screens, the largest in the country. It would be hard to avoid Blackadder now. Atkinson's own fear was being trapped for all eternity with his retarded retainer. He said he was 'extremely worried at the prospect of travelling through time with Baldrick.' Times had certainly changed since their days at the BBC in the 80s, as Tony Robinson acknowledged: 'I am sure Rowan will have a huge Winnebago trailer, and I'll get a small carved turnip.'

15

The Alien Comes Home

So who is Rowan Atkinson? Is he merely the sum of his parts? The cynical Blackadder? The eternal loner Bean? The punctilious Fowler? What about the obsessive Henry Birkin? Or Rick the nerd? Sometimes the skins of his creations fit so snugly that the inevitable conclusion is that there is a part of Atkinson in all of them.

But in 1999 he added a new character to his repertoire. Or at least a new, old character. Back in 1983 on *Parkinson* Atkinson had admitted that he hankered after the role of Dr Who; 16 years later, it was announced that he would appear as the latest Timelord in a one-off special for Comic Relief on 12 March. It seemed to make perfect sense. Suddenly here was another character who fit Atkinson like a glove. Unlike Blackadder who only seemed like a Time Traveller, Dr Who really did have the ability to exert an influence on temporal matters. Since his inception on BBC1 in 1963, he had been constantly reinvented, though in his case played by different actors. Atkinson would be the ninth Dr Who and had performed alongside a couple of the previous Dr Who incarnations: Tom Baker had been the legless Captain Redbeard Rum in *Blackadder II*; and far back in the mists of time, Sylvester McCoy had been in the line-up of the 1979 *Secret Policeman's Ball* as a member of Ken Campbell's road show. It seemed that every actor might get the chance to play Dr Who if his career lasted long enough.

But Atkinson was better placed than many to play this cult hero. He was a great fan of Dr Who and could really bring something new to the role. Like the science-fiction series, his work as a performer appealed to both children and adults. But most importantly, Atkinson had the correct scientific qualifications. Those six years of studying electrical engineering were the perfect grounding for this master of space-age mechanics. Even as a child Atkinson exhibited the technical wizardry necessary for the part; on Hole Row Farm he liked nothing better than playing with machinery. As a young man, his wire-filled room at Oxford had sometimes resembled a huge electronic circuit, and he never went anywhere without one special item – his screwdriver. In a similar fashion, Dr Who would never be seen without his own upgraded model – the sonic screwdriver.

Naturally the Dr Who Appreciation Society was excited about the prospect of Atkinson playing the part. Then again, they would have probably been excited about anyone playing the part. They had always felt that the BBC had a grudge against bringing the series back, and excitement mounted in the run-up to transmission. In the event, the *Dr Who* segments were broken up into three parts, retaining the show's traditional cliff-hanger endings. It was a shrewd move to keep viewers watching all night, but one that did not quite work. When the viewing figures came in, *Dr Who* was the most-watched element of Comic Relief, but dips in the ratings suggested that viewers had been switching channels in between instalments.

The Comic Relief special was written by Steven Moffat, better known to date as the writer of the children's journalism drama *Press Gang*. He was approached by the producers after ideas for Rowan had been knocked around and the Timelord seemed to strike a chord. The challenge, however, was to write something that would appeal to viewers who were not *Dr Who* obsessives. At the same time, the obsessives had to be catered for as well – *Dr Who* fans had plenty of disposable income and it was important that they did not change channels out of anger at the way their hero was being treated. The difficulty was getting the balance right.

The story was filmed during February and at times there were amusing difficulties. The Daleks, for instance, were just as awkward to manoeuvre as they seemed. But the real organizational problem was getting all the people that would play Dr Who when Atkinson regenerated himself into the studio at the right time. In the end Richard E. Grant, Hugh Grant, Joanna Lumley and Jim Broadbent all did their bits within three hours. Richard E. Grant was reportedly bemused by the whole thing – having grown up in Swaziland without *Dr Who* he had no idea what was so funny about Rowan Atkinson turning into him. While Richard E. Grant was confused, Atkinson handled the pressure of quick filming well. The chance to play a hero rather than a villain seemed to appeal to him.

Inevitably, the one-off was something of an anti-climax. Purists were disappointed because of the comedy element. The bewigged, waistcoated Atkinson seemed to be sending up the genre as much as celebrating it; as a running gag he kept telling his assistant Julia Salwalha that he would explain various complicated matters at a later juncture. Maybe Atkinson's old fans would rather have seen Baldrick as his assistant. For *Dr Who* fans, there were not the chills of old that would send them running behind the sofa. Jonathan Pryce was an unusually camp version of his adversary The Master. When Dr Who regenerated himself during the finale and returned as Joanna Lumley, there was some thought that if *Dr Who* was about to make a come-back, maybe it was time we had a female Timelord. But the *Dr Who* episode proved a number of things about Atkinson. It showed that even in middle age he was still prepared to put himself on the line. Hell hath no fury like a *Dr Who* fan scorned, and Atkinson was really going into the lion's den by taking on the role.

It was also notable that, although his collaborations with Richard Curtis were becoming fewer and farther between as their careers diverged, the one time they could be guaranteed to get together was for a charitable cause. While Curtis may have been the great behind-the-scenes motivator of Comic Relief, Atkinson has always been a tireless supporter of the organization. Often people without problems soon forget those worse off than themselves, but Atkinson had always been involved in charity work, even before Comic Relief, dating back to *The Secret Policeman's Ball* in 1979. A decade on, when Comic Relief was established, Atkinson was still happy to oblige. Even when he was not able to appear live he would pre-record contributions. After *Bean – The Ultimate Disaster Movie*, he had planned to take a year off; he first resurfaced for his Blackadder turn at The Prince's Trust Birthday Gala, but Comic Relief 1999 marked his real return to the fold.

Live work is something Atkinson seems less inclined to do. When filming, his desire for perfection has reached such a peak that he can be difficult to work with. This need for perfection, doing countless takes even when to others the early ones seem fine, may be the reason that his live appearances have been limited during the 1990s. How can he hope to emulate his television appearances in one take? Back in 1976, John Lloyd said Atkinson had the potential to be like Chaplin – he is certainly as much of a perfectionist as Chaplin was.

Yet by the middle of 1999 Atkinson's profile was probably as high as it had been in recent years. Following his Red Nose Day *Dr Who*, BBC2 started to repeat *Blackadder II*, while ITV seemed to have a habit of dusting off old *Mr Bean* episodes whenever the early evening schedules needed pepping up. And in June Atkinson appeared live for the first time since Prince Charles' birthday gala. Comic Relief had teamed up with the Jubilee 2000 campaign to cancel out Third World debt and mounted two shows, *Comic Relief – Debt Wish Live*, at the Brixton Academy in south London. Atkinson appeared on the first night to show his support alongside younger stars such as Steve Coogan and David Baddiel. It seemed as if things were coming full circle again. Angus Deayton opened the show and the first guest he introduced was Atkinson, playing a priest once more. 'The Vicar of Brixton' proceeded to bless the show. With his eyes barely open he delivered a sermon which compared God to those about to perform. The Holy One had also done some big gigs in his time, we were informed. And if he could knock out the Ten Commandments without recourse to swearing then the acts tonight ought to be able to avoid it too. In closing Atkinson seemed to be genuinely praising God for the whole concept of comic possibilities. Without them 'John Cleese would just be a tall bloke with a small psychological problem.' And without John Cleese, of course, Rowan Atkinson might have been an electrical engineer.

Despite his contribution to showbusiness, Atkinson certainly has not become a part of showbusiness. If many of his friends – Richard Curtis, Stephen Fry – come from the entertainment world, it is because that is the world Atkinson has lived in throughout his adult life. He also has friends in the motor industry, but these alliances are less well publicized. Atkinson's world seems to be filled with continued success.

Riches did not seem to matter to Atkinson, that much anyway, otherwise he would not turn down work to spend time with his family and cars. According to his brother Rodney, quoted in *Cable Guide* in August 1998: 'The money Rowan has made doesn't lessen his hunger for success. He doesn't have to work but money isn't important to him. He is a very normal person – and a genius.' 'Reserved and very English,' added Peter Bennett–Jones. Sometimes it seems that Atkinson's only true passion, besides his family and work is cars. He could be as precise about his motoring requirements as he could be about his performances. In September 1998 there was a story in the *Mirror* that he sent one of Mel Smith's coffee cups to the Ferrari garage in Italy, saying that he wanted his next Ferrari painted the same shade of speckly blue.

What he really wants, though, is to be left in peace, whether in his west-London house or back in Waterperry, where he might read the lesson in the ancient village church of St Mary or attend parish council meetings. Give him cars, good food, good wine, holidays, some Gershwin, Mozart and Fleetwood Mac's *Rumours*, but, above all, give him privacy. Atkinson's rectory has been his pride and joy, but over the years it has also caused him some problems. Because it was a listed building, alterations invariably meant that planning permission was required. The irony was that every time he did something to protect his privacy, a story appeared in the papers telling the public what he was doing. Shutters, fences and hedges were installed to help protect his personal space. In the autumn of 1998 though, it seemed as if Atkinson was looking for another more exclusive bolt-hole. A story in *The Sunday Telegraph* in October suggested that he had been viewing property in Cornwall, in particular the Bonython Estate, on the Lizard Peninsular, formerly the home to Lord Wyatt's brother, Robert Lyle, priced at £2.4 million and boasting a wind farm armed with 14 turbines.

This need for privacy and a wish that people would not probe too deeply has also manifested itself in Atkinson's dealings with the press when they mention his family. Atkinson is the kind of star that would probably consider it a gross invasion of privacy to report that he was married and had two children.

Atkinson is shaping up to be a strange old – and very English – cove, brimming over with contradictions as well as talent. He does not seem to want to be a star, but believes in the power of populist comedy – this, remember, is someone whose family did not acquire a television until he was 14.

As time went by though, Atkinson did occasionally open up about his craft, but it was not necessarily for widespread consumption. On 22 May 1997 he gave a talk in the Old Library at All Souls College in Oxford. It was part of a series of eight lectures on the subject of humour. Most of the other speakers were less well known outside the world of academia, and spoke on topics as varied as the Philology of Chinese Laughter and Totalitarian Humour.

Though veteran satirist John Bird also took part, the organisers were clearly aware that Atkinson would be the biggest draw and they contrived a plan to stop the event being swamped. His talk was scheduled to be the fourth in the series and to obtain tickets interested parties had to have attended two of the three previous events. This way, it was theorised, only genuine fans of the subject matter would attend.

Atkinson's talk was viewed by an audience of around seventy. In it he talked about his early, formative years, how his school experiences had helped to define his sense of humour and his approach to comedy. One of those present felt that Atkinson suggested that the harshness of his school experiences had contributed to the cruelty of some of his comedy.

The real question is, is his best work now behind him or will he go on to greater things? This has been a problem of a number of comics in the last couple of decades who came through with a bang when they were relatively young. The anarchy of Rik Mayall and Ade Edmondson is particularly suited to youth, and their careers have had difficulties maturing. Lenny Henry has tried to diversify, but the further away he moves from stand-up comedy, the more his career becomes problematic. Jennifer Saunders dealt with growing up by not growing up and behaving like a superannuated teenager in *Absolutely Fabulous*.

By contrast, Atkinson has handled growing up in public very well. He has made the right career moves, nurtured characters, seen them blossom and never outstayed his welcome. The temptation now, of course, will be to do another *Bean* movie; but the way the first movie seemed to be, at times, a summary of his career to date, suggests that there is limited mileage left in the character. There are rumours that

Hollywood stars are clamouring to work with him. Tom Cruise is said to be a fan; Woody Allen is reputed to possess a set of *Bean* videos (as well as a shared love of corduroy trousers). Bean may have started off as an expression of English middle-class repression but it has taken on global proportions. Atkinson has turned acting dumb into an art form, selling it to countless countries – including Bahrain, Venezuela and Zimbabwe. You could almost imagine Atkinson reworking the old Schoolmaster sketch to list the countries Bean had conquered. Over two million videos sold in Britain alone making it the bestselling television-related video release ever.

Atkinson is a funny creature, but funny peculiar as much as down-right funny. In *The Times* in August 1997, Mel Smith called him 'very sanguine, very intelligent, very slow and measured', but he is more complex than that. Mr Bean, for instance, is Rowan's funny coat. He puts it on when he wants to be a funny person, then he takes it off and he is himself again. It's a nice trick and one that keeps him sane in a world populated by fruitcakes. Tony Robinson thinks that there are definitely two sides to Atkinson, according to a quote in *The Guardian* in 1997: 'I think Rowan is the nearest thing we've got to a great clown, and like all the great clowns he seems to me to be constantly walking the tightrope between really painful, dysfunctional isolation and one of the lads having a good time.'

Yet much of the time Atkinson just seems like a normal, regular man. His mother, Ella, certainly didn't think there was anything in his personality that singled him out for the kind of stardom he has achieved. In 1997 when she was asked by the *Newcastle-Upon-Tyne Journal* which of her three sons she thought would be most likely to blossom in the limelight, she quickly replied: 'I don't think I would have chosen any of them.' Whereas Ben Elton had been something of a junior motormouth as a child, Rowan Atkinson had been a quiet child at home.

Until Ella died in 1998, she still lived in Stocksfield with Atkinson's older brother Rodney. Rowan used to phone her regularly and tried to visit every Christmas. She was certainly a fan, though she preferred the more sedate, less rude work. She would usually ask her son whether he thought she would find his latest work suitable before she would watch it.

But what does Rowan Atkinson want? Sometimes it seems as if he performs as much out of politeness as out of a career strategy – take that Prince's Trust *Blackadder* revival for instance. He certainly does not seem to perform for honour. It would be no surprise to discover that he has declined an OBE. It seems strange that Richard Curtis has received one, and in 1999 Lenny Henry received a CBE, yet Atkinson – a huge star, a tireless contributor to charity – has not received one. An eventual knighthood is surely not out of the question. It is an intriguing prospect, but not a ridiculous one given that he clearly has fans in high places.

There will always be critics who will say that if Atkinson is so talented why doesn't he stretch himself by doing something more dramatic. He could be a bank manager in everyday life but those early straight performances suggest a breadth of emotion his comedy has rarely hinted at. But with each success, moving on becomes harder. The baggage becomes heavier. It's like walking through tar; you can move, but every step is slower.

Atkinson is really a unique talent in the 1990s, drawing on ancient traditions, often unwittingly. Much has been made of the influence of Jacques Tati and silent comedy on Atkinson's work. But even if his material has its source in this tradition, there was hardly a copyright on it. The idea that any gag is original is unrealistic – if a gag was done in the silent movies, it had probably also been done in the theatre since the days of commedia dell'arte. There are huge similarities between the silent comedy of Ben Turpin, Buster Keaton and Rowan Atkinson. But that is not a case of plagiarism; it is rescuing the art form. Besides, as Atkinson said himself on *Parkinson* in 1981, he hadn't done anything consciously: 'It all just drifted into the subconscious.'

Atkinson is, in fact, now at a stage in his career where his work is exerting an influence on the style of younger performers. In 1998, Lee Evans performed a musical act in his live show without any instruments, miming percussion sounds, and it recalled nothing so much as Atkinson at his imaginary drum kit two decades earlier. Sometimes the influence is unwitting. Adam Bloom's 1999 Edinburgh Festival show is called *Beyond A Joke*. The more things changed, it seemed, the more they stayed the same.

Critics tend to categorize comics. As a result Atkinson's eventual success in America is compared to that of Benny Hill. After all, don't they both do silent comedy? But Atkinson is much more sophisticated than Hill. Even the stupidity of his slapstickery is clever. And as well as the fastidiousness in the editing process, his sense of timing is acute. They say jazz musicians make great joke-tellers because they have a sense of rhythm; Atkinson the rock drummer seems to possess that talent too.

Take that sneeze in *Bean – The Ultimate Disaster Movie*. The fact that the audience can guess the visual pay-offs doesn't diminish the humour. In fact, it can even increase it. Atkinson is a master at using that principle of anticipation; he knows that part of the joke is that you know what is going to happen next. The build-up can be more funny than the punchline, and the longer it lasts, the greater the intensity of the joke. The obviousness and superficial simplicity of *Bean* conceals the fact that Atkinson works as hard at it as he ever did with the verbal gymnastics of *Blackadder*. Everything – both good and bad – that Atkinson does have its antecedents. Aristophanes's writing was more vulgar than Blackadder; Falstaff was more scheming.

There is no doubt though, that Rowan Atkinson is now at a turning point in his career. At 44 he is entering middle age. The physical pyrotechnics may soon be a thing of the past and he will have to depend more on that face. But what a face. He has the kind of face that will age superbly, whether he wants to continue in comedy or maybe do Beckett. There is something profoundly funny about that physiognomy. In *The Thin Blue Line* it looks as if he is barely moving his face, but every muscle is working to sustain that look of desperation. And yet he tried to leave that face behind. He tried to move away from using his looks and got more into verbal comedy with *Blackadder*. But that face is hard to leave behind. It has been the making of Rowan Atkinson. It may change, but it can only change for the better.

Somewhere out in space maybe there is a race of Rowan Atkinson lookalikes. Maybe on that planet everything is reversed. Maybe there are children who look like the young Harrison Ford who get given strange nicknames. Maybe there is a blond, blue-eyed child light-years away who has been cruelly dubbed 'earthman' or 'pinkboy'. Maybe one day that child, too, will see his face on billboards everywhere. With a face like Rowan Atkinson's, and a huge helping of comic talent, it is hard not to get noticed.

Index

In the index R.A. stands for Rowan Atkinson